PRAISE F
LITTLE GIRL CRYING

"Contemplative prayer is a journey into the heart of God, where we find true healing from the pain, trauma, and wounds of our lifetime. That is the essence of *Little Girl Crying*. Belinda Rose gives testimony with her life story to the work of divine love, mercy, and amazing grace, and to the power of contemplative prayer to transform, restore, and even resurrect the most broken of lives. A compelling and inspirational memoir, *Little Girl Crying* offers hope for a suffering world."

— Fr. Richard Rohr, OFM, Center for Action and Contemplation, author of *Falling Upward* and *Immortal Diamond*

"Belinda Rose takes us on a powerful journey as she travels a tortured path toward healing and transformation going through the pain of trauma and abuse to discover the experience of ultimate love. A modern *Pilgrim's Progress*."

— Janice Morgante, Executive Director, Riverwalk Eating Disorders and Wellness Centres • www.riverwalkwellness.ca

"*Little Girl Crying* is an unforgettable memoir of hope and great faith. It is impossible to put down and the compelling writing takes you deeper and deeper into Belinda's heart, and her quest to find solace and comfort in contemplative spiritual life-saving messages. This book will enlighten everyone who reads it as it is a story of great courage and potent miracles. It is not just a portrayal of a woman with an eating disorder but an inspirational journey for everyone who encounters human suffering and seeks to be healed. This book will help millions of lost souls become whole again."

— Gail McMeekin, LICSW, Creative Success LLC, author of *The 12 Secrets of Highly Creative Women*

Little Girl Crying

BELINDA ROSE

Little Girl Crying

My life-long struggle with anorexia nervosa
and the *prayer* that saved my life

ADORATION
PRESS

Cover design and typesetting JD Smith Design

Author's note: The following account is a true story, based on my own experiences and my life. I've done my utmost to share these memories and the facts
surrounding them with honesty and integrity according to my recollection of
them, but it is still my memory of events as they unfolded. All names and locations have been changed; some locations, characteristics and personal descrip-
tions have been partially altered to protect the privacy of all concerned. Because
the memory of conversations dim over time, all dialogue has been recreated. Any
resemblance to any person, setting, or location is purely coincidental due to text
alterations to protect the privacy of all concerned.

Eating disorders are a serious illness and should be treated as such. This book
is not intended in any way to be a substitute for the medical advice of a licensed
mental health practitioner. Readers should consult with their doctor in any matters relating to eating disorders or indeed any other aspects of their health.

Biblical quotations were taken from the Douay-Rheims 1899
American Edition Version, The New Heart English Bible,
The World English Bible, and the King James Version.

Visit the author's website at www.belindarose.com

Visit the author's fan page, Illustrated Devotions at:
http://www.facebook.com/illustrateddevotions

Printed in the United States of America
First Printing April 2018
ADORATION PRESS LLC

ISBN: 978-0-9988401-0-9 (hardcover)
978-0-9988401-1-6 (paperback)

DEDICATION

For You, Lord ... and Your glory.

Without You, this victory would have never been won.

C O N T E N T S

PREFACE   1

INTRODUCTION   Falling Down the Rabbit-Hole   5

PART ONE
THE LORD IS MY SHEPHERD

Chapter 1	Little Girl Crying	13
Chapter 2	Broken	37
Chapter 3	A Sinking Ship	63
Chapter 4	Lord, Rescue Me	81

PART TWO
FEAR NO EVIL

Chapter 5	Abandoned	97
Chapter 6	Captive	107
Chapter 7	Shelter Me from Evil	117
Chapter 8	The Darkest Valley	129
Chapter 9	A Doubting Heart	141
Chapter 10	Lord, Have Mercy	151
Chapter 11	Aftermath	161
Chapter 12	Going Home	171
Chapter 13	Ill Intent	181
Chapter 14	The Perfect Storm	191
Chapter 15	An Evil Whisper	205

Chapter 16   The Voice of Despair   215
Chapter 17   Hopeless   225
Chapter 18   A Flicker of Hope   235
Chapter 19   The Darkest Night   247
Chapter 20   Have Mercy   259
Chapter 21   Fear No Evil   269
Chapter 22   Breakdown   281

PART THREE
THOU ART WITH ME

Chapter 23   Sayonara   295
Chapter 24   Disgraced   305
Chapter 25   In Sunshine or in Shadow   315
Chapter 26   Saving Grace   329
Chapter 27   On Wings of Light   341
Chapter 28   Angels Unaware   351
Chapter 29   My Darling Child Within   365

PART FOUR
HE RESTORES MY SOUL

Chapter 30   Redemption   381
Chapter 31   A Time to Die   389
Chapter 32   Seventy Times Seven   397
Chapter 33   Love's Pure Light   409
Chapter 34   All Is Well with My Soul   427

EPILOGUE   453
Be Love   458
My Beloved   462
Acknowledgments   465
About the Author   467

PREFACE

Is anyone among you suffering? Let him pray.

James 5:13

I came very close to never writing the book you now hold in your hands. Looking back can be painful, especially when reflections of the past are as horrifying as mine. War is never pretty, especially when that war is so intimate and personal. This war addresses the emotional, physical, mental and spiritual battle that raged within my soul for decades against two powerful dark adversaries – anorexia nervosa and depression. My war stories tell of past events that are often almost too bitter, too painful and too difficult to recall, much less share with the world. As an introvert, I cherish my privacy, and so, I struggled not knowing if I would ever find the courage to fully share this story. To do so meant I had to share the Voice that was the command center of the eating disorder's power, and which assumed control over my entire existence. Doing that might mean some would think me crazy. After all, that Voice is what coerced me into behavior no rational person would deem sane. But the Voice wasn't the voice of insanity; it was the voice of the eating disorder itself. I can only describe it as a kind of possession by a twisted, sick, sadistic inner critic gone wild. For me that voice was beyond loud – it was deafening. Yet I knew – I knew in spite of my fear and any stigma that might attach to me for speaking out – that it was specifically the

1

Voice, the key component of my eating disorder, that needed to be addressed so that families whose own loved ones are suffering from eating disorders might understand this illness on a more profound level. Knowledge is power, and hopefully with it comes a better understanding of eating disorders in order that greater compassion may be given those suffering with ED. It is my belief that the more compassionate family and friends can be, the less alone the sufferer will feel amidst their inner torment. But it wasn't just the courage aspect of sharing my story. There were also other major concerns that gave me pause.

My life has been difficult, dark and depressing. Why would others want to read about it? And how could I possibly divulge my deepest secrets, exposing myself to a harshly critical and judgmental world? I knew that to tell this story in the way it must be told meant baring all. There were times when the thought of writing this book left me overwhelmed and paralyzed at just how daunting it would be to tell a story spanning decades. Yet, something deep inside kept nudging me. I knew that despite my fears the day would one day come when I'd face that blank sheet of paper in my typewriter, and I'd struggle to muster the courage to face the long-buried memories of a forbidding past. Over the years I've had many people – from the director of a national eating disorder association to my own Mom – encourage me to write this book. But the truth was that the time wasn't right; the battle had not yet been won, and ultimately this was meant to be a story of God's light triumphing over darkness, and not simply the story of the trials and sufferings of a woman with an eating disorder.

So why tell my story at all? Why not allow all those dark secrets and hurtful memories to remain locked safely away where they can never harm me again? The answer is simple; this is, at its core, a story about Divine Love. The dark history of my life is merely the backdrop to that story; a story that in the end proved to be a spiritual journey about surviv-

2

al, transformation, miracles, the power of prayer and God's grace. After my incredible encounter with God – the miracle that healed the eating disorder – I knew this story *had* to be told, that at last it was time. This story had now become so much bigger than just me. My experience of God – my own personal miracle, that touch of God's grace – was a testament of His amazing love, goodness and mercy that needed to be shouted from the rooftops. In that moment of grace when God gave me the ultimate victory over the dark forces of anorexia and depression that had dominated my life for so many decades, I realized my story was a message of hope and light from a loving God to a suffering world. Suddenly all the fears and insecurities I'd had about sharing my life story fell away, and the courage and strength to write these words replaced them. I knew I wasn't alone in this task, and that my loving Heavenly Father would guide me through it, because in the end this book is for His glory.

And guide me He did! Whatever and whomever I needed to help me write this book just seemed to come into my life. Each day before I sat down to write, I prayed for His guidance that I might tell this story in a way that it would not only help others, but most of all glorify Him. I have to say that I have never felt His presence with me any more powerfully than when I was writing this book.

I don't know why God chose to heal me after all those years. I don't believe for one second that He healed me because I am any more deserving or special than the next person. But I'd like to believe that just maybe it was because He knew that as a writer I would go forth and share this story of His amazing love and grace with you, so that in your suffering – no matter what form that suffering takes in your life – you too might find yourself being led by grace into a divine intimacy with Him – a journey in prayer unlike any you've ever experienced. It is my hope that in sharing my own experiences of the contemplative path, that you might come to see contemplative spirituality for what it is – a gift that leads us into the heart of God and His transforming love.

Contemplative spirituality has brought untold blessings into my life, not the least of which is love. After searching all of my life – literally dying to be loved – I found that love I'd so long ached for resting in God's everlasting arms in the Prayer of Silence. Then there is the incredible blessing – the miracle of resurrection that I experienced deep in the Prayer of Silence. Here, resting in God's presence, my heart, mind and soul were healed, the Voice stilled and my life transformed. This is the healing and transformational power possible on the path of contemplative spirituality – this is the good news I'd like to share with you. For me, the Prayer of Silence is truly the prayer that saved my life, and I will be eternally grateful for the heavenly grace that led me into its depths.

INTRODUCTION

FALLING DOWN THE RABBIT-HOLE

*"The rabbit-hole went straight on like a tunnel for some way,
and then dipped suddenly down, so suddenly that Alice had
not a moment to think about stopping herself before she
found herself falling down a very deep well."*

Lewis Carroll, *Alice's Adventures in Wonderland*

*I*n sixth grade I landed the lead role as Alice in our grade school production of *Alice in Wonderland*. Though much of that childhood performance has now long since faded from memory, I still vividly recall the scene where Alice fell down the rabbit-hole. I can still see my twelve-year-old self trying to simulate Alice tumbling down that rabbit-hole by swaying to and fro, like a tree bending in the wind and repeating the lines, "I'm falling ... falling ... falling."

The truth is, I was about to fall to the bottom of my very own and very real rabbit-hole. But unlike Alice, my Adventure in Wonderland wouldn't contain magical characters. In my land of fantasy there would be no wonder awaiting me. This would be a much more sinister adventure than Alice's. Mine would be a crazy, mixed-up world, where the skinnier you got, the fatter you felt. Here you avoided food at all costs, yet obsessed so much about it that it followed you into your dreams. Hunger pangs were power and control and being able to run five miles while feeling them was a state of bliss. This was the Land of Anorexia Nervosa, and once you arrived there your life would change forever.

My journey to Wonderland began innocently enough. I just wanted to lose a few pounds because I thought my stomach was too fat. In truth, it wasn't. At nearly 5'7" tall and 112 pounds, I wasn't even overweight. My distorted thinking was a coping mechanism for a young girl who had been dying inside for a long time. I thought I wanted to be as skinny as my best friend, Valerie. "If I could just be as skinny as her, if I could just get rid of this fat stomach, everyone would like me too!" I reasoned. So, the dieting began. You have to understand that in the 1970s, eating disorders weren't the epidemic they are today. In fact, they were for the most part unheard of, the exception being case histories in the medical literature covering this bizarre illness of self-imposed starvation. In the small town where I lived, there weren't eating disorder units, there were just mental wards in psychiatric hospitals. I had never heard of anorexia nervosa. I had no way of understanding what I was getting myself into at the time. I didn't foresee that the rabbit-hole I'd just fallen into would take me nearly forty years to climb out of and would nearly cost me my life many times over.

The twists and turns of my Adventures in Wonderland led me to dark and chilling places, the like of which I thought only existed in scary movies. There were thirteen hospitalizations that included everything from ER visits to critical care to mental hospitals, and each one was a story in itself. Along the way there were forced feedings and painful potassium drips that made my arms ache, burn and throb. There were suicide attempts when I could no longer endure the depression from being trapped in this frightening netherworld at the bottom of the rabbit-hole. There were psychoanalysts and psychiatrists with their array of drugs, which not only caused life-threatening adverse reactions that included tremors, debilitating anxiety and a constant state of being drugged, but even went so far as to cause a psychotic breakdown. There were psychologists, one of whom even attempted to sexually assault me. There were social workers, dietitians, priests and nuns, all well-meaning but clueless as how to understand anorexia enough to help me. None of them would be able to rescue me or help me climb into the freedom I so desperately sought. That's the thing about anorexia, you might think you have control over it, but once this illness sucks you in, it has totalitarian power over you.

Then there are psychological issues regarding why I ever became anorexic in the first place. For me, that list was long and complex. There was no single issue or person; there were many factors that played a part. A childhood of abuse and bullying led to a constant state of fear with only one safe place of refuge – the divine arms of my imaginary friend Jesus. He alone was my solace from the frightening world of a dysfunctional home where I felt abandoned by a father who was abusive in almost every sense of the word and by a mother who was emotionally closed off, shutting down when everything hit the fan. But my home life wasn't the only issue. As well as the long line of bullies at school – beginning in second grade and continuing through high school – there were the betrayals, such as the ill-fated night I was raped by someone I knew, cared for and trusted, that plunged me even deeper into the depths of the rabbit-hole.

It appeared that the cards had been stacked against me from an early age, and I spent a lot of time growing up asking myself why. I was a good girl; kind, sweet, thoughtful, quiet and always trying to please everyone. I was a young, devoted Catholic girl who loved the Lord more than anything in my life, even to the point where I considered a religious vocation. "Why me?" became the question I often asked God. Or was life just not fair? Was I just a victim of circumstance or was there something deeper, something spiritual at work in my life?

I would have to endure many, many years of living with an eating disorder and a deep, immobilizing depression, both of which seemed intent on destroying me physically, mentally and spiritually, leaving me with just one weapon to fight my battle ... prayer. For years I felt lost and abandoned by a God I still loved deeply. I didn't understand. I couldn't make sense of it all. Why had He left me in such darkness? Where was He? Yet it would be that deep devotion I continued to feel for Jesus through the dark nights, and my relationship with Him, that would in the end save my life ... banish the darkness ... still the Voice of anorexia ... and heal me in a most miraculous way.

While this story is about my long dark decades of struggle to survive the ravaging effects of anorexia, bulimia and suicidal depression, I need to say right from the start that this is not intended as a tale of woe. This is not a misery memoir. In truth it is a message of hope and a story of God's love for us all. It is a story of great suffering, yes, but from that suffering God created something good. Mine is a story that speaks about surviving the odds through the grace of God's love, the power of the Prayer of Silence, and the miracles possible in God's loving presence. At its core it is a love story between a soul and its divine creator. Because it would be that deep love and devotion I always held for the Lord and the unfailing love He has for each one of us that would eventually heal the decades of battling against an eating disorder that left me isolated and alone, and led the medical profession to declare me a lost cause.

Through God's grace, I came to know His love not just as something I read about, but something I felt and experienced as real and tangible. In one life-transforming moment, He lifted the veil just enough to allow me to truly experience that divine love – just enough to let a sad, broken soul know how deeply and truly loved she was – just enough to heal and transform my life. He gave that wounded inner child – the little girl crying – the thing she'd been dying for her entire life. Love.

Along the way, I discovered that prayer wasn't just about talking to God, but about *listening* to Him and resting in His presence in the quiet. When I became silent, turning within to seek Him, I came to know my Creator intimately, not just as a God who was out there somewhere in the great beyond, but as "Abba", my Heavenly Father whose presence was not just with me, but within me ... and would remain there always. He is the Father who was everything I'd ever dreamt of in a father and more.

Into the stillness – the quiet I go.
Seeking the One who loves me so.
I hear Him beckon, I hear Him call...
Into arms of love I surrender, I fall!
O let Thy gaze of love smile upon me.
Let my spirit be healed – transformed in Thee!
O sweet divine presence draw ever near.
In perfect peace banish my every fear.
Arise O my soul – rejoice in the beloved!
Be restored – be renewed – in divine love.

All things are possible through prayer. I pray that in sharing my journey you too may find through God's grace and love, the comfort and healing you seek in your pain and suffering. Never doubt for a second the power He has to restore and renew a life, or that such miracles don't include you. I am living proof that miracles happen – and if they can happen for me, they can happen for you, too.

PART ONE

The LORD is my shepherd ...

Psalm 23:1

CHAPTER 1

LITTLE GIRL CRYING

I have heard thy prayer, I have seen thy tears: behold, I will heal thee.

2 Kings 20:5

LITTLE GIRL CRYING
Little girl crying, heart broken in two
Little girl crying, no one loves you
Little girl crying, so lonely and blue
Little girl crying, no one to hug you
Little girl crying, so battered and bruised
Little girl crying, no one to save you
Little girl crying, go on ... just fade away
Little girl crying, no one cares anyway
Little girl crying, so much anger inside
Little girl crying, no one in whom to confide
Little girl crying, a child begging to die
Little girl crying, no one hears her cry
Little girl crying, will she ever be heard?
Little girl crying, no one listens to a word
Little girl crying, aching just to be loved
Little girl crying, no one calls her beloved

I was praying to die, and God didn't seem to be listening. Although God had graciously blessed me with His most precious of all gifts - life - by the age of twelve, I was ready to give up on that life. Like a Christmas present I didn't want, I chose to return the gift, and said a polite prayer of "Thanks, but no thanks, Lord." Why would a child so young have lost the will to live? Why would a child wish to die? It is simple really, that child was starved of the one thing we all need in order to grow and thrive – love.

I've heard it said that eating disorders are often about starving for attention. But for me it was much deeper than that, because I was literally starving to be loved. Oh, I got plenty of attention – just the wrong kind. Bullies teased and taunted me on a daily basis. My dad ranted and raved and abused me, and through it all Mom pretended not to notice. She too was afraid of the monster that was Dad.

I was only five years old when I first learned the horrible and undeniable truth that monsters are real. They aren't fictional creatures from fairy tales and movies, they're living breathing people. Sometimes, these monsters turn out to be people we believed we could trust – such as friends and family. Sometimes, they are even our parents.

I held my breath and kept motionless, my eyes wide open, staring at the red-faced beast just beyond the kitchen window. There was a monster in my backyard! It looked remarkably like my daddy, but it wasn't acting like Daddy at all. The monster was really, *really* angry. At just five years of age, I didn't know a lot about monsters, but I knew what I'd learned in fairy tales. Monsters huff and puff, and stomp their feet, and he was doing all of those things.

Paralyzed, my heart pounded as my eyes remained fixed on the beast's every horrifying move. What was he doing? I looked on; the creature seemed to be taking his time choosing a switch from the maple tree he was circling so furiously. With his powerful hands he ripped a branch right off the tree in one quick loud snap. But wait! He was turning. Oh no, he's making his way back through the yard, and heading straight toward the back door – and *me*!

"Mommy! Mommy! He's coming!" I shrieked. Panicked, I tried to hide, burying my face between her knees. "Mommy, I didn't mean to wake him up!"

The monster stormed through the door in a wild frenzy. His face was flushed, his teeth were clenched and he was swinging the tree switch in his hand in a violent whipping motion. This wasn't a make-believe monster, like in the old Boris Karloff movies my big brother and I watched on Saturday afternoons; this was a real living, breathing monster!

Everything in me screamed, "Run ... flee from the monster!" But I couldn't. I don't know why, but it was as if my feet were stuck to the brown and white kitchen tiles beneath them. Perhaps I knew that I wouldn't be able to get away, that running was futile and would only serve to make the monster madder, make him want to hurt me even more. Perhaps it was simply fear that kept me rooted to the spot, clutching Mom's pant leg between my sweaty little palms. I thought Mommy would protect me. After all, wasn't she supposed to keep me safe? But I stood there, and waited ... waited for the monster to get me.

The monster roared, "When I take a nap I expect this house to stay QUIET! DO YOU UNDERSTAND ME?"

Mom spoke up, pleading my case. "Bill, she was only playing!"

The monster didn't seem to care what she had to say. He

wasn't listening to her; he shoved her out of his way with one powerful hand and yanked me from the safety I so desperately clung to. His large, crushing hand was now firmly wrapped around my tiny arm, and I felt myself lifted off my feet into mid-air. The monster swung the switch across my legs in one stinging blow after another.

I screamed. I wailed. "Don't, Daddy! I'm sorry!" But the monster said nothing. He didn't seem to hear. He was intent on doing what monsters are meant to do – hurt you.

Then as abruptly as it had begun, it ended. The beast released me, bellowing, "Go to your room – and STOP THE CRYING!"

I did as I was told. I went to my room, but I couldn't stop the crying. That much was impossible. So I hid beneath my bed to cry, hoping and praying the monster wouldn't find me there. Huddled beneath the safety of my bed, I dared to let the pain escape. I cried because the red welts on my legs stung. I cried because I was scared. I cried because my heart was broken. I cried because I thought Daddy didn't love me. Daddy was mad at me because I woke him up playing. I hadn't meant to wake him up or be a bad girl. I hadn't meant to make him so angry ... so scary ... so mean. Mommy had always told me monsters weren't real, but she was wrong, because I'd just had an encounter with a real live one. If Mommy couldn't save me from the monster, then who could?

Rooting through the small box of prayer cards I kept stashed beneath the bed, my eyes fell on an image of Jesus, the Sacred Heart. I pulled it from the box and gazed through my tears at the image of His heart bound with thorns, and I thought, *Do those thorns hurt, Jesus? Is your heart broken, too?* Holding the prayer card close to my chest I cried out, pleading with Him, "Make it quit hurting, Jesus. Make the mean monster go away. Make Daddy stop hurting me. I'm afraid of him." Closing my eyes, I imagined Jesus was with me, and suddenly I no longer felt so afraid and alone.

Soon after that I began having night terrors. As clichéd as it sounds to call your abuser or persecutor a monster, in my eyes as a little girl, that is precisely how I saw Dad. I was as terrified of him as I would have been of Frankenstein's monster had he walked in through the front door. Even in my dreams, I couldn't escape the monster or the fear he instilled.

The dreams were the same night after night – a mummy chased me relentlessly. But the mummy of my dreams wasn't slow and plodding like the mummy in the movies. This one ran fast. He'd chase me round and round the house with his arms outstretched. In a last ditch effort to hide I'd make a run for my favorite hiding place beneath my bed. But even there I wasn't safe from this monster, because he'd always find me. His frightening, bandaged arm seemed to grow longer and longer and longer as it inched ever closer to me, and just as he was about to snatch me from under the bed I'd wake up scared to death, crying out in the night for the safety of my mom's arms. But the truth was there was nowhere to run and hide. Nowhere was I safe. No one was there to rescue me from his clutches. I was simply the prey, the victim; I had no choice but to endure whatever the monster had in store for me at any given moment. I craved a safe place, so I created one in my imagination with Jesus as my imaginary friend. It was here in a child's land of make-believe that my life-long friendship with Him began.

I don't remember ever not holding a deep devotion and affection for Jesus. I don't know why this was – only that it was there, as if innate. My dad wasn't religious in the least. He used to say that his many years of army service during the war had turned him into an atheist. My mom raised my brother and me as Catholics, and we went to Mass every Sunday. But there were never parochial schools for us. We stayed in the public system. Catechism classes on Saturdays were the most instruction we'd received in Catholicism. Even though Mom always kept a St. Jude Novena prayer card close at hand, she rarely spoke about religion, or about Jesus, the saints or the angels that were such a dynamic part of our faith. Yet those same saints and angels that graced the face of my prayer card collection or stood as beautiful statues in our church always fascinated me. I was in awe of the beauty of the angels, and dreamt of them often. They arrived in my dreams as beings of radiant, golden light – a light that felt like a warm hug.

As a Catholic child I knew the importance of having a guardian angel. This was an angel we could call on to guide and protect us, as I so often did in my prayers before bedtime each night. As for the saints, I looked up to them often, thinking that because they'd lived their lives in love and service to Jesus He must love them very much. I too, loved Him, and I would strive to please Him in everything I did, just like the saints did. I would be a good girl. In fact I didn't get into trouble very often, and my good behavior wasn't just because I feared Dad's wrath, but because of Jesus and my love for Him. I never wanted Him to be angry with me ... angry like Daddy so often was. Imagining His face scowling at me like Dad's so often did, or seeing Jesus sad because of something I'd done, broke my heart.

It was in catechism school when I was seven years old that I first learned the exciting news that nuns became the brides of Christ. I was elated! I couldn't wait to share with Mom the good news that I could marry Jesus.

"I can marry Him, Momma! I can marry Jesus! I want to be a nun when I grow up!" I could hardly contain my glee. But it was an idea Mom would have no part of.

"Belinda, where did you ever get that idea? Why would you want to be a nun?" she said, giving me her look of stern disapproval.

"Because I love Jesus, Mommy. Didn't you marry Daddy because you loved *him*?"

"Of course I did. But that is a very different kind of love, Belinda. One day you'll grow up, get married and have a family, too. Now, put that idea out of your head. I don't want to hear about it again."

That was the end of the story. My heart dropped. It seemed as if I'd made her angry, and as I always wanted to be a good little girl and please her, I didn't bring it up again. Instead, I felt I had no choice but to repress all my love for Him and my desire to serve Him and store it away as a safely guarded secret. I trusted Mom more than anyone, and if I couldn't share my feelings with her then I couldn't share them with anyone. I would never again speak of my deep devotion for Jesus, or tell her that He had become the center of my life, my imaginary friend. Instead, I would keep my world of make-believe private. It would become a sanctuary for me alone. No one would ever know of it, and I could go there whenever my heart was broken or I was terrified of Dad. Into Jesus' loving arms I would run for shelter. You may say it was only my imagination, but to that scared little girl, Jesus could not have been more real.

GENTLE JESUS BY MY SIDE

O gentle Jesus by my side,
In Thee alone I can confide.
Savior, Lord and forever friend,
My one true light till I'm home again.
With Thee so near I'm never alone,
Thou has made me Thy very own.
May Thy love and grace rain down on me,
Sheltering me on life's stormy seas.
For here in my private reverie,
I'm safe and loved alone with Thee.
In Thy embrace let me abide,
O gentle Jesus by my side.

The best thing about hot summer nights was that Dad would leave the window fan on all night long. I loved lying in bed listening to the constant hum of the fan's motor. Like the soothing beat of a mother's heart, the white noise of the fan soothed me. I found it helped my nighttime reveries. I kicked off the covers to let the warm summer night's breeze coming through the open window next to my bed cool me. The house was quiet now. The monster was at last asleep, and I could spend some time with my imaginary friend Jesus.

As the breeze drifted across my face, I closed my eyes to play my favorite game of make-believe. It had been an awful day. I didn't want to think any more about the horrible spanking Dad had given me that day, or how mean he was, or how much I hated him for being so mean.

From under my pillow I pulled a prayer card. It showed an image of Jesus as the Good Shepherd. He sat beneath a majestic tree with a shepherd's staff in his hand. The sheep that dotted the surrounding lush green hillside and valley reminded me of my Grandma and Grandpa's farm, one of my favorite places in the world. Sometimes Mom would read the verse on the card to me. She said it was from the 23rd Psalm. But it wasn't the verse that comforted me so much as the gentle expression on Jesus' face, and the serenity the image evoked. I wanted to be there with Him on that hillside, and in my imagination I could go there. So I shut my eyes.

In my mind's eye, I was instantly transported onto a narrow dirt path that led up the hillside to the sprawling tree beneath which Jesus sat. As fast as my legs would carry me, I ran the short distance to the top of the hill.

As I neared my destination, I saw my friend sitting beneath the shade of the majestic oak. For a brief moment I stood gazing at Him as the gentle breeze danced through His dark shoulder-length hair and caressed His long flowing white robe. In that moment my fear and my discontent dissolved.

Unafraid, I ran toward Him. His welcoming smile lit up my heart. His arms opened wide and I flew into them, where He caught me up in a big hug. If only my daddy would hug me like this – just once.

From a sturdy gnarled branch of the oak tree hung a plain wooden swing. Here, in my imagination in this make-believe sanctuary, Jesus and I could play for as long as I wanted. My hand firmly planted in His, I pulled Him towards the swing. Like a loving Father, He steadied the swing as I climbed on.

"Are you ready?" He said, grinning ear to ear. I nodded my head and He pushed me high into the air, so high that I was given a bird's-eye view of the sheep that dotted the hillside. Sometimes I imagined the same beautiful angels of my dreams with their golden wings of light. They sat upon the puffy, marshmallow clouds that floated across the beautiful Caribbean blue sky. Here I was free and happy. Here I was loved and cared for. This was our private meeting place and my safe place from the world and from the monster. I loved Jesus more than anything or anyone in my life. I could come here in my imagination anytime I wanted to, and Jesus would always be waiting for me.

"I'm sleepy now, Jesus. Will you stay with me while I go to sleep?" I said, barely able to keep my eyes open.

"Of course I will," He replied softly, smiling. Stopping the swing, He scooped me up in His arms. As I looked into His face, I was caught up in His radiance – the light that danced in His deep sea-blue eyes and the love I felt in His presence.

My thoughts returned to my bedroom, where the warm summer breeze still blew gently across my bed, but in my imaginary world I was no longer alone. Jesus had returned with me. Content, I pretended I was nestled safe in His arms with my head against His chest where I could hear the steady, rhythmic beat of His divine heart and His soothing voice whispering, "It's all right, Belinda. Don't be afraid. I'm here. I promise. I'm always beside you, My child."

By the age of eight, I had learned that life was all about fear. Dad seemed addicted to anger, and he could snap at any moment, becoming the wild beast that lurked within him. I had every reason to be petrified of him, and I was. But the other bullies in my life were schooling me in fear and intimidation, too. I was learning from an early age that monsters came in every shape, size and age range.

The fledgling second-grade bullies had already labeled me ugly, and who was I to think they weren't right? I had precious little self-esteem already. It wasn't only their mantra, the way they chanted "Cooties" when I passed them on the school playground, but the way they looked at me as they chanted it that screamed *Ugly!* I couldn't say I blamed them for thinking such mean things about me. When I looked in the mirror, I could see what they meant. I had what my pediatrician called early onset acne. I may have only been seven, but I already had the problem skin of a fifteen-year-old teenager. It had become so troublesome that when my parents went for teacher-parent conferences, my problem skin was the topic, not my stellar grades or my excellent conduct. But even the nastiness of the kids in my second grade classroom couldn't match the cruelty of Mr. Mike, my best friend Deanne's grandfather.

Deanne lived two houses down from me. We had been friends from the first day she moved in. I was immediately drawn to her, because she looked so much like one of my childhood idols, Cher. Dee had that same long, flowing black hair. She was tall and willowy. In fact, "You look like Cher!" were the exact words that began our first conversation and our new friendship.

Deanne had tragically lost her parents in a car accident at the age of twelve, and had since been legally adopted by her grandparents. She was now fourteen, and although she was six years my senior, the age difference never seemed to matter. Everyone always said I acted older than my age. Maybe that was because living in an abusive home had forced me to grow up faster than most kids. I loved hanging with Dee. It felt a bit like having the older sister I had so often longed for. Our friendship would have been perfect except for one thing – her mean grandpa.

Mr. Mike was a frail, elderly seventy-something man who had retired early because of a heart condition. He spent his days in his old ragged recliner watching game shows and soap operas. Whenever Dee and I walked through her front door, Mr. Mike would greet us, a greeting that will forever remain etched in my mind and heart.

"Did you take your ugly pills today?" he'd chuckle. Too embarrassed to look him directly in the eye, I'd hang my head and gave him a barely audible, "No, Mr. Mike."

But Deanne had no problem at all speaking up on my behalf. "Stop it, Grandpa. Leave her alone!" she'd say, rebuking him in her protective older sister tone. Then we'd scurry off to play.

For as long as Dee and I were friends this scenario played itself out, day after day, over and over again. Never did Mr. Mike miss his opportunity to ask me if I'd "taken my ugly pills." It was as if he waited breathlessly for me to walk through the door and make his day. It all came to a devastating climax on my ninth birthday.

"Grandpa and Grandma have a birthday surprise for you!" Dee seemed as excited as I was to see what that surprise was.

As my girlfriend and I walked through her front door, Mr. and Mrs. Mike began singing an off-key rendition of *Happy Birthday*.

"Thank you," I replied, blushing.

"I have something for you," Mr. Mike said. Tossing a small plastic bottle at me from his seat in the recliner, he snickered, "Here, happy birthday, kid!"

Eager to know what my first present of the day was going to be, I reached out to catch the small package. But my excitement soon turned to horror. What I held in my hand was an old prescription bottle filled with jellybeans. My eyes filled with tears as I read the label: *Ugly Pills. Take one per day.*

My newly nine-year-old heart sank. I didn't speak. I couldn't. I was trying with all my might not to let the tears that blurred my vision escape. Dee, clearly seeing the expression on my face and the tears in my eyes, snatched the bottle from my hand. Outraged, she spoke up once more on my behalf. "Grandpa! That is so mean! Why would you *do* something like this?"

His laughter echoed in my head. Realizing I was about to fall apart in her living room, Dee grabbed me by the hand, pulling me out the front door and onto the porch. I tried to put on a brave face. I didn't want to cry. I didn't want her to think I was acting like a baby. Seeing through my false bravado, she threw her long, willowy arms around me in an enormous hug. "I'm so sorry, Belinda. Don't pay any attention to him," she said.

I was too upset, too hurt and too embarrassed to listen to her kind advice. I just wanted to retreat. I *had* to retreat, because these tears were not going to be denied for much longer. *Run away. Hide. Seek out the comfort of Mom.* Those were my only thoughts. I told Deanne I'd see her later, and made a run for it.

As I burst through our front door sobbing, the sweet scent of cinnamon told me I'd find Mom in the kitchen. Breathless, I threw myself into her arms with the plastic bottle of jellybeans clutched in my hand.

"What's wrong?" she demanded.

Unable to speak, I put the plastic bottle in her hand, and uttered between sobs, "Mr. Mike ggg-ave me th-is!"

Mom silently read the hateful words scrawled in red marker across the label. She gave me a blank, expressionless stare. She was speechless. She didn't seem to know what to say, and so, she just held me for the longest time as I cried. Her only words of comfort were, "Oh honey, that wasn't very nice of him."

Deanne and I saw each other less and less after that. I missed my friend, but I think she realized that I couldn't bear the thought of walking through her front door and seeing her grandpa ever again, much less having him taunt me with his cruel and insensitive comments.

Now the thought that I was ugly had been reinforced in the most brutal way – not just by another mean kid at school, but by an adult. If an adult said it, it must be true, my child-like mind reasoned. The damage had been done. My young heart had been wounded deeply. This nasty and insensitive man had done more harm than perhaps he'd ever intended by his cruel prank. I didn't just think I was ugly anymore; I believed it to my very core.

In an effort to keep the monster within Dad at bay, Mom and I constantly walked on eggshells at home. Conflict was avoided at any cost, because we lived in dread of his next violent outburst. Because I feared him so much, I rarely spoke to him. I avoided him like the plague. If I needed to ask Dad anything I wrote him a note and asked Mom to play messenger, which infuriated him. "Why can't she just ask me herself?" he'd say, as if he was offended and his feelings were hurt. He simply never understood how completely petrified of him I was.

My sense of self-worth was nonexistent. I craved love and affection more than anything, but there was little of either to be found in our home. Hugs and kisses weren't given freely, and love was a missing ingredient. Fear swallowed us whole, and it was that fear that dictated our behavior and the secrets we were forced to keep.

What went on within the four walls of our tiny home stayed inside those four walls. Ours was a house of secrets. Dad never turned into a monster in public, and Mom pretended to everyone that all was well at home. We maintained this phony façade so well that no one knew about the violence and abuse we lived with. Were friends, neighbors, or relatives suspicious of the horrors that went on within this tiny four-room house? If they were, no one let on and none of them dared to ask. Mom was too afraid to speak or step up and do anything, that much I did know. Maybe she just found it easier to deny reality. Maybe as long as she wasn't the one taking the beatings, as long as her 'secret' that Dad was abusive was safe, she could pretend that all was well and endure the horror silently.

Mom once told me that her dad had warned her on her wedding day, "You made your bed. Now lie in it." What did that mean exactly? It seemed an odd thing for a father to tell his daughter on her wedding day. Had Grandpa gotten a glimpse of the monster that lived within Dad all those years ago? I tried to make sense in my mind of why Mom had stayed with Dad all these years, or how she could love him when she saw what he did to me. Perhaps Mom was simply too ashamed to admit she'd made a huge mistake in marrying him. Perhaps she was frightened of trying to make it on her own with two kids, or maybe she was too afraid of what Dad's reaction would be if she left. But whatever her reasons for staying were, not a single one of them was solid enough for her to keep us all stuck in this web of abuse. Nothing seemed to matter as long as no one outside our house knew, as long as Dad's temper and rage remained a secret.

My brother, who was seven years older than me, was rarely around, choosing to be off with his buddies, anywhere but home. I often wondered if he knew the way Dad was hurting me. But how could he know? He was seldom home to witness it, and even when he was no one ever said anything.

Oddly, the abuse and the secrets bonded Mom and me tightly, even neurotically so. Although she didn't protect me from Dad's wrath, it became my purpose – albeit subconsciously – to protect her. I often found myself deflecting his anger onto myself to spare her the grim repercussions. No matter how noble, it was an idea that was utterly ridiculous.

But it seemed natural to want to protect her from Dad, because she was the only love, the only warmth, available to me in that house. In protecting Mom I was protecting myself, and Mom and I shared something that no one apart from the two of us knew. When we were alone together we talked openly about Dad and his rage. But it was always in secret. In those private conversations I would plead with her to leave him. Her answer was always the same: "How would I take care of you and your brother?" I was just a kid and I didn't have the answers to that, but I didn't care. I just wanted to be somewhere the monster didn't live. I wanted to feel safe. I wanted not to be so afraid all of the time. I hadn't yet realized how afraid she was of Dad too, until one horrible evening when she tried to rescue me from the monster's hands.

It began as an ordinary Sunday evening. *The Ed Sullivan Show* blared on the old black-and-white Philco television in our living room. Ed had just stepped out on stage and opened the show with his familiar catchphrase, "Tonight, we have a re-e-ally BIG SHEW!" But the "re-e-ally BIG SHEW" had already begun moments earlier between my Mom and Dad. Tonight the tension was palpable. My parents were arguing again, and it all centered on my seventeen-year-old brother, Darryl.

I had always thought of my brother as a rebel. I understood even as a kid that he was just kicking against Dad's tyrannical rule. But Dad saw Darryl as a troublemaker, a word he liked to use in the heat of an argument with Mom. I was only ten, and my parents didn't tell me everything that went on, or much about the specifics of the trouble he frequently got into. For some odd reason all my brother's troublemaking was kept hush-hush, as if he'd done something to be ashamed of. I didn't know a lot about the current trouble he seemed to be in, except that my brother had broken out of a mental hospital with a group of kids around his age. Their first stop had been my Grandma's house, where they'd failed to coerce her out of her blue '57 Chevy to make their getaway. Now Darryl and his band of friends had been gone for weeks. Where they were was anyone's guess. When I asked Mom why he was in a mental hospital, she had explained to me that my big brother wasn't really crazy, he was just a troubled kid. She said the juvenile authorities seemed to think psychiatric intervention would help him. I wished he would get his act together because it was difficult seeing Mom so overcome with worry that she needed to start taking anti-anxiety medication. During the period of my big brother's disappearance she hardly ate, complaining her stomach hurt. Her hands trembled nonstop, and she rarely slept. As for Dad, he was just plain mad all the time.

"Bill, I'm scared for Darryl," Mom lamented. "He's been gone for weeks. He could be lying on the side of a road dead. He has no money. How is he even eating?"

"I guess he should have thought about that before he ran away!" Dad snapped back as the tension in the room grew.

"How can you feel that way? He's your son!" Mom said, clearly hurt by his insensitivity.

"He's seventeen years old now. He needs to grow up and be a man. I'll tell you what that boy is, Dolores, he's a troublemaker. Look how he tried to steal his grandmother's car!"

Dad's cold, heartless comments elicited only silence from Mom. I glanced over at her, catching the hurt look in her eyes and seeing the tears that had begun to fall from them. I may have been only a ten-year-old kid, but I wasn't stupid. I knew how much she wanted Dad to do something to encourage Darryl home, to console her, or at the very least *pretend* that he cared. Her heart was broken and she was beside herself with worry. But she should have already known that kindness, concern, sympathy or love weren't what she was likely to get from Dad.

I had no particular opinion about my brother and no deep affection for him. He and I were never close. Most of the time he was out with his friends. When he was around all he did was pester me. It was never a loving big brother-little sister type of relationship. All I wanted was for Mom to stop being so upset all the time, for the arguing to cease or for me to be invisible in the midst of it all. I was desperately trying to stay out of it, keeping my eyes on the Ed Sullivan Show. But the quarreling was making that impossible, and I was becoming more unnerved with every passing minute.

"What is it you want me to do, Dolores?" Dad's voice had reached a powerful crescendo, a clear indicator that he was getting near boiling point.

Anxiously fidgeting with the end of my long ponytail, I was unaware that I'd begun chewing on it.

"Get your hair out of your mouth, Belinda!" Dad snapped at me.

Dad was angry, and he meant business, so I did as I was told immediately. But like any nervous habit, I had trouble controlling it, and within minutes I had unwittingly begun chewing on my hair again.

I didn't get a second warning. Jumping up from his chair, Dad glared at me with a look that made my blood run cold. His ice-cold stare was always the first sign that he was morphing into monster mode. I watched horrified as his hand jerked open the buckle of his belt. In what seemed like a split second, his belt was off and doubled over in his hand. I shuddered. "No, Daddy! No!"

I knew what was coming, but why? What had I done? The answer came swiftly as he roared, "How many times have I told you NOT to chew on your hair?"

I looked helplessly up at his crimson face, speechless. I hadn't even realized my hair had been in my mouth again. I cringed in anticipation of his next move. He snatched me by the arm in a violent fury, yanking me from the chair. I dangled from his grip in mid-air like a rag doll. I didn't want to look, and so, I scrunched my eyes tight, and waited for Dad to deliver the first strike. The sting of the leather took my breath away as he smacked my bare legs, over and over and over again. "Daddy, don't! Don't! I'm sorry!" I wailed at the top of my lungs. I screamed from sheer terror and in response to the painful bite of the strap against my bare skin, but my screams did nothing to end the pain.

Amid his fury and the burning sting of the strap repeatedly striking me I had but one awful thought: *I just want this monster to die!* Perhaps Mom could read my thoughts, or perhaps she was appalled at the rising red welts already forming on my legs, because she did something she'd never done before. She intervened.

She leapt up from her chair. "Bill, you're hurting her! Stop it! You're going to kill her!"

He put me down, and paused for a moment. She'd gotten the beast's attention, and he seemed to be listening. But his rage was now aimed at Mom. Towering over her, his face but inches from hers, Dad roared, "Do YOU want some of it too?"

Mom recoiled immediately, her big blue eyes widening and her face stained with tears. She glanced down at me, curled up like a small quivering ball on the living room floor. I didn't need words to understand what her apologetic expression was saying: *I'm sorry. I can't do anything to stop him.* She too was helpless in the face of the fury of this beast before us; that much I understood. If she had even attempted to pick me up off that floor, Dad wouldn't have hesitated to hit her, so she stood silently by and watched.

Stunned that she'd mustered the courage to confront him in the first place, I only wanted her to back away, to be safe. The last thing I wanted was for her to get hurt trying to defend me. But her valiant effort to protect me from him, at least this once, made her a heroine in my eyes.

Dad, no longer distracted, wasn't through with me yet. He smacked me several more times before his lust for violence was satiated. "GO TO YOUR ROOM!" was his final command. I bolted for the sanctuary of my bedroom.

Shaking and sobbing hysterically, I lay curled up in a fetal position on the floor beneath my bed, nursing both physical and emotional wounds. My anger towards him boiled over inside of me. "I *hate* him!" I whispered. "Why does he have to be *my* dad? Why does he always have to be so mean? I wish he'd just die!"

The bedroom door burst open, interrupting my thoughts. My eyes were nearly swollen shut from crying, but I peeked out from beneath the bed to see Dad's hideous form in the doorway. There in the shadows, he still appeared every bit the towering monster. He'd come to deliver one last verbal blow from the top of his lungs, just the way he always did: "STOP THE CRYING UNLESS YOU WANT SOME MORE!" It was a cold, heartless and impossible command, and I hated him all the more for it.

How was I supposed to stop crying when I was hurting so much? I didn't know, but I didn't want him to come back and hurt me even more. I had to find a way to stop the tears, to stop the shaking, to shove all the terror, all the pain and all the anger back inside me. Stuff it inside and be a good girl, I silently commanded myself. Don't make waves. Don't cause trouble. Don't speak. Don't cry. If I could just be better, if I could just be perfect, maybe he'd love me, maybe he'd quit hurting me.

It was a terrified and desperate little girl's ill-fated and illogical plan to seek her Daddy's approval by being perfect at all costs. This was my plan for survival, my plan for keeping the monster at bay and keeping the little girl safe. My plan just to stay alive.

Belinda Rose

Heavenly Father,
My wounds are deep, but not so deep that
Your divine love can't heal them.
I give You my wounds ... my pain ... my suffering.
I pray that You will restore me.
Lord, make me new again.
Amen.

JESUS, HEAL MY BROKENNESS

There is a place inside of me only You can see,
A place of painful memories that long to be set free.
A place old wounds and bruises long buried now reside.
Each wound a tale of terror for every tear I've cried.
A place that knows the horror of living every day in fear.
A place so dark and forbidding no one dare come near.

I know You were a witness to the abuse I had to bear.
I know You heard my cries and every silent prayer.
I know Your sweet presence was beside me ever near.
Just as it was You, Lord, that wiped away each tear.
Only You can see this place buried deep inside of me.
I'm asking for Your grace to finally set me free.

Jesus, heal my brokenness with Your golden light,
A light that is pure love, so radiant and bright!
May Your love, the healing balm, soothe every wound I bear.
May my broken spirit be restored in Your tender loving care.
May these wounds no longer sting – no longer pierce my heart.
May I find freedom from my past – through grace
a brand new start.

CHAPTER 2

BROKEN

The Lord is near to those who have a broken heart,
and saves those who have a crushed spirit.

Psalm 34:18

*O*t was the beginning of seventh grade, and I was overjoyed to be done with grade school and leave the bullies I'd faced daily behind me. No more chants of "Cooties"or "Four-Eyes". I was hoping junior high would be a fresh start, but the bullies I'd dealt with every day in grade school were nothing compared to the ones I'd soon find myself facing.

The events of my childhood had shaped me into a timid and introverted young girl who lacked any vestige of self-esteem or self-worth. It really didn't matter what the reality was – whether I was in fact ugly or not. What mattered was that I believed I was ugly. I felt ugly, and that belief was evident in my demeanor. This all-pervading sense of insecurity and worthlessness was the ideal set-up for the perfect storm that was soon to break over me.

If you remember the fictional bully Eddie Haskell from the much-loved vintage television show of the '50s and '60s *Leave It to Beaver*, you will also undoubtedly recall that, although irritating, he was relatively harmless as bullies go. Unfortunately, the Eddie that sought me out and bullied me in high school was anything but harmless. His greatest joy was my humiliation, and very soon his greatest joy became my greatest pain. Eddie had all but tattooed the name "Freak" on my forehead for everyone to gawk and laugh at. Freak: a humiliating name bestowed on me because of a deep, dark secret that had always been a source of profound shame.

I had vowed that this secret could never be revealed. No one outside of family would ever know the dark truth about me, because it set me apart from my friends. It made me odd – a misfit, even repulsive, I thought. If my friends knew my secret, I would be teased, ridiculed, humiliated and turned into an outcast. I would never learn to swim, because then I'd expose my secret. I would never wear sandals, for that would also expose my secret. No one would ever know that I had been born with six toes.

Having extra digits runs in Dad's side of the family. He had extra toes on both feet, but they were removed in the military. My brother was born with an extra finger on each hand, which were removed at birth. I had an extra finger on my right hand and an extra toe on my left foot. The finger was removed at birth, but the pediatrician adamantly refused to remove the toe. "It will never harm her," he told my parents. He couldn't have been more wrong.

My secret was safe all through grade school, but when I reached seventh grade everything changed. The rules in junior high were different. Now we had gym class with showers afterwards. My secret would be exposed, and I was petrified. I worried about how I would manage to keep my toe hidden and my deep, dark secret buried. When I asked Mom for advice she said in a matter-of-fact tone, "It's nothing to be ashamed of. Quit worrying so much. It's only a birthmark."

No, Mom. It is so much more than that! You just don't get it, I thought angrily. To my already fragile ego it was so much more, it was something she could never understand. Although my extra toe had always been a source of deep shame to me, even I didn't realize how deep it was until the day my secret was finally revealed.

What had begun as an ordinary afternoon in art class would soon become a living nightmare with me center stage. Mr. Hastings, the seventh grade science teacher, entered the room and approached the desk of my art instructor, Mr. Hathaway. I didn't give it much thought until my art teacher called me to his desk.

"Belinda, Mr. Hastings wants you to go to his classroom with him for a few minutes. Do you mind?" I had no idea what this was about, but I liked Mr. Hastings, and I had no reason to distrust his motives. Good girl that I was, I didn't ask questions. I simply complied.

Following Mr. Hastings into the science class, I stood beside him at the front of the room, as requested. He went to the blackboard and wrote a word across it in large letters with yellow chalk: 'HEXADACTYLY'. *What's that?* I wondered. But the bigger question in my mind was why I was here at all? Moving his chair to one side of the desk, he asked me to sit down.

Speaking to the class he said, "Hexadactyly is the scientific term for having an extra finger or toe."

It was as if the air had been sucked from the room ... as if someone had just punched me hard in the gut ... I couldn't breathe. I was disoriented. Did he just say what I thought he'd said? Then he turned to me and said, "Belinda, I've been told you were born with extra digits. Did you have extra fingers or toes?" He inquired as if he saw no wrong in doing so, as if my feelings counted for nothing.

I'm pretty sure that the blood I felt rushing to my face gave my shame away. I felt as if I was going to pass out. How did he know? How *could* he know? I didn't want to answer him. I wanted to just make a run for the hallway, but I was a good girl. I was an obedient girl, and I wouldn't allow myself the luxury of that kind of rebellious behavior, and so I stammered, "Uh ... I had an extra finger and toe." I hung my head in shame. Then came the most dreaded question of all.

"I understand, Belinda, that you still have the extra toe," Mr. Hastings began. "I wonder if would you mind showing the class?"

What was I going to do now? How was I going to get out of this? Of course I would mind showing my extra toe to the class. I would mind very much. But such words were only thoughts, and I could never have brought myself to actually stand up and say them out loud. I could hear the kids snickering already as I forced the tears back. I wanted to run and hide, but Dad had taught us in not-so-subtle ways to always respect authority, and so reluctantly I did what I believed a good girl was supposed to do – I complied. My hands shaking, I slowly took my left shoe and sock off, fighting back the tears. I was determined I wasn't going to let Mr. Hastings or these snickering kids know how upset I truly was. Mr. Hastings tapped the top of his desk with his hand. "Sit your foot right here," he said.

I didn't think it was possible this day could get any worse, until it did. Mr. Hastings motioned to the class with his hand and said, "Come on up, class!"

Mr. Hastings might just as well have shot me dead, because my life ended in that moment as one by one his entire seventh grade science class walked by his desk to get a better view.

Eddie and several of his friends giggled as they walked by, and Mr. Hastings gave them a stern look of disapproval. As he went further into the scientific discussion of hexadactyly, my mind slowly faded from the room. I was trying desperately not to let anyone know how I was feeling inside. I had become adept at repressing my feelings over the years just to survive, but the overwhelming humiliation and sheer terror I was now experiencing took my breath away. I was crushed. My long-held secret had now been exposed to the world in the worst possible way. I felt like a circus sideshow attraction for the cruelest possible audience – my own classmates.

Mr. Hastings' hand firmly resting on my shoulder brought me back into the room. I was aware he was speaking, but his voice seemed a thousand miles away. "Thank you, Belinda," I heard him say. To this science teacher, I was nothing more than a specimen; a means to show his classroom this genetic anomaly. He, like Mom, saw nothing to be ashamed of in having such a despicable birthmark, but these snickering kids told me that he and Mom were wrong.

I couldn't get my shoe on fast enough. I bolted for the door and straight for the girls' bathroom, where I melted into a pool of tears. I hadn't felt so humiliated and disgraced since Mr. Mike gave me the bottle of 'ugly pills' three years before, and even that wasn't as bad as this. I had just been disgraced in front of an entire classroom of kids I knew! How could I ever face them again? I thought at that moment my life couldn't get any worse, but this day was going further downhill by the second.

From my bathroom sanctuary, I heard the bell ring. Thankfully, it signaled the end of the school day. I just wanted to go home and get as far away from school as I could. I never wanted to go back there again. Hoping to slink out of the building, I made my way to my locker. I didn't get far before I heard Eddie's loud voice ring out through the hall. "Hey, Freak!"

I pretended not to hear. My eyes were swollen from crying, but I didn't want anyone to see, so I faced my locker in an effort to appear busy with my books. Was he speaking to me? From the corner of my eye I saw Eddie walking toward me, and he had that nasty smirk he wore so well on his smug face. As he got closer and passed by with his little band of buddies his voice echoed in my ears, assuring me his cruel words were indeed meant for me. "Hey Freak! I'm talking to *you.*"

I kept thinking about what Mom had always told me when my big brother teased me to tears: "Don't let him know he's bothering you." But that never worked at home, and it wasn't going to work here either. Still facing my open locker, I entertained the idea of just crawling inside until he was gone. Since I couldn't do that, I just kept ignoring him and his hateful words. I continued shuffling my books in and out of the locker, my guts churning and my heart breaking. I forced back the next round of hot tears. I couldn't believe what I was hearing; Eddie had now branded me as a freak.

A tap on the shoulder startled me, shifting my attention. "Ready to go home?" It was my best friend Valerie, ready to make the walk home. She was unaware that my entire world had just come crashing down around me. As I turned to face her, my eyes still filled with tears, her jaw dropped. The first words out of her mouth were, "What's wrong?" But I couldn't tell her. I didn't want to tell her, not even Valerie whom I'd been so close to since first grade. I was too embarrassed. I was too numb. But not telling her wouldn't be an option. Eddie would make sure of that, because as luck would have it, he walked the same path to school that Valerie and I did every day.

Although there were days we never crossed paths, tonight he'd made an effort to wait around for us. What I remember most about the walk home that afternoon was Eddie's big mouth taunting me all the way. "Freak," he'd roar and then he and his friends would laugh hysterically. They were having the time of their lives.

Valerie wasn't going to put up with any of Eddie's foul comments, so she suggested we take a detour through a park close to our respective homes, a path Eddie wouldn't be on. There we sat on the swings together, the same ones we had so often played on as little girls a few short years before. I had no choice but to tell her everything. I made her swear to tell no one else – not that it mattered, because the entire seventh grade class would know soon enough. Her reaction was typical of the great friend she'd always been. It was not one of horror or repulsion, but one of compassion toward me, and red-hot anger towards Mr. Hastings and Eddie. I knew she wouldn't speak a word to another soul. I could trust her. I always had. It was never the case that I didn't trust her with this particular secret, it was just that it humiliated me so deeply that I couldn't even face it myself. I didn't want anyone to know, not ever. In the days, weeks and months ahead, Valerie would prove many times over what an incredible and trustworthy friend she was, for not only would she keep our conversation that day to herself, but she would do her best to defend me from Eddie and his vicious, hateful bullying every chance she got.

So it began. I was now officially branded as the school Freak. The minutes between classes, lunchtime and that walk home from school became moments of terror and dread. My big, deep, dark secret was a secret no more and it had turned out even worse than I ever could have imagined. I didn't know how I could possibly keep facing the kids at school. As far as I was concerned, my life had ended. I wanted to quit school. I wanted to die, and while suicide *per se* didn't cross my mind, somewhere beneath the surface, deep in my psyche, a sinister means of achieving exactly the same result was brewing. Perhaps it was an unconscious death wish, but it was a death wish just the same, because I was about to slip and tumble down ... down ... down ... just like Alice in Wonderland into a 'very deep well', a rabbit-hole where only darkness and suffering waited.

My spirit was broken. The old childhood nursery rhyme *Humpty Dumpty* I had chanted so often as a little kid kept reverberating in my mind:

> *Humpty Dumpty sat on a wall,*
> *Humpty Dumpty had a great fall;*
> *All the king's horses and all the king's men*
> *Couldn't put Humpty together again.*

That was exactly how I felt, and I didn't know how to fix this unshakable sense of brokenness any more than I knew who could help me put the pieces of my shattered spirit back together again. What was I going to do?

I had attempted over the years to devise ways of coping with the abuse at home and the bullying at school by losing myself in music, writing, imagination, prayer, my circle of close friends and even my schoolwork. But I was only fooling myself if I thought that such strategies were anything more than an avoidance of the deep psychological issues that lurked beneath the surface. This latest debacle was too much. I couldn't deal with it. I couldn't cope. I didn't know what having a nervous breakdown was, or if kids my age had such things, but I felt sure I was nearing some sort of point of no return.

My usual coping strategies simply weren't cutting it. I found my thoughts scattered, my nerves shattered and my stomach hurting most of the time. There had been many times I'd felt myself emotionally teetering on the edge of a cliff. Now my seventh grade science teacher and a big-mouthed bully had pushed me over that edge. I had landed hard at the bottom of that emotional cliff, my spirit crushed. The pain of the humiliation I bore at school every day was unbearable. I felt an unlikely kinship with Hester Prynne, the ill-fated heroine of *The Scarlet Letter*. While I had committed no sin and wouldn't be forced to wear a scarlet 'A' across my chest, my badge of shame was just as humiliating; a scarlet 'F' for FREAK engraved on my soul.

Other than Valerie, I didn't speak to anyone about the nightmare that had unfolded in Mr. Hastings' science class that day. I didn't run home and tell Mom. What would have been the point? When I'd told her about Mr. Mike a few short years ago, she had said and done nothing. She never did have a word with him. She didn't even have a talk with Dad. As always she just stayed silent and pretended nothing was the matter. No one was going to rescue me. As usual I was left to deal with my problems alone. Only this time I couldn't.

I still had a deep relationship with Jesus, at least that

hadn't changed. I had cried buckets of tears as His imaginary arms held me close. I confided in Him that I just wanted to die and that I couldn't live with this pain and humiliation. Despite the comfort my childhood friendship with Him had always provided, I needed something more at this moment. I needed a living, breathing human being to hold me, comfort me, and most of all guide me through this dark period, but there was no one like that in my life. I didn't want to cause trouble at home for fear I'd anger Dad and the beast would emerge once again. So I stayed quiet and suffered in silence.

It wasn't long before that silence sought a means of expression. I was a young girl literally dying from the inside out. The fear and abuse I'd lived with since I'd been a small child, coupled with the humiliation I'd experienced at the hands of a few cruel and heartless individuals, had broken me at last. Psychologically, I didn't understand anything that was happening to me. I was still just a child and I didn't know how to cope, so my psyche, unbeknownst to me, began creating an outlet for my pain, a new inner critic that wouldn't be silenced. It would become a loud, strong and almost demonic voice that loathed everything about me. *"You ugly fat FREAK!"* it roared inside my head.

I agreed whole-heartedly with the Voice. I was 5'6" tall and weighed 112 pounds. I had begun to see myself as fat, an idea first implanted by a casual remark a classmate made in sixth grade.

We had been to the school nurse that morning to get our annual height and weight taken down for the school record. The teacher had sent us in pairs. I went with my friend Susie. Just over four feet tall, Susie was the tiniest girl in the class. I, on the other hand, had the dubious distinction of being the tallest. On the way back to class from the weigh-in, Susie remarked, "Gee, you weigh 112 pounds. You're big!"

Big? What did she mean by big? Did big mean fat? Was she insinuating I was fat? That is what I *heard*. In retrospect, I suppose compared to her petite sixty-five pounds I was pretty big by her standards. I was nearly double her weight and far taller than her. But that wasn't what my twelve-year-old brain was thinking at the time. It had been a silly, childish remark, but it stuck in my head. I couldn't forget it no matter how hard I tried, because it had for the first time in my life made me *feel* fat.

Now, a year later, I still couldn't get that stupid remark out of my head. Only now, instead of being something that came to mind every so often, it was there all the time. The Voice had picked up on it and it ran through my head as a tormenting echo that cried, *"You weigh 112 pounds! You fat slob! Just look at that fat stomach! You're disgusting!"* Yes, I agreed, the stomach had to go. I thought of my friend Valerie, and her flat, concave stomach. I wanted one just like hers. Perhaps then I'd be as popular as she was.

I knew that dieting in order to achieve a new svelte body wouldn't be easy. Not in our home, anyway, where every meal was large and you were expected to eat every bite on your plate. Nevertheless, I was determined. The next morning at breakfast the diet began. It was a defining moment in my life, one that would set me upon the slow road to self-annihilation.

It began with a pop tart.

Breakfast was always a big meal in our home, and it was the first meal that had to go. There would be no more waffles slathered with butter and grape jelly, no more bowls of cream of wheat swimming in extra cream. To Mom, these were the breakfasts of champions. I knew she wouldn't let me skip her usual robust breakfasts easily, so I'd have to be a wee bit cunning and come up with a plan.

Fortunately that plan fell right into my lap, and I didn't

have to make something up, because the stomach pain I'd been experiencing recently gave me all the excuse I needed. I honestly didn't feel like eating such big meals most days, so that morning, I told Mom I didn't feel like eating breakfast because my stomach hurt. Of course she insisted I eat 'something', and my 'something' became a brown sugar cinnamon pop tart and a glass of milk.

At first I ate the entire pop tart and didn't give it much thought. Just avoiding Mom's king-sized breakfasts each morning seemed like a hard-won victory. But as the weeks went on I began whittling that pop tart down until I was taking only one or two bites of it. I folded the rest into a napkin and hid it in my purse when Mom was busy elsewhere in the house. It was a much-appreciated daily treat for Duke, the neighbor's dog that Valerie and I passed every day on the way to school. No one was any the wiser except the dog, and he wasn't going to say anything!

Lunch at school was easy to avoid if I chose to, but I was new at this dieting thing, and I was honestly hungry by lunch. So, rather than skip it altogether, I elected to eat a lighter lunch than normal. Besides, I didn't want my girlfriends questioning my new eating habits.

Supper was the meal that proved the biggest challenge of all. We always had big dinners and we were again expected to finish everything on our plates. I tried taking smaller portions but Dad noticed, insisting I finish what was on my plate. So I took larger portions of less fattening items such as vegetables and smaller ones of meat and potatoes. Desserts were forbidden.

My weight began dropping quickly, and within a couple months I was down to ninety-nine pounds. I was happier with my new thinner image. The curves I'd once had and had come to see as fat were all but gone now. But when I looked in the mirror, the Voice would make itself known, berating me for still being too fat, eating too much, exercising too little, and not yet being perfect. No matter how many sizes I dropped or how flat my stomach may have appeared to others, all I saw was a bulge – a protrusion that needed to go, no matter what I had to do to make it happen. Being 'fat' was now worse than having an extra toe. More disgusting! More vile! More hideous! There had to be something more I could do. Exercise was the answer.

I began riding my bike more. On those occasions when Mom and Dad left to run errands I ran laps around the backyard until I was exhausted. This newest strategy proved effective, giving me wonderful results in no time at all. Soon, I was down to ninety-two pounds.

No one really seemed to notice my weight loss, or if they did no one said anything. My grades were still high enough to keep me on the honor roll, and that kept my dad contented and thinking everything was fine. Mom had become accustomed to my new eating habits, or at least she didn't complain about them, which was all that mattered to me. I thought my new dieting plan was going swimmingly. But what I didn't realize was that the better the dieting went, the more I was losing something much more precious than another pound: I was losing every part of me that mattered. I had unknowingly entered into a competition with myself, a competition where winning it all meant losing it all – and that my life was the ultimate stake.

I turned fifteen in December of my ninth grade year. It had been two years since the mortifying experience in Mr. Hastings' science class that had set my life onto this dark path of self-destruction. That path I was now walking had not only changed my eating behavior, it had also affected my personality. I had gone from being just a quiet kid to being a recluse. I'd always preferred one or two close friends to a group, but now I chose solitude over any friends outside of school at all. I refused their offers to hang out, because hanging out often meant eating, and by this time I was avoiding food at all costs, even if it meant losing my friends. I just wanted to be alone.

Even without my friends outside of school, I still had plenty of things to keep me busy at home, because I had a lot of responsibilities there. I helped Mom with the housework, and more so with cooking the meals. She was working full-time again and when I came home from school it was my job to prepare the evening dinner.

Mom was a fabulous cook, and she must have taught me well because Dad was in awe of how I could cook "just like her". It was a sure-fire way to get his approval, and it always worked like a charm. So I took great care to prepare every meal to his liking, complete with pies, cakes and fancy pudding dishes for dessert. I loved cooking and baking for my family. I loved feeding them. I just didn't eat any of it myself. In fact, cooking and baking became new obsessions right alongside my dieting.

When I wasn't helping out around the house, I spent most of my free time alone in my bedroom playing records, reading, writing, studying or exercising to the point of exhaustion. No one seemed to notice that my behavior had changed and that I'd become reclusive, preferring isolation to anything else. No one seemed to notice that my eating habits had changed either, or that I now weighed only ninety pounds, or that I had sunk into a deep depression. Maybe no one cared. Maybe everyone just wanted the status quo maintained and conflict avoided so desperately that they were just pretending I was fine. I could be okay with that too, if it meant being left alone. The fact that no one was paying attention gave me more freedom and more control to do the things I wanted to do without interference, like read up on the latest dieting fads or memorize caloric values I'd found in nutrition books from the library or the bookmobile. I had committed to memory the calories contained in every food imaginable, but I didn't stop there. I knew the calories expended by a half hour of bike riding, an hour of calisthenics, fifteen minutes of jumping rope or a dozen other such activities. I also loved cookbooks. Even though I didn't eat, I still loved poring over Mom's old cookbooks in an effort to uncover new and tasty dishes to create for my family. Food became my preoccupation in every conceivable way, and that preoccupation didn't end when I closed my eyes to go to sleep at night. I dreamed of food; it occupied every waking and sleeping moment.

I'd dream of sitting at the head of an enormous banquet table, tempted by every food imaginable. In some of these dreams I stuffed myself like the victim of starvation I had become, only to awaken drenched in sweat with a sigh of relief that it had just been a dream. At other times I sat in proud defiance at the head of that table as the tantalizing aromas of some of my favorite foods wafted past my nose. I took great satisfaction in the face of such temptation, for now I could prove my unyielding self-control by getting up and walking away from the table. But no matter how in control I felt in these dreams, they too felt like nightmares.

'Nightmare' was the best way to describe my life. The nightmare that was my dad was still as real and vivid as it had ever been, but in keeping myself locked away in my room or doing chores I found a way that kept me from becoming the target of Dad's fury for the most part. He would still morph into monster mode from time to time, but I was fifteen now, and no longer did I find myself dangling from his powerful grip when his rage erupted. Being older had its advantages. But just because the whippings had stopped didn't mean his violent anger and rage ever did, and the fear I felt in his presence that had been ingrained deep in my psyche as a young child had never dissipated. Dad still dominated everyone, holding all the power in our home with his icy stares and un-controllable outbursts. Trying to always please him and lying low in my bedroom as far away from him as possible seemed to be the ticket for staying out of harm's way. My system worked well until my health began to deteriorate.

My stomach had been hurting on and off for the past couple of years, but now it hurt constantly, and it wasn't just pangs of hunger. The discomfort became so severe that Mom decided I needed to see the doctor. The tests he ordered to determine the problem revealed a stomach ulcer. But it wasn't the stomach ulcer he was most concerned about, it was my mental and emotional health.

After he had given us the results, he asked Mom and me to come into his office to talk further. Looking my mom straight in the eye, he said firmly, "Get her some psychological help now or you are risking her becoming a psychological cripple."

If he had recognized I was in the early stages of anorexia nervosa, he didn't say as much. Such a diagnosis was never made. It was the early 1970s and anorexia was not a wide-ly-known or accepted illness. But the stomach ulcer and the dramatic weight loss had given him a clue that something was terribly wrong in my world. Someone at last was paying attention.

Mom said little in response. It was a typical response on her part. Instead she looked at me with an expression that seemed to question what it was he meant. I stayed silent. The doctor's warning went unheeded, and instead became a prophecy.

Instead of us discussing what the trouble might be, we went quietly home with not a word said. She went back to pretending all was well, while I retreated to the safety and iso-lation of my bedroom. Tucked away in my self-imposed iso-lation I thought I was protected, safe from the monster in the house and the monsters at school. But I wasn't safe from the monsters at all, for there was an even more threatening monster inside me that was growing stronger and more powerful with each passing day. My bedroom sanctuary was only giving the eating disorder and depression an opportunity to thrive, drawing me deeper into the illusion that I at long last had at least some degree of control over one small aspect of my life. Here, undisturbed, the Voice was given free rein to take total control of me – and I didn't even hear it coming.

The end of freshman year in junior high meant big changes all around. No longer would I have to walk to school and endure the tormenting chants of "Freak" from Eddie and his gang, because sophomore year meant a bus ride to a new high school. I should have been excited about the new adventure that was about to unfold, but I wasn't. Yes, I was glad to be rid of Eddie on the walk home each afternoon, and I was hopeful that because high school was so much larger I might even get really lucky and avoid his big mouth altogether. But I was a recluse now, and I found the thought of meeting new kids and socializing awkward and uncomfortable. I didn't fit in, no matter how hard I tried. That realization became more acute as the new school year began and I watched my girlfriends each with their new boyfriends – something I wished I had. But boys weren't for me. They didn't look at me. I wasn't *that* girl, no matter how much weight I lost or how perfect I tried to be, and the more that realization set in the more painful school became.

I still saw Valerie at school and on the bus ride to and from it, but she had a steady boyfriend now, and it changed everything in our relationship because she spent all her free time with him. It was clear that she was growing up while my own growth was stunted in comparison. Locked inside a prison of my own creation there was no room for growth, at least not the normal healthy growth one would expect of a young teen-age girl.

I made a handful of new friends in my classes that year, but none would become as dear to me as Pamela, a big-hearted redhead who sat beside me in Music Appreciation. Pam was funny and easy to talk to. But even the close bond that she and I formed and having her to hang with at school didn't take the sting out of getting onto that bus and facing that school full of kids amongst whom I felt so out of place. My deep sense of not being good enough and never fitting in made school intolerable.

I rarely saw Eddie at school now, but it didn't matter. The past three years of daily bullying had already done its dam-age, convincing me that I was an ugly, hideous freak that no one could ever love. So it didn't matter if I never saw Eddie again in my lifetime, I wore the stigma of being a freak re-gardless. Such deep feelings of inferiority and low self-esteem prompted almost daily arguments with Mom over getting on the school bus each morning. I won a lot of those arguments and stayed home, taking my absenteeism off the charts. But my parents couldn't complain too much, because my grades still placed me on the honor roll each semester. But it wasn't only my emotional state that kept me from getting on that bus each morning, it was the state of my physical health too, which was beginning to deteriorate at an alarming rate. This time it wasn't just my stomach giving me problems, it was something much more dangerous – my kidneys.

I began to have severe kidney and bladder infections. Some days the pain and burning were so intense that I could hardly stand it. Mom knew I was having problems, but she didn't offer to take me back to the doctor. Perhaps she didn't want to face him and the threat of another scolding. He might ask her if she'd gotten some psychological help for me. Was she going to embarrass herself by admitting she hadn't? Perhaps she didn't realize how severe the pain was or how ill her emaciated ninety-pound daughter had become. Maybe she thought that if I felt so poorly I'd be begging to go see him myself. Little did she know that Dr. Freeman's office was the last place I wanted to visit. He was the one who had been paying attention, after all, he was the one who could find me out, and I was content to be left alone. But my days of obscurity were coming to an abrupt end.

By the end of my sophomore year my repugnance for high school had become so great that I'd sought out and found a method to end the torture sooner rather than later. With the help of my guidance counselor, I discovered a way to graduate early. He told me all I would need to do was take a couple of correspondence course classes from a local university over the summer break. Doing this would give me the credits I needed to completely eliminate my senior year and graduate at the end of junior year instead. I was over the moon that such an option was available to end my misery. But as much as I hated high school, I still dreamt of going to that local university to become a doctor – and not just any type of doctor, but a psychiatrist. It seemed so ironic that the girl with all the problems was the one the other girls came to for advice. They always said I acted so much older than they were and so much more mature. I seemed to be pretty good at helping others with their troubles. How unfortunate I couldn't help myself with my own.

My dream of college was really nothing more than wishful thinking, and my rapidly deteriorating health would soon shatter any expectations I might have had. I'd been living on 200-400 calories a day for nearly five years, and my starvation diet was taking its toll. I was cold nearly all of the time. In an attempt to protect itself and stay warm my body had grown a fine, thin hair known as lanugo. I felt faint, dizzy, and tired most of the time, but that was the least of my problems. The issues I had been having with my kidneys accelerated. I began passing blood – lots of it. Fear finally drove Mom to make that inevitable call to the doctor for the chronic infections I'd had for the past two years.

Dr. Freeman didn't waste any time in calling in a specialist. The day after I saw him, I found myself sitting in the office of a nephrologist having tests, and the day after that I was in the hospital. The nephrologist was very concerned, so he ordered an entire battery of tests. It was determined that I had interstitial nephritis, and then the nephrologist repeated the ominous warning that Dr. Freeman had given my mom a few short years before.

"Your daughter's weight is extremely low, as is her blood pressure," the nephrologist began. "She isn't just malnourished, but dehydrated, which I believe is the major component of her current kidney dysfunction. My deeper concern beyond the issue with her kidneys is the underlying cause of why she is dehydrated in the first place. Have you considered getting her some psychological help before she becomes psychologically crippled?"

There it was again, that same dire warning. There was no diagnosis of anorexia nervosa yet, just a doctor's recommendation that I needed psychological help or my parents risked my becoming a 'psychological cripple'. What exactly that meant I wasn't sure, but this time the warning had been given to both Mom and Dad, and that changed the outcome dramatically. Dad listened, and he heeded the warning. The search for a psychologist began in earnest.

After a short hospital stay I was released, but because my health was so fragile by that point, the doctors wouldn't release me to go back to school for finals week. As luck would have it, my grades had been so good throughout the year that my teachers decided to allow me to skip final exams alto-gether. They graciously averaged my grades and let me follow through with early graduation in the spring of my junior year. I was elated. Finally, I was OUT! The misery was over once and for all. No more school!

I spent most of that summer after graduation under the scru-tiny of my dad, which I found unbearable. Thankfully, he spent long hours at work and our only family meal was dinner. Much to my dismay, he paid careful attention to what was on my plate – and, worse than that, how much of it was eaten. The Voice wasn't happy with the situation either. *"Are you going to let him ruin it all? Are you going to let him make you even fatter? Do you want to be that cow with that disgusting fat stomach?"*

No, I didn't. So I took small portions and ate slowly in an attempt to eat as little as possible and stretch supper out until he left the table. Then I could discard what was left on my plate in the trash when I cleaned up the kitchen. After the kitchen cleanup, I took long walks to burn calories. When the lights went out at night and I was sure my parents were asleep, I'd quietly get up and do hundreds of sit-ups or jumping jacks in the privacy of my bedroom just to be sure that the evening meal hadn't added a new and unwanted pound of flesh. No one was any the wiser.

But Dad wasn't just focused on what I was eating at this point. Summer was drawing to a close, and he wanted me to do something with my life – like go back to school. Brighton Business College was his school choice. They served up two-and four-year degrees in Fashion Management, Retail, Tour-ism, Interior Design and the Public Relations industry. It was no secret in our home that I had long been a fashion addict.

Mom and I loved to shop and I had a closet jam-packed with clothes to prove it. So when Dad mentioned sending me to Brighton to get a degree in Fashion I was over the moon.

My parents and I made the trip to the city to meet the college director, Mrs. Clay, the following Saturday. It was a relatively small school located on the upper floor of one of the city's loveliest high-rise buildings. Mrs. Clay was cordial. She took us on a grand tour of the school and patiently answered all of our questions. By the time we left three hours later, I was enrolled and majoring in Fashion Management and Retail. School would begin the day after Labor Day, which was just three weeks away. But going back to school wasn't the only thing Dad wanted me to do – he also insisted I begin seeing a psychologist.

Dr. Freeman was finally asked for that recommendation that he'd wanted to give Mom all those years before. That fateful first appointment was made with a young psychologist in his building for the following week.

Dr. Tully was a tall, handsome dark-haired man in his early to mid-thirties. He had not yet received his Ph.D. in psychology, and was working as an intern under the head psychologist, Dr. Bingham. He was friendly enough – charming actually. But I wasn't talking – at least not about all the things that needed to be talked about, like the abuse, the bullies and the Voice that was driving my incessant dieting.

I felt awkward and uncomfortable in the presence of this attractive man – doctor or not. Besides, I wasn't used to opening up about my problems with anyone, and I wasn't about to give up my secrets. So what was I supposed to say to this stranger sitting across from me? I certainly couldn't tell him our family secrets, all about Dad the monster or the fear I lived in. Dad might find out and that would be certain disaster. I wasn't about to share with him how fat and ugly I felt or how skinny I longed to be. So why was I here?

The first few sessions were hard to get through. Dr. Tully would ask questions and I'd evade them with small talk. I was determined that he wasn't getting into my head or my life, and because I was being so stubborn he seemed to be struggling to understand what was going on with me or how to make a diagnosis for my parents.

Then, as fate would have it, I was flipping through a teen magazine at home one afternoon when I stumbled on an article about young women with a rare illness called anorexia nervosa. The article spoke about several girls – each in different parts of the country – who had an extreme fear of being fat. Chills went down my spine as I read how they too starved themselves and exercised to an extreme in the relentless pursuit of thinness. I couldn't believe what I was reading. *This article was talking about me!* Every word rang true. I could feel my heart pounding inside my chest as the realization hit me that I'd just made my own diagnosis. I had anorexia nervosa!

I was anxious and excited to speak to Dr. Tully about my discovery at my next session with him. I thrust the open magazine onto his desk and said, "Read this! This is about me. This is what I have."

Intrigued, he picked the magazine up, read every word, and then looked across the desk at me and said, "Can I keep this? I want to confer with Dr. Bingham."

"Sure. But what do you think? Those girls do what I do. They think what I think. That article is speaking about me."

"I don't know, Belinda. You may be onto something. That's why I need to speak to Dr. Bingham before I say anything more."

But I knew he knew I had hit the nail smack dab on the head. As if I'd opened Pandora's box, Dr. Tully now began asking me all kinds of questions about my eating habits and my weight.

"How much do you weigh now, Belinda?"

"I don't know ... somewhere around ninety pounds, I guess." I wanted to avoid the subject. The Voice, in total agreement with me, sounded off in my head with, *"That's none of his business. Keep your mouth shut!"*

"Tell me about your eating habits. What do you eat in a normal day?" he said.

"I don't know. Fruits ... vegetables," I said, squirming in my chair, wanting desperately to avoid this entire line of questioning.

"Do you exercise?" Dr. Tully continued, in what to me was becoming more like an invasive interrogation.

"Sure, I walk a lot." That was all he was getting. Those forty-five minutes seemed like the longest forty-five minutes of my life. I watched the timer on his desk tick away the seconds, each seeming longer than the last. Finally the timer chimed, signaling my freedom. I jumped up from my chair, thrilled that the grand inquisition had ended, at least until next week.

But the week flew by, and once again I found myself in the hot seat. Last week's interrogation had surely held me over the fire, and I'd certainly felt the heat, but this week's session would all but throw me into the pit itself.

On his desk were the teen magazine and an apple. On the floor beside his couch was a typical bathroom scale.

"Belinda," he began, "I spoke to Dr. Bingham, and he concurs that what you have is definitely anorexia nervosa. So, I'd like to try something new this week. I'd like our weekly sessions to begin with a weigh-in so I can keep track of your weight."

Terrified, the nagging shrill Voice in my head angrily protested. *"No! Don't let him do it! Don't let him know what you weigh. Tell him right now that you're not doing this. All he wants to do is make you eat ... he wants to make you fat."*

"I can't," I said sheepishly, looking down at the floor.

"Why can't you?" Dr. Tully said.

"I don't know. I just can't." I knew he was looking straight at me, but I couldn't look him in the eye.

He didn't push me. Amazingly, he just let it go. But even more terrifying were the next words out of his mouth.

"You said you like fruit and vegetables, and you're clearly quite thin, so I brought you an apple," he said.

I felt a bit like Eve being offered the apple by the serpent in the Garden. I could be stronger than she was, though. I could say no. Did he think he could tempt me with that gorgeous smile?

I didn't respond. I uttered not one word. I just sat there motionless, my stick-thin frame all but swallowed up in Dr. Tully's big cushy black leather chair. For the remainder of the session, and many of our subsequent ones, this was how we spent much of our time together. We sat in silence, a silence that made confrontation all the more uncomfortable. All eye contact with that shiny, red apple on his desk was avoided as if it were a dead maggot-infested rodent he was asking me to eat. Dr. Tully could quit asking, because my answer wasn't changing. I wasn't getting on his scale and I wasn't eating the forbidden fruit. Not now ... not ever!

Heavenly Father,
I give You my brokenness.
Restore me.
Make me anew according to Thy divine and perfect will.
Amen.

CHAPTER 3

A SINKING SHIP

Blessed are they that mourn: for they shall be comforted.

Matthew 5:4

> *My soul is as a tiny ship lost on a stormy sea;*
> *Fierce winds moan and howl to threaten me.*
> *Raging waters spill over every side*
> *The night's darkness leaves no light to guide.*
> *My sail's torn and battered as my little ship's tossed;*
> *Amid this growing tempest I now find myself lost.*
> *All alone and abandoned, oh, how frightened am I!*
> *I fall to my knees. "Dear Lord, save me!" I cry.*
> *"Why did You leave me?" my troubled soul pleads.*
> *"Have mercy O Lord, for my wounded heart bleeds!"*

By mid-September I had settled into college and had even made some new friends. I enjoyed my classes, although I found it hard to concentrate. No matter how hard I tried to divert my attention away from the eating disorder, the Voice was always there in the background. When the other girls went out for lunch every day, I tagged along but never ate. Instead, I always came up with some excuse as to why I couldn't. Some of them praised me for my thinness. Others said they wished they had my willpower and self-control. Hearing these things made me feel all the more in control of my utterly out-of-control life. But it was the comments of my new friend Cindy that would send me in a new, and unexpected, direction.

"You need to try out for the Fashion Board, Belinda. You're so tall and skinny. You already have that model look going on!" Cindy said.

"What's the Fashion Board?" I asked.

"It's a modeling tryout. The girls that are chosen will be models that represent the college at area department stores and publicity events. You'd be perfect!"

I loved the idea ... but me, modeling? I was never *that* girl – the pretty or popular one – although I was intrigued by the whole idea. Cindy wouldn't let it die, continually encouraging me over the next week to go to tryouts. She was so confident I was a shoo-in that she came along with me to the tryouts.

The all-girl college had roughly two hundred students, and about half of them were there to try out for Fashion Board. Only five would be chosen. Tryouts consisted of simply walking a runway that had been set up in the school auditorium, where we were judged by a panel of three teachers and the director, Mrs. Clay.

Two days later, Cindy grabbed me enthusiastically by the arm, dragging me all the way to the student lounge where the results were posted. She pointed her finger to my name – second on the list. "Belinda! You made it! You were picked! See, I told you so! I told you you'd be perfect!" she said, hugging me.

I stood there, transfixed, staring at my name. It *had* to be a mistake! I was not the pretty girl. I was never the model type. How had this happened? How was it even possible?

"Say something!" Cindy said.

"I don't know what to say. I can't believe it."

That evening, after the initial shock had worn off, I eagerly told my parents that I'd been chosen to be a model for the school's Fashion Board. Dad was especially proud of my achievement. If I'd wanted his approval, this certainly hit the spot. Dad's glowing face confirmed one thing for me, anyway – I had finally done something to make him proud, and that felt really good. I didn't want to let him down now. I had to excel at this new opportunity, and to do that I had the Voice to guide the way.

"You're a model now. Models are skinny. You need to lose a few more pounds and be the best – look the best you can. Don't mess this up!" the Voice said.

"I won't! Just show me what I need to do," I replied. This amazing achievement had only given the Voice even more clout in my mind. The Voice was right, models were indeed skinny, and with its help I would achieve perfection.

In spite of Dr. Tully's subtle coercion tactics to eat or step on the scale, I had grown rather fond of him. I didn't see him backing off with trying to persuade me anytime soon, any more than I would back off in standing my ground and saying, "No!" But he was winning me over with his gentle and kind persona, and to top it off he acted as though he genuinely cared about my well-being. That was something I wasn't used to, especially from males. Even though I couldn't open up about my life and my newly diagnosed eating disorder, I felt as if I was in friendly territory – as if I was safe with him.

In November of my eighteenth year, Dad's mom, my beloved Grandma Ruby, passed away suddenly. She had been one of the most important people in my life. Every Sunday afternoon after dinner for as long as I can remember we had visited her. In my mind's eye, I could still see her standing at the front door of her small brick bungalow, arms open wide, ready to swallow me up in one of her warm and wonderful hugs. In my imagination, I could still place myself in that hug, and hear her say "I love you." But such warm and fuzzy memories weren't going to help my aching heart at that moment – they only served to make it ache all the more. Devastated wasn't a strong enough word to describe my emotional state. I treasured both my grandmothers. They were among the few people in my life who made me feel loved, and now I had lost one of those treasures. I had never experienced the death of a loved one so close to me before. I was lost as to how to deal with the grief that now consumed me.

But I wasn't the only one consumed with grief; Dad was, too. It was the first time I had actually seen him cry. It seemed odd to witness the monster tamed in this way. All vestiges of his hard, abusive side had disappeared, leaving a sad middle-aged man that I no longer recognized. This man was weeping as if his heart was broken ... as if he'd known how to love all along. Who was this stranger? I felt so sorry for him that all I wanted to do was run and put my arms around him. But I didn't dare. I was too afraid. So was my mom, and so, he cried in the dark alone.

We weren't the only ones who loved Grandma Ruby. Her funeral brought out a steady stream of people who had loved her as well, and who wanted to pay their final respects. She had attended a strict Charismatic church for years, and although she didn't practice everything they preached, the congregation didn't seem to love or respect her any the less. Instead, they packed the funeral home to honor and remember this amazing woman who had touched all of their lives in ways I hadn't been aware of.

It was at her funeral that I met a young man who introduced himself as David. He knew Grams from church and had a personal story about her of his own to share with me. Caught up by his charm and the humor of his story, I momentarily forgot my grief. I was grateful for the diversion and genuinely touched that he'd taken the time to stop and share his personal memories with me.

I went through the next few days and weeks with my heart shattered and with a deep longing to feel myself in the midst of one of Grandma's warm and loving hugs. If only I could have had just one more hug to say goodbye; if only I could have one more chance to tell her how much she had meant to me. I had never told her that. Did she know? I cried until no more tears would come.

At last, I had something I could open up to Dr. Tully about besides school. It was the first time I'd openly shared my feelings with him about anything, and it felt good to express my grief in this way. But no matter how much I cried and no matter how much he counseled or consoled me, my heart continued to ache. I just wanted to be near her, and that need prompted me to make a life-altering decision to begin attending her church. I didn't make this decision with the intention of taking an active role in this other church, because I was still very much a Catholic. I just wanted to feel closer to my beloved grandma. I thought this gesture would make her happy if she was watching from her new heavenly home, and that being near the people who had adored her so much would make me feel closer to her as well.

At the end of the first Saturday evening service I attended, David was waiting in the church vestibule to greet me. Our conversation was easy, and it was only a matter of minutes before he invited me to go out to eat with him and a few of the other young people from church. While eating wasn't on my agenda, I was attracted to him and I didn't want to say no to his invitation. He came off as friendly and easy to talk to. In my mixed-up state, and in my need to be close to someone who had known Grandma Ruby, I hung on his every word. I wanted to get to know him better, so I fibbed and told him I'd already eaten, but that I'd enjoy the company and the chance to meet some of the other young members of the congregation.

But the David I met that night in the church vestibule wasn't who he appeared to be. He was, as they say, "too good to be true". Underneath that smooth and charming demeanor was a cold and heartless predator lying in wait, and I would be his prey.

David was the only son of one of the most respected families in the congregation, and he appeared to be every young girl's dream. At nineteen, he was good-looking, funny and charming, and he had a smile to die for. I attributed his strong and muscular physique to the years of martial arts training he talked so much about. In fact, he seemed quite proud of the fact that he had a black belt in karate. And if all this wasn't enough to make a teenage girl's head spin, he drove the most gorgeous red convertible! He could have had any girl he wanted, so why choose me?

At first, our dates consisted of socializing before and after church with a small group of kids there. But it wasn't long before we became inseparable. Our budding friendship blossomed quickly, and it seemed no time at all until we "officially" became boyfriend and girlfriend. I thought I'd found love at long last, and I felt as if I was walking on air.

It was summer vacation, and my first year of college was behind me. David and I could now spend every free moment together. He said he loved me; he spoke about our getting married in a few years; my desperate-for-love inner child soaked up every last scrap of the attention he offered. I was too inexperienced to see through his charming lies, and that his protestations of love were merely the cries of a predator to his unsuspecting victim. Soon this young man that I believed to be "the one" would begin revealing himself. Hidden beneath that captivating, well-dressed exterior was a troubled young man who was much darker, colder and more violent than I had ever dreamt possible. He was a devil in disguise.

In my naïveté, I thought expressing love for a boy meant merely displaying affection. I didn't grasp that anything more would be asked of me. Because I had been starved all my life of affection, I ate up the hugs, kisses and hand-holding. I loved having his arm around my shoulder during church services. I didn't figure into the equation that having a relationship with a boy – especially a Christian boy – would mean sexual pressures, and it was something I was totally unprepared for. I was still a virgin, and my virginity was something I clung to and considered precious. The deep devotion I'd had for Jesus all my life coincided with a deep desire to remain pure and chaste until I married. I held on to this belief fiercely and no one was going to talk me out of it – not even David, this young man I thought I was so head-over-heels in love with. In my heart, pleasing God still came first.

So, when David initially began making moves on me in his car, I wasn't quite sure how to react. This was foreign territory. I was shy and intimidated by anything even remotely sexual. Other than Mom kissing Dad when he came home from work at night, I had never seen so much as a hint of anything sexual between them. The word "sex" was never spoken in our home. The only time Mom and I had ever had a conversation about sex was when I was in fifth grade and I'd pulled her into the privacy of our tiny bathroom to ask her if what I'd heard that day at school was true. My girlfriend Nancy had told me in the playground that she knew how "It" was done. I shared with Mom every detail Nancy had shared with me. I studied Mom's face in the bathroom mirror as she pulled the comb through her soft brown curls, looking for some sort of reaction before I popped the question, "Is she right, Mom?"

Expressionless, Mom replied, "Yes, sweetheart, she is."

That had been the end of the conversation: there was no explanation, nothing more was added. Was sex bad? Was it wrong? Was I a bad girl for asking? I couldn't tell by Mom's response, but at the very least I got the message that Mom was uncomfortable having this conversation with me. She never spoke of such matters again, leaving her little girl to grow up believing that such things weren't spoken of.

So when David wanted to go beyond kissing I rebelled, no matter how pressured I felt. I really, really liked this boy and I didn't want to lose so quickly the love and attention that I'd dreamt of for so long. But in the end I knew it wouldn't have mattered how much coaxing or pleading there was on his part, because the strength of my inner convictions wouldn't allow me to cross the line that went beyond "making out". I wasn't ready for more than that, and although he always seemed disappointed and even hurt at my refusal, he'd always come around in the end, saying he understood. But that understanding was short-lived.

After a brief period, David's insistence to take things a little farther than merely making out became nonstop. He began asking me to do things I knew nothing about, and which I flatly refused. Just the mere thought of his ideas made me feel dirty, ashamed, and disgusted. I'd vowed long ago to be pure and chaste until marriage and I wouldn't hurt Jesus by betraying that vow. But this young, innocent, naïve and, love-starved girl didn't heed the warning signs that were being given off by David's pushy and aggressive behavior. I needed so desperately to be loved by someone, even the wrong someone, and my inability to just walk away would prove to be a mistake that in the end would nearly cost me my life.

Our dates soon took a darker turn. No longer did he want to go out with the other kids after church. Instead every moment together was about finding a quiet parking lot, somewhere that we could be alone – something I resisted with every fiber of my being. I was scared. I could feel that something dark and ominous was waiting for me. Yet my fear of losing him and of not being loved always won out, convincing me not to walk away.

He was becoming more and more aggressive every time I saw him. When I wouldn't do what he asked, he became angry and would promptly drive me home as if to punish me. I was torn. There was a part of me – that love-starved inner child – that knew full well what the outcome of refusing his demands would be; I'd lose him. But there was another part deep inside me that had a stronger pull, the part of me that insisted I wouldn't displease or hurt the Jesus I so loved. The deep abiding love I'd held since childhood for my friend Jesus, the one who had been there for me through so many dark times, was stronger than my feelings for this boy or anyone else in this world. No, I would not – I could not – give in to David's demands, for then I'd betray the one I loved the most.

It began as an ordinary Saturday evening. From my open bedroom window, I heard David's sports car pull up in front of our house. I glanced at the clock on my dresser: 6:00 p.m. Church services began in an hour and I was running late. Mom kept David occupied with small talk in the living room as I rushed to finish my makeup.

After church services, a young couple we were good friends with asked us to join them for the rest of the evening. But David had seemed edgy all through the church service. He declined their offer, saying he wasn't feeling well. We thanked them for the invitation and left. I assumed he would just take me home that evening if he wasn't well, but that wasn't what he had on his mind.

It was a perfect summer evening to have the top down on David's little red convertible – the perfect evening for a long ride and for looking at the starlit night sky. David chose a secluded spot at a nearby park with a beautiful view of a lake, an ideal spot to look at the summer sky. Maybe he'll relax now, I mused. Maybe he'll tell me what's wrong with him and why he's so on edge tonight. He suggested we climb into the back seat. I didn't think this anything out of the ordinary because the gear stick in the front seat made sitting together impossible. I hoped I could get him to open up and share whatever it was that had seemed so off with him by spending some quiet time with him. But he wasn't talking tonight.

There wasn't the usual chitchat about church, the youth ministry we belonged to or even the kids we hung with, not tonight. There was only that uncomfortable stillness – a stillness David broke with his first move. I thought he was pulling me in to kiss me, but instead he pushed me down onto the seat of the car, throwing his full body weight on top of me and pinning me there. I was stunned!

"David! What are you doing? Stop it! You're *hurting* me!" I shouted, struggling and squirming beneath his weight. He said nothing, instead allowing his actions to speak for him.

My slight ninety-pound frame was helpless to escape from under the weight of his muscular 190 pounds. It seemed the more I struggled, the angrier and more violent he became. "David! Get off of me! Stop it! You're hurting me! I can't breathe!" I cried, still trying to wriggle out from beneath him and get myself free.

Like a wild man, he began yanking and pulling at my clothes. Reaching his hand up my dress, he ripped off my underpants, tossing them to the rear seat foot-well. The horror of what was about to occur hit me like a ton of bricks. My heart pounded wildly inside my chest, but I was powerless against his weight and strength. I could do nothing to stop him. I pounded on his back with my fists. At the top of my lungs

I yelled at him, "GET OFF ME! PLEASE DON'T DO THIS!" I tried desperately to push him off, but to no avail. It was as if David had left, and his body had been taken over by some violent sub-human beast. Resistance was futile, because the more I fought, the rougher and more violent he became, the more intent on getting what he was after. Hysterical, shaking and crying uncontrollably, I cried out one last time in desperation, "NO! NO! NO!"

Pain shot through my abdomen as he penetrated me, and then I just switched off. I, too, had left my body. I was numb. I couldn't think. I couldn't fight. I couldn't move.

Immediately afterwards, all I felt was shock; I was totally unable to grasp what had just happened. In the next moment, as if my soul had abruptly re-entered my body, hysteria returned full-force. I found myself once again in the front seat with no idea how I'd gotten there. The next thing I remember was that we were driving down my street. Almost as if I was in an altered state of awareness, I heard him say, "If you get pregnant, I've got a plan!"

In my frenzied state, I just stared at him in dazed disbelief. I just wanted out of that car and as far away from him as I could get. He acted as if he'd done nothing wrong, and as if nothing was wrong with me. How truly delusional he was became crystal clear when he calmly and politely opened my car door to help me out and insisted on walking me to the front door. My only thought was to get inside my house and as far away from him as I could.

Trembling, I fumbled in the darkness to get my key into the front door lock. But before I could open the door, and make my way to safety, he had one last thing to say as he plunged the cold, sharp blade of betrayal deep into my heart.

"What are you crying about? You can't stay a virgin forever!"

It was way past midnight when I walked through the door. My parents were already in bed, but Mom wasn't asleep yet. She'd heard me come through the door crying and jumped out of bed to see what was the matter. She came into my bedroom quietly, shutting the door behind her so as not to disturb my dad. Sitting beside me on the bed, she put her arm around me. "What happened? Why is your dress torn, Belinda? What in the world is going on?" she asked, her voice expressing her concern.

I was crying so hard it was difficult to reply. I didn't know if I even wanted to reply. So many thoughts raced through my mind. How could I tell her what had happened? Would she be as ashamed of me as I was of myself? I felt filthy, vile and disgusting. Would she think the same of me? We had never had the "talk" so many parents have with their kids. How was I supposed to open up about something like this with her? What if my crying woke Dad? Oh goodness, what would *he* think? More importantly, what would he say and do? So many thoughts bombarded my frenzied mind. Part of me just wanted to crawl beneath my covers and never wake up, to pretend it had all been a horrible nightmare. But it wasn't. It had been real. I had to tell her something. So I told her everything between sobs.

She listened to every word just as she had the day I ran home from Deanne's, a humiliated nine-year-old with my bottle of Ugly Pills clenched in my hand. If I'd needed the comfort of her arms then, how much more did I need Mom's love now? But solace wasn't what I would receive from her. Her reaction to the horrific events of this night was no different than her reaction to Mr. Mike and his hateful birthday prank all those years ago – apparent indifference. Her response spoke volumes about the dysfunction in our family.

"Don't tell your dad," she said, then she stood up and left the room.

That was it. Nothing else. No words of comfort or solace. All that mattered was that Dad didn't find out. The events of the night were to be swept aside forever, as if they had never happened. Keep the peace in the house at all costs, no matter how high that cost might be. After that night my mom never spoke of what had happened to me again, and neither did I. I obediently toed the line like the good little girl I was and did what she had asked. I was to repress every last detail of that terrible night forever. That was her plan.

Her reaction stunned and disappointed me. I needed her to be my mom. I needed her help, and yet in that moment I realized she'd done what she always did as far as I was concerned: she turned a blind eye and pretended nothing was wrong. Once more, she had abandoned me when I needed her most. It wasn't only David who had betrayed me that night; my own mother had betrayed me too, with her cold and heartless reaction.

I couldn't stand how dirty I felt, so I went into the bathroom to wash. I needed to get *him* off of me. I couldn't take a bath because it would wake Dad who was sound asleep in the next room, so I filled the bathroom sink with steaming hot soapy water, and began to scrub. I scrubbed and scrubbed and scrubbed in a frantic attempt to get every vestige of David off of me. I tried to shut down the sobbing that now seemed beyond my control. I didn't want my sobs to wake Dad up, but as I washed away the blood that stained my inner thighs, I was faced with the cold, harsh reality that I was no longer a virgin, and with that realization my sobs could no longer be contained.

I struggled to wrap my head around all that had happened over the past few hours. Thoughts flickered through my mind like flashes of lightning. How could he do this to me? *Why* would he do this? I thought he loved me! How can I keep something like this quiet? I had known he was getting more aggressive weeks ago. If only I'd broken up with him then. He should pay for what he did! What if I'm pregnant? Could I have fought harder? But the most devastating thought of all was the realization that I had lost my virginity in such a way. Something I considered so precious and so sacred had been ripped from me in the most violent and disturbing manner imaginable. I felt I had let Jesus down. I felt used and filthy. No longer was I the pure and virtuous young woman I wanted to be – needed to be – for my Lord. I didn't know how I was ever going to deal with all the emotions I was now feeling. I had no one to talk to. I was alone in this – all alone except for Jesus. But I had let Him down. Perhaps He was upset with me now too. Perhaps Mom was upset with me and that's why she'd reacted as she did. I needed help desperately, but there was no one.

I washed and scrubbed every square inch of my body over and over and over, only stopping when I saw that I was starting to rub my skin raw. I slipped into my pajamas and crept across the hall to my bedroom. Curling up beneath my covers, I was too ashamed to even speak to the Lord I had always so counted on. I simply wanted to turn and hide my face from Him. I told myself I didn't want to live anymore, and I cried myself to sleep.

In the days that followed that night it seemed as though part of me had left the planet. I walked around in a daze, my mind in a fog, not knowing what to do with all the tumultuous feelings I was holding inside. If I had to stay quiet and maintain the status quo, did that mean I had to pretend I was still seeing David so Dad didn't ask questions? How could I do that? I loathed him. The thought of being anywhere near him made me physically sick. How would I even handle being in the same church as him? I didn't know how, but I knew I had to try to keep that peace Mom spoke of for all our sakes. Not knowing what else to do, but desperately needing to tell someone trustworthy what had happened to me, I made an appointment to visit our parish priest. But when the time came to see him, when we sat face-to-face in his office, the words wouldn't come. I couldn't tell him what had happened. I was much too ashamed.

David called later that week to see if I was still riding with him to church Saturday night. How could he be so stupid to think I ever wanted anything to do with him again? Maybe he was just checking in to see if I had snitched, and given him up to the authorities that needed to bring him to justice. I wasn't about to tell him that I would never tell a soul about that night, and that his heinous behavior would be yet another secret I'd be bound to keep for the sake of peace in our home. Let him sweat. I hoped he was sweating bullets worrying about what I was going to do next. He had to be worried somewhere deep within that evil, warped mind of his that his own parents would find out – those same parents who were such stellar members of their church. Such a scandal would ruin his privileged family – and not only at church.

The anger and rage I felt towards him took my breath away just hearing his voice on the other end of the phone. But rather than express my rage then and there and risk Dad overhearing, I simply stated, "No thanks," and abruptly hung up. I vacillated between feelings of intense rage towards him, feelings of being frightened of him and feelings of being deeply hurt by him, and in the end the rage won out. Perhaps that rage would help to fuel the courage I'd need to muster in order to see him just one more time. Why? I needed to ask him. How could he hurt me like this? What was wrong with him? Did he understand what he'd done? I'd wait for that confrontation for the next time I saw him face-to-face.

I spied him in the hallway of the church basement after Saturday services. Most of the congregation was still upstairs, and it was a perfect opportunity to confront him. Everything I'd rehearsed saying in the face-to-face showdown escaped me, and instead I blurted out, *"You raped me!"* Tears filled my eyes, and it took every ounce of willpower I had to keep them from spilling over and losing all control. Whether from fear or anger or a little of both, I trembled at being in his presence. All I knew was that I wanted to lash out at him and hurt him as much as he'd hurt me. If only I could have shouted what he had done from the pulpit to the whole congregation, if only I could tell them all what a vile and evil person he was. But that was just a fantasy. I would never intentionally make such a scene at church. His reply to my declaration was as cold and callous in that moment as his words had been the night he attacked me:

"Go ahead, tell someone. No one will ever believe you," he said. He turned on his heel and left.

I was certain I had come face-to-face with pure evil. How could I have ever been so taken in by his charm? How could I ever have believed he loved me? Taken aback by his response, I felt my courage disappear, and I ran like a frightened rabbit. I might have to stay silent about that night but I didn't have to put myself in his presence ever again, and I didn't have to go back to that church – my own beloved grandma's church, I reminded myself. I was done. I quit church, and I quit life. I never saw David again. I withdrew further into my own little world – a world of self-starvation, suicide-by-numbers, and deepening depression. I had made a silent wish to die the day I'd been so humiliated in front of my seventh grade class; now that death wish was stronger than ever. I meant business. I had reaffirmed my wish to die the night I was raped, and now I'd do my best to turn that wish into a self-fulfilling prophecy.

All the years of feeling abandoned by my mom and abused by my dad, being humiliated by bullies at school, and now being raped and betrayed suddenly erupted, unleashing the full-on fury of anorexia nervosa, the savage beast that had already taken up residence within me years before. My soul was a little ship lost on a stormy sea ... a little ship sinking ... swallowed up in the depths of the dark ocean of depression and anorexia. I'd starved myself for the last six years. Now, simply starving wasn't enough.

> *Heavenly Father,*
> *Tonight, my sorrow is too bitter, and my cross too heavy.*
> *I cannot find the words or the strength to pray.*
> *Draw near, O Lord, and search my heart*
> *For the words I cannot find ...*
> *For that prayer I cannot say ...*
> *Is crying out to You, O Lord, in every teardrop that falls.*
> *Amen.*

CHAPTER 4

LORD, RESCUE ME

O God, come to my assistance.
O LORD, make haste to help me.

Psalm 70:1

EVERLASTING ARMS

Into Thy everlasting arms I flee.
Lord, make haste to rescue me.
Bow down Thine ear and hear my plea.
Lord, make haste to rescue me.

In arms of love all sorrows erased.
Lord, make haste to rescue me.
All-sufficient is Thy grace.
Lord, make haste to rescue me.

O everlasting arms, my resting place.
Lord, make haste to rescue me.
Comfort me in Thy embrace.
Lord, make haste to rescue me.

*I*f ever there had been a time in my life when I needed God to rescue me, this was it. But rescuing me didn't seem to be part of God's plan. Why had He allowed this heinous thing into my life? I was confused and angry with Him. I felt betrayed by the God I had always loved and adored so much, the God I'd always believed to be my dearest friend. I just didn't understand why He would allow such a horrible thing to happen to someone who loved Him as much as I always had. Is *this* how He treats His friends, I wondered? You bet I was mad, and the confusion and red-hot anger I felt wasn't only towards God.

I was angry and confused by Mom's reaction to the rape. I felt as if she'd abandoned me at a moment when I desperately needed her, and I was furious with David too. He had violated me in an unimaginable way and stolen something that was irreplaceable – my virginity. But my anger wasn't just directed at Mom, David and God: I was also angry with myself.

I loathed myself for being so needy that I hadn't had the courage to walk away when I began to see David's behavior becoming more aggressive. How could I have been so stupid? But there were countless other emotions I needed to find a way to deal with too.

As well as the all-consuming anger, there was the unbearable pain of being so deeply hurt by those I loved the most. Perhaps this betrayal was the deepest hurt I had ever felt. David, Mom and Jesus – all of whom I thought truly loved me, had between them shattered my heart into a million pieces. There was no doubt in my mind that they had betrayed me, and if I couldn't trust them to do right by me, then whom could I trust? But there was one more emotion that I was experiencing in equal measure to the anger and the hurt – shame.

I was so ashamed. I felt so dirty and impure. I kept thinking perhaps Mom had reacted as she did because I had been bad or that it was somehow my fault this terrible thing had happened to me. If I hadn't gotten into the back seat with

David that night, perhaps none of this would have happened at all. If I had broken our relationship off the moment he began getting aggressive then maybe I'd still have my virginity and my life wouldn't feel the way it was now – spiraling out of control.

I had no outlet for the flood of pain and the emotions I was experiencing, not even my kind and caring psychologist Dr. Tully. He too was off-limits. Mom had told me not to tell Dad, and I was afraid that if I told Dr. Tully, he might tell Dad or the authorities. Even if Mom hadn't sworn me to silence I could have never told him about the rape, because I was just too filled with shame. So I remained silent. Instead of expressing the raw emotions I was feeling, I repressed them. I went numb. I stuffed them down inside as deep as I could in an effort to pretend that terrible night had never happened. I would try to forget it all like a bad dream, push it out of my head along with all the emotions that went with it.

But Dr. Tully wasn't stupid. I didn't need to tell him anything for him to pick up on the fact that something was very wrong in my world: my uncontrollable bouts of crying, my rapid weight loss and my haggard appearance gave me away.

Dr. Tully's office almost seemed like a home away from home by now, a place of refuge almost as safe as my bedroom sanctuary. The only monsters I found here were a scale and a piece of fruit; they were monsters I could handle. Dr. Tully was a gentle and kind soul. I wanted desperately to open the floodgates and tell him everything, even how Mom had told me not to tell a soul. But I couldn't. I just couldn't. It was as if some powerful force beyond my control had sealed my mouth shut. As I sat once again in the now familiar black leather chair, all I could do was cry ... and cry ... and cry some more.

Stepping out from behind his desk, Dr. Tully stooped down beside my chair. Placing a handful of tissues in my hand, he looked up at me and said, "Can you tell me what these tears are about?"

He didn't know how much every fiber of my being wanted to tell him all of it, right down to the last sordid detail. He didn't know that I couldn't because I might disturb the monster at home that he knew nothing about. "I can't," was the only response I could muster.

"Why? Why can't you? I want to help. But I can only help if you talk to me, Belinda."

The depth of his sincerity touched me deeply. I knew he wanted to help. I could feel it in his demeanor, hear it in his voice and see it in his warm chestnut eyes. But if Dad found out and World War III erupted at home I would once again have to face the tyrant's fury, and I'd be disappointing – perhaps even betraying – my mom because I'd broken my silence. Just because she had let me down didn't mean I wanted to do the same to her. No, I couldn't speak up, as unfortunate as it might be for me. Dr. Tully wasn't at home to protect me from them, he was here in this sanctuary, this home away from home, this place of safety that was no longer safe. So I once more tearfully whispered, "I just can't."

He didn't push me, and perhaps that was one of the reasons I'd grown so fond of him. He didn't try to control me. But it was obvious he wasn't going to let this go. "I want to set up a family session," he said. "I want your mom, dad and your brother to be here."

I gulped, but said nothing. Did he know what he was doing, asking for us all to be in the same little space together? What if all hell broke loose?

"Belinda, your depression is obviously getting worse, and you look thinner to me. I'm concerned."

"Dr. Tully, asking them here won't do any good."

"How do you know that?"

"Because I know them."

"Well, I think we have to try," he said. "These tears are about something – something really important. Something is ripping you apart. All that pain that you're holding inside needs to be expressed, but so far you've not been able to do that. Would you like to tell me what is hurting you like this?"

There was no way I could tell him about the rape, but my mind searched frantically for an answer – something to appease him, something that might get him to forget about this family get-together. So, I took a deep breath and said, "Part of it's my dad."

"Your dad? What do you mean?"

"He's mean." There, I'd said it. Maybe I'd let the cat out of the bag, or maybe speaking up would prevent him from calling my family in here. It was a risk I'd take.

"How is your dad mean? Tell me about it," Dr. Tully said.

"He hits me. He always has. He's a monster." As the words spilled from my mouth I could feel the emotion beginning to rise up like a tidal wave from deep inside. I'd never told a soul that my dad hit me, or that I thought of him as a monster, and the repercussions of doing so frightened me as much as it felt good to finally say those words out loud.

"Tell me about him, Belinda. When did this begin?"

"When I was just a little girl."

"And why does he do this? What provokes him?"

"Anything can provoke him. Little things. He just gets angry. It's like he's a raging beast sometimes."

"And then he hits you? With his hand, or with something else?"

"No, not his hand. He uses a tree switch, or his belt mostly. Sometimes he uses a wooden paddle he keeps on top of the fridge. He doesn't do it as much as he used to, 'cause I'm older, I guess."

Dr. Tully sat back in his chair, obviously disturbed and surprised by my revelations.

And then I surprised myself by passionately blurting out, "I HATE him!"

"Yes," Dr. Tully began, "I think you have every right to be angry, Belinda. You need to let this anger out. Remember this:

anger turned inward leads to depression. Part of getting you well means expressing all that pent-up anger. Get it outside of yourself. I'm really glad you felt you could share this with me. It's a good step forward."

The timer on his desk rang, signaling our time was up for this session, but Dr. Tully wasn't through. "I want you to think about your feelings towards your dad before our next session. You may feel hatred and anger towards him for what he's done, and rightly so, if he's hurt you physically and emotionally. But I bet you have conflicting feelings towards him – some part of you loves him too. Feelings aren't always so black and white. Just think about that."

Did part of me love Dad? I had always been so frightened of him that I'd never really thought about whether I loved him or not. I was too angry with him to consider feeling anything but hatred. Was it possible I could love him and hate him at the same time? I was still reeling from my unexpected admission. Emotion overcame me. My face felt hot – flushed. I tried to steady my shaking hands. Had I revealed too much?

Unfortunately, it wasn't enough to prevent Dr. Tully from insisting on that family session. Perhaps it only made him want it even more. He called Mom in from the waiting area to make the arrangements.

I knew he meant well, that he was trying to help me. But he didn't know my family and I couldn't foresee any good coming out of this little family gathering. Our family simply didn't communicate, and bringing us together as a group wasn't going to change those dynamics.

After that session with Dr. Tully, the Voice inside me began to make itself heard in new ways. Had unleashing long-buried secrets about Dad the tyrant and giving expression to just a small part of the anger I'd held inside for so long given the Voice a new sense of power? Could it be I just couldn't cope any longer with the pain and trauma I'd stuffed inside for years? Maybe the Voice was simply a way of anesthetizing it? Could it be that the rape had finally sent me over the edge into a land of no return? Was I going crazy? I didn't have the answers to these questions; all I knew was that the Voice was becoming louder, stronger, more demanding and so much nastier. It had come up with a new and grander scheme to lose all that unsightly fat on my ninety-pound body – purging. Purging had a whole new set of benefits, because now I could eat and eat and eat, and all I'd need to do is throw it all up again. Purging was easy for me which made the idea all the more desirable. I didn't even need to stick my finger down my throat; I just had to bend over the toilet and up it came! *"Easy-peasy,"* the Voice assured me.

But it wasn't through with introducing new and innovative ways of losing those extra inches and pounds. There were diet pills, diuretics and laxatives the Voice told me to buy at the corner drugstore. Soon I was purging even water. Nothing was allowed into my stomach but the laxatives, diuretics or diet pills, and the Voice was right: the weight began falling off in record time. Within a week my weight had fallen to eighty-five pounds.

With every pound I lost I felt stronger and more powerful, and that strength and power made me feel even more in control. If I could get down to eighty-five pounds, could I reach eighty? I was intent, focused, driven, and the relentless Voice of the beast within cheered me on every step of the way.

Weighing myself became my newest obsession. After every purge the Voice demanded I weigh in to see if I'd gained an ounce. If the needle on the scale moved in the slightest I felt compelled to bend over the toilet and purge whatever else remained until my stomach was completely empty. The purging went hand in hand with bingeing. When my parents left to go shopping or run errands I was free to use my culinary skills for my own benefit for once. Now I could fix stacks of blueberry, chocolate chip or buttermilk pancakes or plates of grape jelly-filled waffles, foods that I adored and had not eaten in years. No longer deprived of these foods I loved as a child, I could now eat and purge and eat and purge again and again without fear of gaining one pound. *"It's a win-win!"* the Voice cried from within.

But it wasn't a win-win at all. The bingeing only served to make me feel guilty, like I'd lost whatever control I thought I had achieved. The purging was my attempt at regaining that control. And it only made me loathe myself all the more. But the bingeing and purging were harder to control than simply starving myself, and were even more dangerous to my health. I would eat and purge until I was exhausted and had to sleep, not realizing – or perhaps simply not caring – about the damage I was doing to my body. After all, I had made that silent wish to die and now, consciously or subconsciously, that death wish was being carried out. No one at home knew what I was up to – not yet, anyway. I made sure of that, and they wouldn't until it was almost too late.

The ill-fated family session with Dr. Tully came around before I knew it, and I dreaded it. Just the thought of putting all four of us in one tiny office together made my skin crawl. Never had we come together as a family in a way that would suggest we might need to actually talk to one another. It was coercion, plain and simple, just like the scale on the floor in Dr. Tully's office or the pretty red apple that sat on his desk begging for me to take the first bite. I would be stubborn today just like

I was with the apple and the scale. I simply wouldn't speak. I wondered if the rest of my family felt the same sense of dread and foreboding?

Dr. Tully was as warm and welcoming as always that afternoon. He had never met my brother or my dad, so he spent a few moments on introductions. He graciously asked everyone to find a comfortable place to sit, and the torture commenced.

"I've asked you here today because Belinda has a serious illness," Dr. Tully began. "I'd like to see how we can all work together to help her through this. Does anyone have any questions or anything they'd like to say?"

No one did. Dr. Tully continued. "So, who would like to open up this conversation?"

No one was taking Dr. Tully up on his invitation to speak. It was as I thought it would be – dead silence.

Mom broke that uncomfortable silence by offering up her usual friendly and meaningless chitchat. I tried to remove myself from the tension that filled the room by diverting my attention to a fly that I'd spied crawling in a crack on the black and white tile floor beneath my feet. I watched mesmerized as it rubbed its tiny legs together, and recalled how I'd read somewhere that this is actually how a fly cleans itself. My eyes fixed, I followed its every move as it abruptly took flight, buzzing past Dad's head. It seemed fitting that it would choose to circle the beast in the room. Finally, it landed on the arm of the leather chair on which Dad was sitting. I kept trying to distract myself; I kept trying to amuse myself. I kept trying to pass the minutes that crawled past like hours, and I kept praying Dr. Tully wouldn't breathe a word of what I'd told him in our last session about Dad's behavior.

My attention briefly came back to the room. Mom had run out of chitchat, and silence reigned. I glanced over at Dr. Tully. He caught a glimpse of the tears that were filling my eyes, and reached over to hand me the box of Kleenex on his desk, and then he spoke, breaking the dreadful silence. Perhaps he'd seen those tears in my eyes as an S.O.S., because he promptly put an end to the torture.

"I appreciate each of you coming today. I'd like to spend the last fifteen minutes with Belinda. So, if you don't mind stepping into the waiting room."

He stood up from behind his desk, made his way over to shake their hands and graciously escorted them from the room. As the door shut behind him, I could no longer hold in my emotions. I could cry now. They were gone. Perhaps it was relief, or maybe it was great sadness at the harsh reality of how deeply my family was broken that set off this newest flood of tears. But it was as if a dam had broken. The tears came rushing forth and I was helpless to hold them back. Dr. Tully sat beside me on the couch and, in a show of great compassion and support, put his arm around my shoulder.

"Go ahead, and just let it out," he said softly.

And I did. I wouldn't have been able to stop myself if I'd wanted to.

"Now do you see? Do you see how they are?" I said between sobs.

He nodded. "You and I will talk all about what happened here today in our next session. Do you need to come back sooner than next week?"

"No, next week is fine. Thank you," I replied, as the crying began to subside. As I stood up to leave, Dr. Tully did something that he'd never done before: he opened his arms to give me a much-needed hug. Perhaps this hug crossed the doctor-patient line, but in the moment it felt appropriate, and it was the best medicine he ever could have given me that day.

Not a single thing was said at home about what a disaster our family session had been. I knew the truth was that neither Mom nor my brother spoke up because they didn't want to infuriate Dad. Speaking or having thoughts or feelings of your own – much less expressing them – was forbidden in our house. It was Dad's way or the highway. We were Dad's little soldiers, not unlike the men that had been under Dad's command during his years in the army. We had all learned over time to keep quiet and toe the line or suffer the consequences. It was always about doing things Dad's way to keep him quiet, to keep the peace. That's all that ever mattered. But the calm atmosphere that we all strived to maintain was about to go up in smoke.

Day by day the Voice became increasingly louder, stronger and more dominating. The bingeing and purging was now an unstoppable force. I consumed laxatives and diuretics daily and my weight continued to plummet. I was now down to eighty pounds – but the weight loss was the least of my problems, because my physical health was rapidly deteriorating.

My legs ached constantly. I felt myself growing weaker by the day. I grew dizzy and faint whenever I stood up. My hands often tingled and twitched uncontrollably, and I was becoming even more profoundly depressed. My long hair had begun to fall out in large clumps when I brushed it. I was constantly cold no matter how many layers of clothing I wore. Sleep was nearly impossible because I hurt so much – everywhere.

I looked over from my bed at the clock on the dresser: 1:00 a.m. I had tossed and turned for hours, unable to sleep because the aching in my legs just refused to let up. Although I had become accustomed to hurting every night, the pain was much more intense on this particular night. I wanted to get up and grab the bottle of liniment from the bathroom cabinet. Sometimes rubbing my legs down relieved the aching enough to let me sleep. But tonight I was in so much agony I didn't think I could make the short walk to the bathroom.

Overcoming my constant fear of disturbing Dad, I finally called for help. I called out for my mom.

She came through and sat beside me on the bed. "What's wrong?" she asked.

"My legs are killing me. Can you get the liniment?"

Her reply wasn't what I'd expected. "Belinda, I think you need to go to the emergency room. This has been going on now every night for a while. You're getting worse. Something is very wrong."

I didn't fight her. I knew deep down inside that she was right. Something was very, very wrong. I felt horrible. I knew I needed help.

She woke Dad, who astonishingly wasn't angry that his sleep had been disturbed. Instead, he seemed concerned. Within the hour, I was on my way to the hospital emergency room.

Mom didn't leave my side as the doctors and nurses took charge in the ER where my vitals were immediately taken. I watched in horror as the blood pressure cuff that was growing tighter and tighter around my stick of an arm made my bony hand curl up in a tight and painful spasm; a hard ball that I couldn't undo. The nurse gave the doctor a look that said she'd not seen anything like this before. He ordered a whole battery of blood tests done – stat. The results were back within the hour, and they weren't good.

I listened, stunned, as the doctor explained to my parents that my electrolyte balance was badly disturbed. My calcium level was so low that it was causing the spasms he referred to as tetany seizures. My potassium was critically low, causing the severe aching in my legs, and there was a heart arrhythmia I didn't even know I had. I was severely dehydrated. My body temperature was below normal and my blood pressure was dangerously low. But it was the last thing he said that really caught my attention: "She only weighs seventy-seven pounds. She is starving to death."

The insidious Voice in my head suddenly emerged, as if this particular news had stirred it from slumber. *"Yes!"* it cheered gleefully. *"Yes!"*

Doctors came in and out of my hospital room in a steady stream the next morning. This was a teaching hospital, and I was apparently an unusual case. I had an illness these young interns had never seen before. Lucky me! Here I was, the uncomfortable object of show and tell yet again, just like I had been on that awful afternoon in Mr. Hastings' seventh grade science class.

As much as I loathed these doctors gawking at me and chattering over me in scientific terms as if I was some kind of medical project, I was too weak to do anything about it. My arm throbbed from the potassium that dripped ever-so-slowly into it from the IV, and I was frightened by the whispers I was hearing of plans for force-feeding. I closed my eyes. Perhaps if I pretended to sleep they'd all go away, or better yet I'd wake up to find this had all just been a bad dream. I guess my odds weren't very good on either count. But wait! I could have sworn I heard Dr. Tully's voice call my name. Perhaps I was dreaming. There it was again! I opened my eyes to see his most welcome face smiling down at me.

"Hey, how are you doing? Your mom called to let me know you were here," he said, pulling up a chair to sit down.

I was overjoyed ... overwhelmed to see him! Finally, I had a friend in the midst of all of these strangers.

We chatted a while like old friends. He seemed genuinely concerned about my condition, and then his voice got serious as he said he had some important news to share.

"I'm sorry, but I'm not going to be able to be your therapist any longer," he said. "You have an illness that might require hospitalization from time to time, and as a psychologist I'm not on staff. You need to start seeing a psychiatrist. I have someone that I am referring you to, and he'll be here later today to meet you. His name is Dr. Kraft."

I didn't want to hear what he was saying. I wanted *him* to be my therapist, and no one else. I liked him. I trusted him. Now he was leaving me too. Tears fell softly down my cheeks and my heart felt as if it was breaking. I hadn't realized how attached I'd grown to Dr. Tully. But it appeared there was nothing I could do to change the situation. The plans had already been set into motion and the deal was sealed.

Our family doctor, Dr. Giles, came in later that morning to discuss my "fragile condition". He made sure I realized what a serious condition I was in, and how close to dying I had come. Dr. Giles hadn't left the room before a short dark-haired man with black thick-rimmed glasses walked in and stood beside him.

"Belinda," Dr. Giles began. "This is Dr. Kraft. He will be your psychiatrist."

Heavenly Father,
My heart is heavy,
My spirit filled with pain, sorrow and grief.
Come Lord, have mercy.
Comfort me.
Lift my spirit up in Your embrace of love.
Amen.

PART TWO

FEAR NO EVIL

Yea, though I walk through the valley of the shadow of death,
I will fear no evil ...

Psalm 23:4

CHAPTER 5

ABANDONED

Hear my prayer, LORD, give ear to my cry.
Do not be silent at my tears.

Psalm 39:12

Little One
I'm here right beside you,
Yet you know it not.
Don't you recall My promise,
Or is it you forgot?
I vowed I'd never leave you,
With My presence ever near.
I said I'd smooth the way for you,
So what have you to fear?
Though you doubt My presence,
Never doubt My love or care.
For when the night is darkest,
My arms embrace you there.
My face shall gaze upon you;
I will not turn away.
My love will never fail you;
My light will guide your way.
Trust that I am with you;
Have faith I hear your prayers.
You'll find Me in the silence –
Be still – I'll meet you there!

"Hello, Belinda, I'm happy to meet you," Dr. Kraft said. He smiled, but his smile didn't feel warm and genuine like Dr. Tully's. It felt faked, and more an attempt to win me over – perhaps to gain my trust. Well, he'd have to try a bit harder than that. Dr. Kraft tucked the clipboard he'd been taking notes on beneath his arm to shake my hand. His hand felt like a limp fish. I wasn't impressed.

"As Dr. Giles told you, I'll be your psychiatrist. You, my dear, are a very sick young lady – a classic textbook case of anorexia nervosa. So, after you spend some time here on the medical floor recuperating, I will be having you transferred to the psychiatric unit. We will work together there to see if we can get to the bottom of the problem."

What? My thoughts ran wild. Psychiatric unit? Why are they sending me there? I'm not crazy! Whose idea was this? Who did this little guy in the expensive-looking black suit think he was? I didn't want to go to any psychiatric unit – I wanted to go home and back to school. It was already the end of September, and I'd missed nearly three weeks. But words expressing my fear and outrage weren't what came out of my mouth. Instead I mumbled a pathetic, "Okay."

"We will be monitoring your food and caloric intake while you are here," Dr. Kraft began. "As long as you eat for us, we won't have to begin force-feeding you. But, if you refuse to eat, we can't risk your health deteriorating any further, and we will have to take steps to prevent you harming yourself any more than you already have. Do you understand?"

I said nothing, but nodded. I didn't like this guy with his limp fish handshake and fake smile. Neither did the Voice in my head that began asserting its opinion: *"Are you really going to let this jerk haul you off to the psych ward? Are you going to let him take away all you've achieved? Are you really going to eat just because he is threatening you, and let him make you FAT? Do you want to be a fat cow?"*

The Voice was loud, mad, and scared. Scared that I was

going to have to eat. Scared that I was going to get fat. Scared that all the control I'd struggled so hard to win was about to be undermined by this smug, full-of-himself shrink!

A week later, my vitals had improved to the extent where they could transfer me to Fairhaven, the psych ward on the hospital's sixth floor. I was totally unprepared for the life-altering experience that was about to unfold.

Mom and Dad had shown up on the day of my transfer to oversee things. I would have liked to believe it was for emotional support, but I knew better than that. Our family had no concept of emotional support. Maybe I should have played nice and given them the benefit of the doubt, but I was way too angry with them at that moment to play nice. In fact, I was just plain furious that they'd signed the papers that would have me committed, and I didn't know if I could ever forgive them. Maybe they really thought I was crazy, or maybe this creep Dr. Kraft had convinced them I was. Whatever their reason was for deciding to 'put me away', I was being kept against my will. I didn't like it, and they weren't about to make me fat. But I wasn't worried; the Voice would help me find a way to win this battle – no matter what.

The ride to hell was a six-floor elevator journey in the wrong direction. Hell was down, and I was going up. I was taken to my new room in a wheelchair with a nurse escort because I still had an IV drip. The painful potassium had been replaced with glucose. *"Pure sugar!"* the Voice shouted. *"Wonder how many calories that has?"*

The elevator doors opened wide and we entered a bright, spacious room. At first glance, the sunshine streaming in through the row of windows that lined one entire wall gave it a warm and inviting feel. But that warmth quickly evaporated as I caught a glimpse of the patients in the big room. One man in particular drew my attention. His expression was vacant, his glassy eyes stared into space. Was this the effect of some medication, I wondered? Would this be me in twenty-four hours?

"This is the solarium," the nurse informed us. "This is where the patients mingle, watch television, and where the meals are eaten." If she was trying to make this place seem more inviting – or at least less intimidating – it wasn't working. She came off like a tour guide on some kind of dream vacation.

She wheeled my chair purposefully down a long corridor to my own private room with Mom and Dad in tow. Dr. Kraft entered a few moments later and wasted no time doling out orders. He handed the nurse a roll of duct tape and instructed her to seal the bathroom door shut before turning to address us.

"Good afternoon!" he said in a chipper voice. "I'd like to outline the behavior modification program you will be on while you are here, Belinda. You will be monitored 24/7. If you need to use the bathroom you are to call a nurse, who will take you there and stay with you until you are finished. You will eat all your meals in the solarium, where a nurse will monitor you for the first hour. You will be weighed daily. If you gain a pound, you will gain a privilege. Likewise, if you lose a pound, you lose a privilege. Privileges will be things like occupational or recreational therapy, a phone call, a visit from a friend or relative, an hour of television of your choice, a day pass home when I've seen visible signs of improvement, or even the simple freedom to shower and use the bathroom without supervision. If you lose a pound after you have begun to gain a little weight, you will immediately lose all privileges that you have earned. Do you understand?"

What I understood was that I was in hell, and this shrink was the devil incarnate. This guy thought he was going to force me to eat and gain weight even without a tube in my stomach! The anger I felt boiled up into rage. I was furious! How could Mom and Dad allow this to happen? I glanced over at the bathroom door, which was now sealed up tightly with gray duct tape, and a pervading sense of humiliation swept through me. I wanted to scream. I wanted to run far, far away. I wanted to lash out and hurt this devil doctor – and my parents for putting me in his charge. I hated them all! But all I could muster was a lame, "Why did you seal up my bathroom door?"

"Because you won't be allowed to use the bathroom without supervision, Belinda," Dr. Kraft said. "Do you understand the rules?"

"Yes, I get it," I replied, struggling to inject a hint of sarcasm.

"Good. Now tell your parents goodbye because you won't be hearing from or seeing them again until you've gained the privilege to do so."

Shocked, I started to cry. I looked at Mom and saw tears falling from her eyes too. Dr. Kraft had left the room. "Mom, *please* don't leave me here. Please!"

"The doctors say this is best for you, Belinda. They say they can help you."

"Mom, this is torture, not help! What about school?" I cried.

"Mrs. Clay has been gracious enough to let you have a leave of absence while you concentrate on getting well. So don't worry. Dad and I will be back to see you just as soon as Dr. Kraft says we can come. I love you, sweetheart," she said, her voice breaking. She bent over to hug me goodbye.

Dad had been surprisingly quiet. I wasn't sure, but wait ... it looked as though he had tears in his eyes too. Standing beside the wheelchair, he touched my arm tenderly and said, "Do what the doctors say, honey. Get better."

And then they left. I was alone, at the mercy of this devil

doctor. I wasn't quite sure what to expect from him. He was a whole new breed of monster to do battle with. But no matter how smart or cunning Dr. Kraft thought he was, he had never done battle with the Voice. He had told my parents he'd never had a patient with anorexia nervosa before, so it was obvious he had no idea what he was up against. *"Don't worry,"* the Voice consoled. *"We'll show him what the word* cunning *really means!*

It rained the next day. The somber fall sky and the cold, incessant rain matched my mood – sad and depressed. Perhaps raindrops were the tears of God and He was as sad and depressed as I was today. Peering out from between the steel bars on my window to the busy street below I couldn't help but feel a hint of jealousy well up inside me as I watched people with umbrellas of every color scurrying up and down the sidewalk seeking shelter from the stormy weather. They were free. I was not. I was imprisoned now in this loony bin. I wept. I hated my life.

"Breakfast!" The nurse's unexpected entrance startled me, interrupting my reverie. "Oh, I'm sorry, I didn't mean to startle you, dear. Everyone eats in the solarium, but first I need to weigh you."

The anger rose up, and the Voice silently spoke, *"No! I don't want to be weighed!"* I didn't want my weight controlled or tracked. It was no one's business but my own. But I didn't have a choice. The nurse walked over and stood beside the scale that loomed like a mechanical nemesis in the corner of my room, an ever-present reminder of why I was here and what they expected of me. She reminded me of a game show hostess standing there grinning ear to ear holding her clipboard at the ready to record today's magic numbers. I grabbed onto the IV stand with one hand to steady myself and rose slowly from my window seat, my eyes fixed on the cold, steel mechanical beast in the corner. If only I had some sort of superhuman powers, and I could just will my adversary to vanish, vaporizing it into thin air. With each step closer the anger and fear became more intense. It felt more like I was walking to the gallows, than stepping onto a scale.

Apprehensive, I watched as the nurse delicately balanced the steel slide. "Seventy-eight pounds," she declared, making a quick note on her chart. "Come on, let's get you down to breakfast."

After the morning weigh-in, there was a breakfast of soft-boiled eggs, toast, oatmeal and fruit waiting for me. I nibbled on the fruit and ate the eggs. It seemed enough to appease the nurses, at least for now. After breakfast came "meds". It appeared to be a morning ritual here. The head nurse rang a tiny silver bell and yelled out, "Med Time!" All the patients rushed to the nurses' station like over-eager little kids running to a kindly grandma whose pockets were bulging with some sort of yummy sweet treat. Well, I never cared for sweets much, and I would have gladly passed on the invitation, but once again they weren't asking, they were telling. I got in line.

Dr. Kraft had chosen a colorful array of odd-shaped little pills which the nurse handed to me in a small white paper cup. I counted four in all. I wondered what each one was for. With one hand the impatient nurse shoved the pills in my face, and with the other a styrofoam cup of water to get them down. From the scowl on her long, sullen face, I'd say she must have been having as bad a day as I was. Her eyes followed my every move, keeping watch until she was assured each pretty little pill had gone down the hatch.

"Open," she said, sternly. As if watching me take them wasn't enough, now she even had to look inside my mouth to see if the pills were gone? Unbelievable! But I played along, giving her a good long look all the way down to my tonsils. "Ahhhhh."

"You have to stay in the solarium and close to the nurses' station for an hour. Dr. Kraft will be in to see you this afternoon," she said, her voice harsh and impersonal.

I obeyed, flopping down on one end of the long, green sofa that was smack-dab in front of the nurses' station and her scowling eyes. I picked up a *National Geographic* from among the dozens of magazines scattered on the end table at the sofa's edge. I couldn't physically escape my prison, but perhaps I could escape into my imagination. I opened the magazine to find incredible images of pristine beaches and a deep blue sea. These breathtaking images transported me to Fiji, of all places, and I was more than ready for my exotic vacation, if only in my mind. Even though I can't swim a lick I imagined floating peacefully upon the limpid blue waters with the sun's warm rays dancing on my skin. Dreaming of this paradise of tranquility made that hour fly by. I was brought back to reality all too soon by a gentle tap on my shoulder. I opened my sleepy eyes to see one of the nurses. This one didn't have a scowl on her face – in fact she was smiling and her voice was pleasant.

"Belinda, you can go to your room now."

Looking at her name tag, I made a mental note: *Karen.*

"How are you feeling?" Karen asked in a voice that showed genuine compassion.

"Sort of dizzy and tired."

"That's the medication. Let me walk with you to your room, where you can rest," Karen said, helping me to my feet.

I was glad she had come to help me to my room. The last thing I wanted to do was flip out on the floor and lose consciousness along with what little control of my situation I had left. But even though I didn't lose consciousness, these new drugs had already begun to usurp physical control over me. I'd never taken psychiatric medication before, and I had no idea what they were peddling. But whatever it was, it was making me dazed and confused. I hated this feeling as much as I hated this place. Karen helped me, wheeling the IV stand down the long corridor to my room at the end of the hall.

She helped me settle into the big, overstuffed chair next to the window. "Ring the bell if you need anything," she said in a cheerful voice as she made her way out the door.

Just as Dr. Kraft had instructed, the nurses watched me like hawks. How was I going to deal with their judgmental eyes constantly upon me, even during my most private moments such as using the bathroom or showering? It was worse than humiliating – it was downright degrading. I loved my privacy, and it had been stripped from me in the most demeaning way I could imagine.

There had been other patients in the solarium that morning, but I was too depressed to mingle with them. Who cared about being social? I didn't want to watch television either, so who cared if I wasn't allowed to? I wanted to be in my room alone. I missed Mom. I was used to talking to her about almost everything, even if she seldom understood my feelings. Now we were cut completely off from one another, and I'd have to earn the right to see her. I wanted to tell her how much I hated this place, how the medications made me feel spaced out, and how forcing me to eat wasn't the solution. But most of all I just needed to hear her voice. I felt abandoned, not only by my parents but by God.

Peering out between the bars on the window I looked up into the dark gray sky once again and I cried out to Jesus. "Where are You, Jesus? Where have You gone? Why did You leave me here? I thought You at least loved me! Why have You abandoned me, Lord?"

Shutting my eyes and forcing myself to remain still, I leaned my head back and sank into the comfort of the soft, overstuffed chair. I tried to let my imagination take me to the place on the hill beneath our giant oak where Jesus always waited for me. I needed to imagine His smiling eyes on me and I needed to feel the warmth of His loving embrace. But the lush green hillside and the familiar dirt path I'd walked upon so many times in the past was no longer there. There was only a black void. I couldn't find Him or that sacred place. Perhaps this really was hell, a living hell, and I was being punished.

Jesus was my light, and that light had been extinguished. Only darkness remained. Perhaps He didn't care at all. Don't give up, I counseled myself. Keep praying ... keep crying out to Him. My tears fell as steadily as the rain that morning, as I spoke from my heart to my beloved Jesus:

Lord,
I need Your help.
I'm not strong enough to face life on my own.
Why are You so silent, Lord?
Why do You hide Your face from me?
Why do You ignore my prayers?
I need to feel Your presence near.
Help me, Jesus.
I love You.
Amen.

CHAPTER 6

CAPTIVE

I will not leave thee, neither will I forsake thee.

Hebrews 13:5

Lord, am I forever lost in the shadows of the night?
Shall I ever see Thy face again, so radiant and bright?
Will Thy gaze of love once more shine down upon my soul?
Am I forever parted from the One who makes me whole?
How I miss Your eyes that twinkle so with heaven's light.
Lord, am I forever lost in the shadows of the night?
I'm begging, Heavenly Father, help me now and set me free,
Like when I was a child and You came to rescue me.
Free me from this prison-mind – release my every fear;
In Your love and mercy cut the chains that bind me here.
I'm begging, Heavenly Father, help me now and set me free.

It was nearing mid-afternoon when Dr. Kraft finally made a brief appearance on the first full day of my captivity. Yes, captivity is the only way I could describe how this felt. For all intents and purposes I was being held captive and something about losing my freedom was bringing out the fighter in me – as this devil doctor was about to find out. He had no sooner taken a seat beside mine when, with righteous indignation, I blurted out, "I really hate this place!"

Did I really just say that? I was taken aback by the ferocity of my outspoken and angry remark. Perhaps it was merely the effect of the cocktail of medication they were giving me three times a day, because this wasn't like my usual shy and docile self. But I had every right to be outspoken and angry! I had been put here against my will. My freedom had been taken away, and this guy had been the one who'd convinced my parents to do it. Dr. Kraft, however, seemed unaffected by my comment or my impolite tone. His beady brown eyes peered over his black, heavy-rimmed glasses. Looking me directly in the eye, he calmly replied, "Can you tell me why you feel that way?"

What sort of a dumb question was that? I wanted to lash out at him, to hurt him, like he'd hurt me with this stupid game he was playing with my life. "Because you've taken all of my freedom away," I retaliated. "The nurses keep tabs on me like I'm a prisoner. The medication makes me feel dazed and dizzy, and there are bars on the windows. I'm not ten anymore! I'm eighteen, and I didn't give anyone permission to put me here. I'm not your prisoner!" Overwhelmed by emotion, I felt the tears begin to fall.

"None of this is designed to make you feel like a prisoner," he said in a feeble attempt to reassure me. "Perhaps you don't realize how ill you really are? If your parents hadn't brought you into the ER when they did, you may have died. And, if you hate this place so much," he continued, "then there is one way to get out of here, isn't there? Eat!"

Eat. He'd said the magic word. I suddenly felt cornered, like the caged animal I was. Infuriated, I shot back, "This whole thing is about forcing me to eat, isn't it?"

"This 'whole thing', Belinda, is about getting you well. Eating is a large part of that, because our work together will only move forward when you are nutritionally balanced and thinking more clearly."

Like a scared rabbit, I backed down, and my tone suddenly went from righteous anger to pathetic pleading. "Dr. Kraft, I want to speak to my mom." My tears now fell in a steady stream, and I reached for a tissue from the box beside my bed. "I miss her terribly. I feel so alone in here."

"I'm sure you do miss her, but speaking to her requires that you gain some weight. Outside contact is a privilege to be earned. If you feel lonely, let me encourage you to spend a bit of time getting to know some of the other patients here."

I had nothing more to add. If I had to play this game of his, then so be it. I'd play it – and I'd win it.

"Let's talk about all that anger you have inside, Belinda. Do you have any idea of where all that anger comes from?"

"No," I said defiantly. I was lying. Did he really think I was going to open up and share my deepest thoughts and feelings with him? Not likely! I didn't even like him – this devil doctor – not one little bit. Perhaps it was just the Voice, the illness itself, but I didn't see him as someone who wanted to help me. I saw him as my nemesis and my adversary – a foe to be defeated.

"I hear a lot of anger in you, Belinda. That needs to be expressed. So, what I want you to do is start writing your feelings and thoughts down in this notebook." Reaching inside his shiny black leather briefcase, he pulled out a small, burgundy spiral journal. Before handing it to me, he opened it and began writing.

"Belinda, do you know what an obsession is?" he asked, handing the open journal to me.

I read aloud what he'd scribbled on the first page, *Obsession = Thought that is unwanted, irresistible, and senseless.*

"Yes, and we are going to begin talking about this in our next session. Why don't you give this some thought when I leave, and write down all the thoughts you have that seem unwanted, irresistible, and senseless. We can discuss them tomorrow."

Did I really want to open up to him about this? What did

he mean by obsession anyway? Was that relentless Voice I heard so strongly merely the voice of obsession? I was convinced he didn't understand what was wrong with me any more than I did. Still crying, my eyes rested on the duct tape that formed a tight and impenetrable seal around the bathroom door. Oh, how I longed for freedom. But the gray steel bars at my window were a harsh and cruel reminder that freedom was a privilege that I was being denied. What had I done that was so horrible to deserve such a punishment? How was any of this going to make me well, or help me heal the pain I felt so deep inside? Didn't they know that I was already a prisoner? I was the prisoner of a Voice within my own mind that was stronger than my will; a Voice that ruled through fear. *"Do this or you will be fat! You fat, ugly cow!"* The Voice commanded, demeaned and berated me, and the good little girl who was crying inside to be loved obeyed its every wish because she had thought once upon a time that by listening to it, by becoming thin – perfect – she would become someone worthy of being loved.

But the Voice had lied, and now it was responsible for my being held hostage. It no longer mattered if at times I longed for freedom from it, because I had become a prisoner of the fear through which it ruled me, the overwhelming fear of being fat. I was trapped, and although I had no idea how it had happened, somewhere along the way this inner voice had gained total control over my life. I was being held captive in a cage of fear. The bars might be invisible, but their effect was no different from the cold, steel bars that barricaded these windows. If I silently screamed, *"Let me out!"* the Voice inside my head screamed back even louder, and more angrily: *"Shut up! No one ever hears your cries!"* Was the Voice right? Would I be its captive forever? Could I find a way to break free from my prison of darkness and fear?

The next morning the solarium was bustling with activity. The television that hung high from its ceiling perch blared the morning news as nurses tended to their duties. I chose a seat in the corner of the room where I could be as inconspicuous as possible. Sizing up the patients who had congregated, I noticed some who seemed lost, deep in their own little worlds. Perhaps their state of mind was due to their illness or perhaps it was the medications they were handling out so freely here. I felt sad for them. I understood emotional suffering. It hurt – badly. No one seemed to understand mental suffering or know how to "fix" it the way a broken leg could be fixed. Instead, they carted you off to a psychiatric facility where they filled you full of pills that made you even more dazed and confused. Oh well, perhaps dazed and confused equaled numb. If I was numb, then maybe I wouldn't feel the pain inside so acutely. But was that the best any of us here could hope for? Being kept comfortably numb wasn't going to fix us. Perhaps there was no fixing us.

Alongside those in the solarium who chose to be alone, there were some who had paired off into groups of two or three. It appeared many of the patients here had become quite friendly with one another. But for now I was content to sit by myself off in one corner of the room and observe the goings-on.

Eventually my eyes met those of a young woman across the room. She appeared to be in her mid-thirties. She smiled. I smiled back. She began making her way through the solarium towards my chair in the corner.

"Hi, I'm Jilly," she said. She had a pretty smile and a soft voice that immediately put me at ease.

"I'm Belinda," I said, returning the smile.

"What are you here for, Belinda? I'm here for depression," she said brushing her long auburn hair from her eyes.

"Anorexia nervosa."

"What's that?"

"It's kind of hard to explain. I'm not even sure the doctor understands. How long have you been here?" I said, trying to change the subject.

"A few weeks now."

"Are you going home soon?"

"I doubt it," Jilly began. "The drugs the doctors are using don't seem to be working the way they'd hoped. They're talking about giving me ECT."

"What's ECT?"

"Some kind of electric current they zap your brain with. They call it Electro Convulsive Shock Treatment."

"It sounds painful."

"I don't know. A lot of the patients here have it once a week on Thursdays. If I knew why I was depressed then maybe I could get better," she said, a deep sorrow apparent in her voice.

"You don't know why you're depressed?" I hardly knew this young woman and yet I already felt a connection to her. Something in me wanted to reach out and lift the great sadness that seemed to weigh her down.

"Nope, and the worst part of being in here is I can't see my little girl, Jenny. My husband comes to visit, but Jenny's too young," she said, her deep brown eyes welling up with tears.

"How old is she?" I asked.

"Eleven," Jilly said, pulling a small snapshot from the pocket of her grey sweatshirt. "This is her school photo."

She handed a much-handled photo to me. The image featured a cute little girl with dimples, long auburn curls and deep brown eyes. She looked just like her mother. "She's really cute! She looks like you."

"Thanks. Hey, you met anyone else here?"

"No."

"Come on. Let me introduce you to Peg," Jilly said, rising from the couch.

Peg was sitting in the chair smack dab in front of the television, her attention honed in on a morning game show.

"Hey Peg," Jilly said, bending over to give the middle-aged woman a warm hug. "How are you today?"

Peg seemed genuinely happy to see Jilly. "I'm okay. Who's your friend?"

"This is Belinda."

"Hi, Belinda. I'm Peggy, but you can call me Peg like everyone else. Good to know you," the petite blonde woman said, rising from her chair to greet me. "Welcome to the funny farm." She grinned.

"Funny farm?" I said, intrigued.

"Yeah," Jilly said. "I really wish she wouldn't call it that."

"Isn't that what they call mental institutions where they put the crazies like us?" Peg said.

"We aren't crazy!" Jilly said, obviously annoyed.

Peg laughed. "No, Jilly, we aren't. Maybe just a wee bit off the rails upstairs. But doesn't everything about this place and the way they treat you scream funny farm?"

"Yeah, sometimes." Jilly nodded in agreement.

"So, Belinda, when did you arrive?" Peg said, abruptly changing the subject.

"A couple of days ago ... and you?"

"Two months. Apparently, it takes a while to recover from a nervous breakdown," Peg said.

"Oh," I said, unsure of how to respond. I wasn't even sure what a nervous breakdown was.

These two women seemed so ordinary. They weren't crazy or 'off the rails' as Peg jokingly put it, they were just troubled – like me. Peg was funny, but I had to wonder if she used her dry sense of humor to hide from her pain. Still, I appreciated the way she lightened things up, made me laugh and helped me forget where I was, even if only for a moment. Jilly was the sensitive one – she was a bit like me. The three of us sat chatting like old friends for the next hour. I was surprised how much I liked chatting with these two ladies. We talked about our families, our doctors, and even the reasons that had brought us there, and I felt something I'd not felt from anyone else in my life – acceptance. We shared a common bond of emotional and mental suffering. Suddenly I didn't feel quite so alone. No, they didn't have anorexia nervosa, but they knew what it felt like to hurt inside. They knew what it was like to cry yourself to sleep at night. They understood the darkness that so often felt as if it would swallow you up, or the depression that sometimes became so heavy it felt like you were suffocating. They knew and they understood. Finally, I had met others who truly grasped my inner pain. I felt blessed to know them.

I wondered if Jesus had heard my cries after all? Perhaps they hadn't been in vain. Perhaps these two women were His reply, so that I wouldn't feel so abandoned, so alone. Perhaps after all His gaze of love was shining down on me and dispelling the long shadows of darkness through the warmth and camaraderie I had found today with Jilly and Peg. I still hated this place, my life and the devil doctor, but my spirits had been lifted and an unbearable situation had been made bearable, because for a few brief moments I had forgotten how abandoned I felt. In that hour of conversation with Jilly and Peg, I forgot my anger and resentment at being held a captive here with no freedom unless I did as I was ordered. Forgetting felt good. How sad that it was to be so fleeting.

Heavenly Father,
Teach me to trust that in life's trials and sufferings
I am never alone or abandoned. For it is in times of suffering
You are closest to me, to uplift, comfort, give strength,
courage and hope. Grant me wisdom to see there is a purpose
to suffering – and the realization that Your presence is
oh so near, closer than my very breath!
Amen.

CHAPTER 7

SHELTER ME FROM EVIL

Deliver us from evil...

Matthew 6:13

BENEATH THY WINGS

Shelter me beneath Thy wings
Where I shall fear no earthly things.
Let shadows draw nigh in the night
The victory's mine in heaven's light!
For nestled oh so close to Thee
From every fear You set me free.
I shall not fear what man can do
I have my hiding place in You.

Shelter me beneath Thy wings
Where I shall fear no earthly things.
Let rain come down and thunder roll,
O Lord and Savior of my soul!
In love with power to transform
I'll find refuge from the storm.
I shall not fear what man can do
I have my hiding place in You.

ithin the first two weeks of confinement, my weight had risen to eighty-two pounds, and I was slowly being given back parts of my life the devil doctor had stolen from me. Dr. Kraft had granted me phone privileges again. I could call Mom, but there was one hitch – my calls were timed. Dr. Kraft gave me fifteen minutes of phone privileges three times a week. "Big of him," I thought. Although I was livid at the injustice of it all, I had other more immediate issues to handle – like trying to quell the internal fear that came with every pound gained.

As my weight began to rise, the Voice chattered incessantly. As the needle on the scale rose, the fear level rose right alongside it. But gaining weight was the only way I'd ever get out of here, I kept reminding myself. In an attempt to allay the overwhelming fear, I told myself over and over again to gain weight – to play the game, because it was the only way to regain control of my life. Besides that, it was going to be the only way to go home and get far, far away from this shrink that I didn't care for in the least.

No matter how hard I tried, I just couldn't relate to Dr. Kraft. He wasn't warm, genuine or compassionate like Dr. Tully had been. I was convinced he didn't care one iota about me. Oh, he tried to be friendly, but it never came off as anything more than an act. I never got the feeling he really understood anorexia – as evidenced by his behavioral modification program, which was doing more harm than good. It was painfully obvious that he had no experience in helping someone suffering from an eating disorder. Unless Dr. Kraft had something up his sleeve that I wasn't aware of, I had no confidence in his ability to unravel the mess of emotions that kept me sick and depressed. I had no idea why I was suffering from anorexia nervosa, but I did know that being committed to this psych ward – and being in the care of a shrink who was delusional enough to believe that coercing me into gaining weight was the answer – wasn't the answer at all. The answer had to lie in all those jumbled feelings and emotions that kept churning away inside me, making me more afraid and more despondent by the day. But I hadn't a clue how to express my thoughts or feelings – at least not in a healthy way. I had spent my life trying to suppress my emotions for fear of provoking Dad's wrath or in an effort to avoid trouble for Mom. Those long-buried emotions were like a volcano that had lain dormant for years and was now threatening to erupt – an eruption that had the potential to obliterate everyone in its path. Yet the fear of facing whatever it was that had gotten me to this point in the first place was too much, so I thought it best to just not think about anything at all.

How pointless it seemed to have a psychiatrist if I couldn't or wouldn't deal with the feelings and emotions that were making me sick in the first place. But hang on, wasn't it his job to help me find a way to open up – to sort through these feelings - to maybe even make sense of them? Perhaps that might have happened with another psychiatrist or Dr. Tully at some point, but it wasn't going to happen with Dr. Kraft. This whole funny farm scenario was a total waste of all our time and my parents' money. The minute Dr. Kraft sealed my bathroom door shut, he had also sealed shut any hope of ever getting me to trust, open up or feel any rapport with him. Heck, I found myself struggling to hold a conversation with him, much less express my deepest feelings. Humiliating and demeaning someone wasn't the way to get into their head, their heart or their soul. So I kept silent – but while we didn't talk about my feelings per se, Dr. Kraft took me by surprise when he asked about the Voice.

"Belinda, do you feel as though there is a part of you – a separate voice, let's say, that controls your actions and thoughts regarding the anorexia?"

"Maybe." I tried to avoid giving him an honest answer. Did I really want him to know about the Voice? I wondered how he knew about it at all, or where he was going with this question.

"If you were to give that part of your psyche a name, what would it be?"

I didn't need to give this any thought at all. It was strange, but I immediately had a name in mind. It was as if that Voice had been waiting for this 'coming out' moment all along. Finally, it was being recognized for the powerful force it was! "The Gobbler," I blurted out.

Dr. Kraft sat quietly for a moment as if deep in thought before he responded. "Perhaps," he said, "we should consider the Gobbler in its verb form. It shows what this illness is doing to you – gobbling you up."

For once there was something he and I could agree on. He was correct. This illness was most certainly gobbling me up – body, mind, and soul.

I wondered what his motives were for wanting to give the Voice a distinct name of its own? It seemed to me that in naming the Voice he was calling it out – giving it an identity that was separate from my own. For years there'd been warring factions duking it out inside my head. But what if naming it somehow solidified it, and perhaps even gave that Voice more power and control over me? Dr. Kraft had given the Voice its very own persona, and it was this persona Dr. Kraft seemed most interested in knowing more about.

"Belinda, I want you to write something in your journal for me about how the Gobbler feels about you weighing eighty-two pounds." He seemed to be talking as if I had a split personality. I didn't. I guess sometimes it certainly felt that way, because the Voice did have immense power over my thoughts and actions and had become the stronger and more dominant part of my personality. I vacillated between loving it and hating it. There were days when I wouldn't have traded the eating disorder for anything in the world, because it gave me a sense of supreme control; it made me invincible. At times like those

I clung to it, ready and willing to defend it – to hold on to it even if it meant my very life. I relished that euphoric feeling of not being powerless, and growing right alongside that sense of power and control the illness had given me something even more unexpected – a new identity.

I had been ill now for roughly six years, and during that time the Voice had slowly *become* my identity. I no longer knew who I was without it, how I would cope without it, how I would *live*. In my mind I was Belinda the Anorexic, and she acted nothing at all like the good girl I used to be. The good little girl I'd always been – the sweet, obedient child who only wanted to please others, who could be so easily controlled – was being overshadowed by this new, strong, manipulative and angry version of me – an ill-mannered and hateful version I really didn't care for. But it didn't matter whether or not I liked my new angry persona, because I felt powerless to resist it.

I could rail against the Voice all I wanted, and I often did in those moments when the other part of me – the good part – shouted at it to shut up, leave me hell alone and let the torment cease. But the Voice was beginning to sound more and more like evil personified, and it had me right where it wanted me – powerless to prevent myself from thinking about food, scales, weight and fat. There were moments when I longed to go back to my life the way it had been before the eating disorder. It would be in such fleeting moments that I felt at my weakest, because I realized my innocence had been lost. I was no longer that same girl. I couldn't go back. Such thoughts pierced my heart as waves of grief washed over me, making me feel as if my life was once more spiraling out of control. It was in this weakened state of vulnerability that the Voice came to my rescue, telling me it would save me – return to me the control over my emotions and my world that I so desperately needed, if I'd only just listen to it – let it have its way with me. So I hung on its every word and obeyed its every command because inside me lived a scared little girl, crying. She was lost in the dark and couldn't find her way back to the light on her own. She needed Jesus for that. He had always been the light in her life, and now that light was gone, like a lamp that had been switched off. She'd been immersed in total darkness with the Voice of an eating disorder bent on her destruction. How unfortunate for her that she didn't realize the Voice was lying, and every pound that fell off, every new bone that protruded and was meant to give her power and control over her emotions, was merely an illusion of the power and control she sought so desperately.

Yes, I *hated* the eating disorder, yet I *needed* it because I believed that I would never be able to deal with life and all the pain I had stuffed so deeply inside without it. Anorexia had become my outlet to cope and survive emotionally, and yet my means of coping was destroying me. I was caught in the middle of this relentless war inside my head, and I had no idea how I'd gotten here, or how – or even if – I wanted to silence the Voice. No wonder I was so depressed. Maybe I really belonged here on this funny farm.

7:00 a.m. The bold black numerals on the clock above the nurses' station seemed to taunt me with the early hour. I just wanted to sleep. The medications I was being routinely given had taken their full effect by now, and being tired all the time was chief among those effects. Yet here I was, the good little girl, once again doing what was expected of me, doing what I was told to do.

In this case I was expected to be up and in the solarium at 7:00 a.m. for my morning feeding. I'd grown to resent the coercion tactics they used here to make me eat just so I might regain my life and my freedom – a freedom they'd had no right to take away in the first place. I laughed to myself. I had to wonder what Dr. Kraft would think if he realized I was playing along with his little game just in order to get out of here and go home. I thought it odd that I wanted to go home regardless of how much I had always hated being there. I was finally out from under Dad's icy stares, his raging temper and his total domination, and all I felt was homesick. But at least home was familiar. I knew what to expect, and I had some vestige of control over my life. Here I was in foreign territory among strangers, and the control they wielded over my life was totalitarian. Why was it everyone, everywhere I went, thought they could control me? And they wondered why I was so angry!

There were patients lined up in the solarium this morning, and they didn't appear to be waiting for breakfast. Then I recalled that it was Thursday, and I remembered what Jilly had told me about Thursday being the day patients had their ECT treatments. That, I assumed, was the reason I was seeing so many new faces. The two large couches held four or five people each, and the chairs that lined the bright, sunny windows seated several more. I watched as the morning nurse with the long, scowling face made her rounds, doling out a familiar little white cup of meds to each of them. She looked like she was having another bad day to me. Maybe she was the one that needed the happy pills, I mused.

I spied Jilly coming down the hall towards the solarium, and I was glad to see her friendly face. She made her way towards me through the maze of patients, couches, and chairs and took a seat beside me at the long dining room table.

"Hey! How are you today?" She tried to sound upbeat, but her swollen, bloodshot eyes told a different story.

"Okay," I replied. I wanted to ask her why she'd been crying but I wasn't sure I should. So instead I just made small talk. "I guess these people are waiting for their ECT treatments?"

"Yeah. It's Thursday." She paused. A look of sadness fell

across her face as her eyes rested on a young man about her age sitting near us waiting for his treatment. His glassy-eyed stare told me his medication had taken effect. Then Jilly continued, "I guess that will be me next Thursday."

Now I got why she'd been crying. "When did you find this out, Jilly?"

"Last night. My doctor came by when Bobby – my husband – was here."

"So, that's who that big guy was I saw you kissing!" I said, in a weak attempt to lighten the mood.

"Yeah," she said with a half-smile. "That's him."

"So, what, the medication isn't working?" I asked.

She looked down at the table-top and shook her head. "It doesn't seem to be."

"I'm so sorry, Jilly."

She nodded, and began to cry again.

"I didn't mean to start you off again. I just had to go and open my big mouth."

"It's okay. I'd have told you anyway. I'm just scared. I don't know what to expect. The doctor says I could lose my memory. That's one of the possible side effects."

I had no comforting words. I knew nothing about ECT treatments. I reached over and put my hand on her arm in a gesture of support. "I don't know what to say, Jilly, except I'd be scared too."

"I don't want to think about it anymore," she said, looking up and wiping away the tears that streaked her pretty, freckled face.

Breakfast arrived. It was the usual: eggs in some shape or form, toast and fruit. That's what I chose to eat anyway. The oatmeal had the consistency of mud, and the sausage patties were always hard or burnt. But on this particular morning neither of our minds was on the food in front of us. We were watching the nurses as they led those awaiting ECT one by one down the hall to a designated room for their treatment.

I wondered what was going to happen to these people. What exactly was ECT? Why did Jilly say she might not have her memory afterwards? I couldn't begin to imagine how frightened she must be.

"You gotta sit here after breakfast today?" Jilly said.

"Yeah, same old same old," I said with a note of sarcasm.

"Then I'll sit with you, and keep you company," Jilly said, smiling more brightly. Who was she trying to cheer up, herself or me?

I was happy to have her there. We chose a couch near the bright solarium windows that morning to spend the hour after breakfast. Already seated on one end of the couch was a dark-haired, middle-aged man.

"Hey, Father Sam. How you doing today?" Jilly asked.

Looking up from the book he was reading, the forty-something man said, "Okay, and you?"

He didn't sound okay. He sounded depressed to me. But then, who wasn't – considering where we were?

"Father Sam, this is my friend Belinda," Jilly said. From across the solarium we noticed one of the nurses beckoning to Jilly. "Let me go see what she wants." Giving Father Sam a wink, she said, "Keep my friend company for me while I'm gone!"

"Sure," Father Sam said, closing his book. "Nice to meet you, Belinda." I liked his voice; it was deep and soft. Then, I noticed he was staring at the cross pendant I wore around my neck.

"That crucifix – are you Catholic?" he asked.

"Yeah. You too?" I replied.

"I was a priest," he said with a note of sadness.

"I suppose I should have guessed that from your title," I said, a little embarrassed. "What do you mean 'was'?" I saw the pain flash through his eyes as soon as I'd asked the question. He looked away. Perhaps I shouldn't have asked. "I'm sorry. I'm not trying to be nosy."

"No. It's okay. I don't mind you asking. It just makes me sad, that's all," he began. "I had to give up my duties because of depression."

"I am so sorry, Father. Can you go back when you are better?"

"I don't know. It's not that simple, unfortunately. Besides, it isn't up to me. I don't really see my return to the priesthood happening. You see – and I don't know why I feel the need to tell you this – but I tried to kill myself about a year ago." He unbuttoned the cuffs of his long-sleeved grey flannel shirt to show me the scars that remained. "Painful reminders," he said.

I was stunned by his candid admission. Unsure how to respond, I simply blurted out what I was thinking, "Why? Why did you do that?"

"Because my faith grew weak. I was weak. I just wanted the pain to stop. I didn't trust in God, as I should have. This illness – this depression – runs in my family. I've always thought I would be strong enough to fight it with God's help. I wanted to be the one to break the family curse. But I allowed the enemy to overcome me in a moment of weakness."

I could see Father Sam's eyes filling with tears, and I searched for some way to console him. I knew as a Catholic that the Church viewed suicide as a mortal sin. I wondered if he was concerned about forgiveness for what he had tried to do, so I said, "God forgives – you already know that. He will forgive you."

"Yes, perhaps *He* will. Perhaps He already has. But I'm not sure *I* can ever forgive myself. I let God down. I let the Church and my congregation down. I let my family, and even myself down." Tears trickled down his troubled face.

"I will pray for you, Father." It was all I could offer him.

He looked up at me and smiled warmly. "Young lady, what are you doing in here? You don't belong here. You are obviously so different from any of us."

I wasn't exactly sure what he meant by this comment, but I took it as a compliment and smiled back. Now my eyes were filling with tears too. This gentle, soft-spoken man carried inside him the shame for what he'd done, and that shame ran as deep as the depression that caused him to do it in the first place. I felt so sad for him.

Nurse Karen approached us. "Father Sam, your doctor is waiting for you in your room," she said in her usual sweet tone.

"Thank you," Father Sam said. We rose together from our seats on the couch. He turned to me to offer a hug. "Belinda, I am so glad to have met you. Perhaps we can talk again soon. Thank you, my dear, for your prayers. Bless you."

Father Sam had made a strong impression on me, and his story had moved me deeply. I didn't understand why God would allow someone who had given his or her life in service to Him to suffer so unbearably. I hardly knew Father Sam, and yet I knew he was someone I'd like to get to know better. I gravitated towards his warmth, sensitivity and gentleness, and more than anything I wanted to find a way to help him. But the only way I knew how to do that was to pray for him. The prayer that kept coming to mind was the one that often brought me comfort, one I imagine as a priest Father Sam had said many times - The Lord's Prayer.

Our Father, who art in Heaven, hallowed be Thy name. Thy kingdom come; Thy will be done on Earth as it is in Heaven. Give us this day our daily bread, and forgive us our trespasses as we forgive those who trespass against us. Lead us not into temptation, but deliver us from evil. Heavenly Father, hold Father Sam close to You. Keep him safe from temptation and evil, be his refuge and hiding place. May he find peace in Your presence where there is only light, love and peace, and may he find victory over his every fear.
Amen.

CHAPTER 8

THE DARKEST VALLEY

Surely goodness and mercy shall follow me all the days of my life: and I will dwell in the house of the LORD for ever.

Psalm 23:6

GOD'S MASTER PLAN

To everything there's a reason and rhyme.
For everything a season and time.
It's not for us to understand,
The purpose behind God's master plan.

Childlike trust He asks of you,
Faith that His presence is guiding you,
Belief a higher purpose is in all things,
Even the suffering and pain life brings.

Just when you think you've got it all figured out,
'Life happens' to fill you with questions and doubts.
In a world of confusion, doubt and despair,
His presence whispers, "Seek Me in prayer.
Lean into My comfort – Trust in My ways,
Let My light and love lead you all of your days."

I woke with a start, my dreams interrupted by the clamor of the nurses in the hallway just outside my door. Groggy, I tried to shake off the medication that made waking up every morning a struggle. Rubbing the sleep from my eyes, I managed to open them just wide enough to see the time on the clock beside the bed stand. The large illuminated roman numerals told me it was 4:00 a.m. It would have been so much easier to just fall off to sleep again and forget the noise in the hallway, but something more than idle curiosity demanded that I rise from the warmth of my bed at this early hour to see what was going on.

Still trying to shake off the medication, I climbed slowly out of bed and made my way to the doorway. As I peeked around the corner, I spied several nurses and doctors in a huddle down the hall. My vision was poor without my contact lenses in, but I got the distinct sense that something was very wrong. I watched as a nurse wheeled a small cart with an odd-looking machine into a room – and it suddenly dawned on me that it was Father Sam's room.

From my hiding place I saw Nurse Karen headed down the hall. Not wanting her to see I was peeking around the corner of the door frame, I drew back for a moment into the shadows of the darkened room as she passed. I had to keep watching, though. I wanted to know if Father Sam was all right.

I looked on apprehensively, hoping for some sign that he was okay or some small clue as to what was going on. A long twenty minutes passed and the small team of nurses and doctors that had been huddled in the hallway earlier finally exited Father Sam's room. Two men in white coats that I didn't recognize were pushing a stretcher – and there was someone on it!

I scrunched my eyes together, hoping it would help me to see a little better, but at this distance and with my lousy vision, it was impossible to see anything clearly. The two men in the white coats were headed towards the elevator, which was at least a little closer to my room. As they stood waiting for the elevator doors to open, I made out the shape of a body lying on that stretcher. If it was Father Sam, I needed to know what had happened to him.

I hardly knew him, yet I was deeply concerned for his welfare. I continued to watch intently until the nurses, doctors, and the unidentified figure on the stretcher had disappeared behind closed elevator doors. Eager to find out what had happened, I no longer cared if the hospital staff saw me. I sprang from my hiding place and ran to the nurses' station. I was in luck; Nurse Karen was on duty. Perhaps she'd give me the answers I sought.

"Nurse Karen," I said anxiously. "The commotion in the hall woke me up. I could see from my doorway that something was happening in Father Sam's room. Is he okay?"

From the expression on Nurse Karen's face, I could see I had taken her by surprise with my question. Busily putting pills into the tiny paper cups for the morning meds, she paused and said, "Belinda, I can't give you information about another patient."

"You can't even tell me if he is *okay*?" I said, nearly pleading with her.

I didn't want to seem too emotional – I was in a psych ward, after all. What if they tried to sedate me to calm me down? I tried to contain my distress, but the tears that were filling my eyes would be harder to hide.

Nurse Karen's green eyes shone with compassion. Walking around from behind the nurses' station, she asked me to sit down on the couch. She stooped down in front of me and held my hands in hers.

"Belinda, I can't tell you the specifics. I might even get in trouble for telling you what I am going to tell you now, but I can see Father Sam meant a great deal to you. Father Sam passed away this morning. I'm so sorry."

I stared at her in disbelief. I had spoken to him only hours ago. I was numb, aware only of the warm tears that now trickled down my face.

"Belinda, are you all right?" Nurse Karen reached up, wiping my tears away with a tissue. She was so kind, and she had the energy of a caring mother.

I nodded. "But I just spoke to him yesterday. He was so sweet ... so gentle. I can't believe this. Why? What happened to him?" I needed to know more.

"I'm sorry, sweetie. That's all I can give you right now."

I knew she would have told me more if she could. I really liked Nurse Karen, and I surely didn't want to get her in any kind of trouble, so I didn't press for more.

"Why don't you go back to bed and try get some rest?" she said. "It's barely five a.m."

"Yeah, okay." I rose from the couch. "Thank you."

She smiled back, squeezing my hands in hers.

I walked slowly back to my room and threw myself on the bed, crying. But these tears weren't only for Father Sam. Yes, I had been drawn to him for some reason, and I felt horrible that something so tragic had happened to him, but the truth was I hardly knew him. These tears were for Grandma. My beloved Grandma Ruby, whom I missed so very much. My grief over her death had still not healed. Father Sam's passing had brought all those feelings I'd stuffed inside to the surface.

Burying my face in my pillow, I turned my thoughts to God. Why, Heavenly Father? Why did Grams have to die? And why Father Sam, when all he wanted was to get well and go back to being a priest? I don't understand. Please Lord! Can't you help me understand?

Nurse Karen came into my room at 7:00 a.m. for the morning weigh-in.

"Did you get any sleep, sweetie?" she asked.

"No, not really. I couldn't stop thinking about Father Sam. You know, I just met him yesterday, and I really hoped to get to know him better. I could sense how sad he was. But there was just something about him that was special. I could feel it."

"Yeah, everybody here said the same thing. There was just something about him," Nurse Karen said, opening the blinds to let the morning sunlight stream in.

"Nurse Karen, how do you do it?"

"How do I do what, sweetie?"

"Get used to people dying around you? Get used to people being in such pain?"

"Well fortunately, as a psych nurse, I don't lose many patients. As a nurse, though, we're trained to not get too involved – too attached. But I admit that is something I personally struggle with." She paused for a moment to motion me over to the scale. "You know, Belinda, sometimes it seems like life has no purpose ... no reason or rhyme. If you believe in God then I think you just have to trust Him, and believe that things happen for a reason. As for death, it's just a part of life we all have to learn to accept. You're just a kid yet, and that's something that takes a little bit of age to understand."

I shuddered as I set my bare feet onto the cold steel platform of the scale. "Eighty-five pounds. Dr. Kraft will be pleased," she said, smiling. "See you down at breakfast."

Neither food nor hunger was on my mind that morning, but I was anxious to get to breakfast so I could talk to Jilly and Peg. I wanted to know if they'd heard about Father Sam. Perhaps they'd even know what had happened to him.

I dressed quickly and made my way down the long hall to the solarium. Jilly and Peg were already sitting at the table waiting for breakfast to be served. I greeted them and sat down in the vacant chair next to Jilly's. Anxious to see if they had heard the news about our friend, I said, "So, did you guys hear about Father Sam?"

"Yeah. It's terrible," Peg said.

"It's hard to believe," Jilly added.

"No one will tell me what happened to him. Do either of you know anything?" I said, hoping they had some information to share.

"I know what the rumors going around here say. He either died from a massive heart attack or suicide," Peg said.

Jilly jumped to Father Sam's defense. "Suicide! I don't believe he'd try that again."

"How can you possibly commit suicide in here anyway?" I asked. "They watch us all the time. We have bars on the windows, and there's definitely no sharp objects in my room."

"I know," Peg said. "You'd think it would be impossible to kill yourself in here, but I guess anything's possible if you want it bad enough. I don't know what's true and what isn't. All I know is that it's tragic. He was a good man. I'll miss him."

We all nodded in agreement.

"Do you think the nurses would allow us to have a little memorial service for him? Just something small to say goodbye?" I said.

"That's a lovely idea!" Jilly said.

"Let's ask," Peg said.

After breakfast, the three of us approached Nurse Karen with our idea. She loved it and told us that she'd call the hospital chaplain to set the wheels in motion.

Peg excused herself. It was time for her morning ritual – the early news shows. Jilly stayed to keep me company. We would pass my hour of surveillance together, and I was grateful for her presence because she had turned that dreaded hour every morning into something enjoyable with her friendship and conversation. From across the room, we saw the elevator doors open. Dr. Kraft emerged and headed straight to the nurses' station.

"He's early today," I said, surprised and disappointed. I would much rather have sat and chatted with my friend than have an early morning session with the devil doctor.

He and Nurse Karen seemed to be going over a chart, and he was smiling. I wondered if that chart belonged to me, and that she was telling him about my weight gain – my "wonderful progress". Eighty-five pounds. Whoopee! Well, at least one of us would have something to be happy about.

Approaching Jilly and me on the couch, he said, "You ready to get started, Belinda?"

I nodded. "Gotta go. See ya later, Jill."

Together we walked down the hallway to my room. Dr. Kraft opened the session exactly as I thought he would – with my latest weight gain.

"Your weight was up today. That's wonderful news, Belinda! That means you've gained additional privileges."

I was glad he was glowing over the news because I certainly wasn't. But I was happy to regain some of the privileges he'd stolen from me.

"I'll be adding Recreational Therapy and Occupational Therapy to the list. You can sign up at the nurses' station for day trips or go down to the OT room daily."

"Great!" I said. I wondered if he'd noticed the tone of sarcasm.

"You don't sound too happy about any of this."

"I'd prefer a visit from my mom."

"That will come in due time – as long as you continue to make progress. How do you feel about the weight gain? What's the Voice saying?"

"It doesn't like it! It's scary."

"Why it is so scary?" Dr. Kraft asked.

"I don't know. It just is."

"Are you journaling like I asked you to?

"Yes."

"May I read yesterday's entries?"

Did I have a choice? I reached for the small burgundy journal beneath my pillow. Handing it to him, I watched his reaction as he attentively read yesterday's entry:

I'm so depressed today. The Gobbler has been scream-ing in my head all day long. I fight the thoughts, but the fear is overwhelming. It is like a little demon inside of me that keeps criticizing me. "Look how fat you're getting! That stomach is going to be the size of Santa Claus's soon! Ho! Ho! Ho! You slob! No control! You're disgusting!" How do I fight against this thing that's so intent on my destruction? It is so powerful! I'm so afraid. I don't know how to deal with the fear. I don't want to live with the fear. Father Sam told me today that he had tried to commit suicide because the pain was too much to live with. I understand how he felt. Sometimes, life makes no sense. Sometimes, life is un-bearable, and not existing seems preferable to this.

"Belinda, are you having thoughts of suicide?" Dr. Kraft said, looking me sternly in the eye.

"Thoughts? Sure, sometimes. But it doesn't mean I'd do it."

"Talk to me about the fear, Belinda."

I looked away and said, "I don't know what to say. It's suf-focating. I don't think you realize, Dr. Kraft, how hard it is for me, gaining this weight."

"So tell me about it. Tell me how hard it is for you," Dr. Kraft said, removing his glasses. Once again, he tried to make that same direct eye contact that always made me so fidgety and uncomfortable.

"What am I supposed to say? It's not as if I understand the fear. I don't know where it comes from or what it's about. It's just a feeling that's there. I don't know why I'm so terrified of being fat." This wasn't a place I wanted to go – not with him anyway. So, I tried yet again to change the subject and avoid trying to express my feelings.

"Dr. Kraft, can you tell me what happened to Father Sam?"

"Father Sam wasn't my patient."

"Yes, but you can find out?"

"It is not ethical for me to do that," Dr. Kraft replied.

It was almost the same answer that Nurse Karen had given me. "Well then, let me ask you this. A few of us spoke to Nurse Karen about having a small service for Father Sam. Can I help with that? Do I need permission to attend?"

"It sounds like he meant a great deal to you."

"Kind of ... yeah. I didn't know him very well. But I did like him, even if I only met him one time. I just felt his pain. Anyway, I'd like to say goodbye. We all would."

"Of course, Belinda. If something is arranged for him on the hospital grounds, you may certainly attend."

"Thank you, Dr. Kraft." I was surprised but thankful that he'd agreed.

He smiled, and for the first time his smile felt genuine. "I think, Belinda, that you have a great deal of trouble expressing your feelings verbally. Perhaps you just don't understand what you're feeling, and that's why it is so hard for you. But I've noticed you tend to avoid my questions. So when I leave I want you to take some time today to write down your thoughts, feelings and emotions. Let it flow. You seem to have a knack for expressing yourself through the written word, anyway. So, we'll try to deal with the feelings locked up inside of you through journaling. I'll let the nurses know you're good to attend a service for your friend, if it's at the hospital, and that you are cleared to go to OT and RT as desired. I'll see you tomorrow."

The memorial service for Father Sam was held a few days later, on a Sunday afternoon in the hospital chapel. Twelve of us – staff and patients – attended the Mass. Halfway through the service, the hospital chaplain invited anyone who wished to speak about Father Sam to do so. We had elected Nurse Karen to speak for all of us. She walked to the front of the chapel to read the short tribute that both patients and staff had written in his memory:

Father Sam,

We thank you for touching each of our lives with your warmth, sensitivity and caring heart. We feel blessed to have known you. In life, you suffered the torment of depression, and many of us here today understand the pain that you lived with every single day. But today is a new day, and your suffering is over, because our Heavenly Father has called you home with Him. Together we pray that as you now spend eternity in His light and love, your soul may find peace and eternal rest in His embrace. Father Sam, we love you, and we will miss you. May His angels guide you safely on your journey home.

There wasn't a dry eye in the chapel when Nurse Karen finished. Jilly had requested the chaplain read the Twenty-Third Psalm, which according to her had been one of Father Sam's favorites. The chaplain read it at the conclusion of the service. It had been a lovely memorial, and one that I was sure would have made Father Sam feel very loved. I closed my eyes to say one last prayer before leaving:

Belinda Rose

Heavenly Father,
Have mercy on Father Sam's soul. Lead him home to You,
that he may dwell where suffering is no more. Let him find
that joy, peace and love that eluded him in life – a joy, peace,
and love that we can find only in You. Let him know how very
much we all cared about him, and that he touched our lives.
Let him know I'll never forget him.
In the Name of the Father, the Son and the Holy Spirit ...
Amen.

CHAPTER 9

A DOUBTING HEART

*Trust in the LORD with all your heart and do not lean on
your own understanding.*

Proverbs 3:5

Jesus,
What's life about?
My spirit is troubled.
My heart's filled with doubt.
A world
of suffering is all I see.
Please help me dear Jesus
I just want to
believe.

By the beginning of the third week of my incarceration I had gained ten pounds, and at a
whopping eighty-seven and a half, I felt a little
like a baby whale. Physically, I felt much better.
My legs no longer ached and throbbed constantly, and I felt
a little stronger, but my mental and emotional health continued to spiral downwards.

The Voice was never quiet now. It droned on and on, and
the more it did, the more afraid and depressed I became. But

no matter how loudly the Voice squealed in my head in resistance to the weight gain, I had no choice but to put on weight if I ever wanted to get out of here and go home.

Being eighty-seven pounds had its perks, I suppose. If I continued on this "forward path", as Dr. Kraft so succinctly put it, I could have a visit from Mom and Dad this weekend. I wanted to see Mom desperately, but Dad not so much. I guess at least the week was starting off with something to look forward to.

But even though the thought of seeing Mom over the coming weekend gave me something positive to focus on, my journal entries had become increasingly dark as the depression grew ever deeper. That darkness had begun to seep onto the pages of my journal and seemed to upset Dr. Kraft very much. My entry for the evening of Father Sam's memorial was particularly disconcerting to him. It was this journal entry that he chose to focus on in our session the following Monday afternoon.

I watched Dr. Kraft's expression carefully as he read over the journal entry, wondering what his thoughts were. He appeared concerned – troubled even. Looking up from the page, he handed the journal back to me and said, "Belinda, read this aloud."

I didn't understand why he'd want me to do that, but I complied.

Why does life hurt so much? When I was fifteen, I had dreams of being in college at this age and studying to be a psychiatrist. But by some sick cosmic twist, I am in a mental ward instead, being treated by one. I thought at eighteen life was about having dreams and fulfilling them, but I no longer have any dreams except one – to get out of here. Dreams are for others, not me. What dreams I might have had were shattered by an illness no one seems to understand and no one seems to be able to help me get over. I don't know how to fight such a forceful enemy from within. I hate my life. Perhaps Father Sam and Grandma are the ones that are better off in the end. Their pain and suffering is over. I wish mine was as well.

By the time I had finished reading the entry, the emotions behind those words had overcome me – the tears flowed.

"Belinda, talk to me," Dr. Kraft said. "Tell me your feelings about why your life hurts so much. You say you hate your life and that your grandma and Father Sam are better off because they are dead. What do you mean? Are you saying you'd be better off dead?" Dr. Kraft's voice was unusually soft.

"I mean what the journal says. What more is there to say?" I looked away, avoiding his gaze. Instead, my eyes fixed on the steel bars that the late October sun was streaming through. "Life isn't worth living. I miss my Grams horribly. If my life is going to turn out like the people in here are leading, what's the point? There's nothing to look forward to. Besides, Dr. Kraft, I can't stand this ache inside anymore. I'm tired of hurting and being hurt. Really, what's the point to any of this? Life ... it's just all pain and misery from where I'm sitting."

"There is so much that you are not telling me, Belinda. I don't know what has happened to you, where all your pain comes from, but I know there is a lot you haven't told me. Do you feel as if you would hurt yourself?"

"You mean, do myself in? I don't know. It's just a thought. That's it." That was as honest as I could be. The more I explored this dark place inside, the more the pain rose up, threatening to overwhelm me. Perhaps I was afraid of facing all the abuse, the rape, the bullies and Grams's death for fear that if I let it all out I would never be able to stuff it away in its safe little storage compartment ever again. That compartment was a Pandora's box that I'd long been terrified of opening. I worried that if it were ever to be opened, I simply wouldn't be able to handle it. Perhaps I was frightened that I'd find myself pushed over the edge, with suicide the only answer.

"I'm really concerned. I feel you are falling deeper into depression. Do you think that is a correct assumption?"

"Yes. I guess so. This place is depressing." What did he expect? Being put in here and forced to gain weight had only made things worse for me. Every morning as I stood on that monstrous scale, I cringed. Every half pound I gained only added to the depression.

"Perhaps I need to consider increasing your medication."

"Please don't do that. I struggle with the dose you have me on already."

"What do you mean, 'struggle'?"

"I mean I feel doped up all the time. I'm dizzy. I have trouble waking up in the morning. It's like my head is in a constant fog. I feel jittery and anxious all the time. I tremble and shake. I don't want any more drugs!"

"Okay. I will leave things as they are for now. Belinda, you are Catholic, correct?"

"Yes."

"Is there a priest that you'd like to talk with? Someone you know and feel comfortable with?"

"Yeah. I suppose."

"Your patient information mentions a Father Campbell. Would you like me to put in a request for a visit with him?"

"I thought I wasn't allowed visits?"

"I think we can agree that clergy is a bit different." Dr. Kraft offered me a thin-lipped smile.

"No. I don't want him to see me in here. Not like this." I wondered what the matter was. Was Dr. Kraft so worried I was going to hurt myself that he thought a visit from my parish priest might save me?

"Are you ashamed of being here?"

"Look, I just don't want to drag him into this." In fact, I *was* ashamed. Just as ashamed as I had been the evening I'd tried to tell him about the rape and couldn't.

"Fine. If you change your mind, let me know. Let me encourage you to spend some time in OT or to go on one of the little day excursions with RT. Keep writing in your journal. Perhaps you could consider writing about all the people and events in the past who have hurt you so deeply? I'll see you tomorrow."

I nodded, but it wasn't in agreement. I wasn't going to be writing about the traumatic events of my life, especially for his eyes. All I wanted was to gain enough weight to go home and get out of this funny farm. That would be my main focus.

At dinner that evening, Jilly seemed preoccupied. Over the past three weeks she had become my dearest ally in this place. Although she was nearly twenty years older than me, the age difference had never seemed to matter. She often joked that she was old enough to be my mother, and perhaps that motherly instinct and missing her own daughter so much was the reason she had taken me under her wing in the first place. Whatever the reason was, I had come to look at my relationship with Jilly as the one thing I had to look forward to here each day. I had grown so attached to her, and I felt as though I knew her well enough now to ask her what was on her mind.

"Jilly, is everything okay? You seem a million miles away tonight."

"Thursday's the day."

"The day for what?"

"My first treatment."

"You mean the first ECT treatment?"

She nodded.

"Oh Jilly." I didn't have the words to comfort her, so I hugged her.

"Yeah. I am so afraid. What if I lose my memory?" she said, trying to force back the tears that filled her deep brown eyes.

"Are you sure you will?"

"Memory loss is one of the side effects, the doctor says. Sometimes, it's only short-term, sometimes not. But it terrifies me, Belinda. What if I don't remember my baby girl or my husband?" The tears that filled her eyes began to fall freely as she continued. "My husband is coming to visit tonight, and I even get to see my little girl before the first treatment. I just don't know what to expect. But I'm not getting any better ... at least that's what the doctor says. This is kind of a last-ditch effort. At least, that's how I see it. I just want to get well and go home to my family."

I didn't really know what to think or say, but I did know that I was as upset about her having to go through these treatments as she was. I had seen the dazed and drugged expressions on the faces of the patients awaiting ECT treatments on Thursday mornings, and I didn't want my dear friend to be among them.

The days leading up to that inevitable Thursday morning passed quickly. Now that I had the freedom to go to Occupational Therapy, I could go with Jilly. I was happy about that because it meant that I could spend more time with her. It was only a few days before Halloween, and the OT staff threw a Halloween party. Jilly and I had fun. We laughed like little girls, almost forgetting where we were or why we were here at all. It felt a bit like being in grade school again when we made Halloween decorations to adorn our classroom. In this case, however, it was the OT room we were adorning. Then we painted scary faces on pumpkins. Prizes were given out, and amazingly I won first prize, which was an adorable stuffed pumpkin.

Occupational Therapy had been a good diversion that week. It had kept Jilly's mind occupied with something other than the fear she felt every time she thought of Thursday morning and the ECT treatment that was looming. But a diversion was all it was. Thursday morning came, and I met Jilly in the solarium that morning to wish her well before her treatment.

As I entered the solarium, I found her sitting by herself crying.

"Hey. How you doing?" I said, leaning over to give her a hug.

"I'm not gonna lie ... I'm terrified," she said. From the look of her swollen, bloodshot eyes she had been crying for a while. I wanted to cry too, because I was afraid for her. But I was determined to stay strong and not shed any tears in front of her.

"I'm praying for you, Jilly. I'm praying it's all going to be okay."

"Thank you, Belinda. You are the sweetest thing."

"Stay positive. I'll be by to see you later tonight if they let me in."

"Yeah. I'd like that."

We sat together as we had so many other times before. Only this time it was different. She wasn't helping me pass the time; this time I was helping her. The morning nurse with the scowling face approached and asked Jilly to sit on the couch with the others waiting for treatment. I gave her one last hug.

I watched as the nurse gave her the medication just as she did all the others, and then I could watch no more. My heart was breaking. I didn't want to witness Jilly being dazed and confused, so I left for my room without breakfast. Let them be mad at me. Let them take my privileges away. I couldn't stand to watch my only friend being led away down the hallway to have bolts of electricity zapped through her brain. It seemed inhumane. Everything about the way they treated us seemed inhumane.

Nurse Karen came to my room a little later to see why I had not been at breakfast. I was glad it was her, because she was the only one I could have told. I was crying when she came into my room. I knew why she was there, and I spoke up before she had a chance.

"I'm not trying to be difficult," I said, "but they took Jilly for ECT this morning. I couldn't stand to watch as they took her down the hall. So I came to my room. I guess I'm in trouble, huh?"

"No, sweetie, you aren't in trouble." She sat beside me on the bed and put her hand on mine. "We were just concerned. I'll have a tray sent to your room. Try to eat something anyway, okay?"

I nodded, but I knew in my heart I couldn't eat a bite. Not today.

It was early evening when I approached the nurses' station to ask for permission to visit Jilly. I was told that her husband was with her, and that I could go in after he'd gone. So I sat in the solarium and passed time with Peg. But Peg's eyes were glued to the television screen, and she wasn't much of a conversationalist that evening. I sat in the silence, nervously looking towards Jilly's room, waiting for her husband to make his exit.

My wait wasn't long. I saw him leave her room and make his way to the nurses' station. My heart dropped when I saw he had been crying. When he got on the elevator, I made my way to Jilly's room, not sure what to expect.

I entered her room and found her lying in bed, awake and alert. I hoped that was a good sign.

"Hey Jilly," I said, edging a little closer to her bedside.

Her pretty brown eyes rested on me in confusion, and then she said, "Do I know you?"

I was caught off guard by her comment. I don't know what I was expecting, but I wasn't expecting this. "Yes, it's Belinda."

She looked at me as if I was a total stranger and said, "I'm sorry. I don't know you."

Emotion overwhelmed me. My heart sank. I turned and bolted for my room. Flopping down on the large overstuffed chair in the corner, I curled up into a fetal position and cried. My heart was broken and my mind was racing with a million questions. Why didn't she know me? Had she lost her memory? Is that why her husband had been crying, too? Maybe she didn't even know him! Would she get her memory back? Had I lost my only friend in this Godforsaken place? Why had the doctors done this to her? How was this helping her any more than taking my privileges away was helping me? But the hurt I was feeling suddenly turned to anger at the injustice of it all. I wasn't just angry with the doctors that treated us like lab rats, I was angry with a God that allowed it.

Why, God? Why do You let things like this happen? Why did Jilly have to lose her memory? What about her little girl? Why did You take Father Sam away ... and Grams? Why did You let Dad hurt me for all those years ... why did You let all those kids torment me? Why did You stand by and allow me to be raped? I have always adored You! I thought You loved me! Is it all a lie? Do You really exist or are you a figment of my overactive imagination?

I cried and vented my anger at God until all I felt was emptiness. It was an emptiness that I'd never felt before – a space with no feelings occupying it. Perhaps this was a good thing. Feelings hurt too much. Perhaps it was easier to just shut down and feel nothing at all. Every night since I'd been a small girl I had faithfully said my prayers to a God whom I thought was always with me, but tonight my heart was full of doubt. Tonight there would be no prayers to a God that I was no longer even sure existed.

CHAPTER 10

LORD, HAVE MERCY

Hear, O LORD, my prayer: and let my cry come to Thee.

Psalm 102:1

I'll keep my pain and anger locked away
Never again to see the light of day
Never acknowledged ... Never revealed,
Deep, deep down where I can't feel.
Hidden away so no one knows
Just how deep down the heartache goes.

*T*he full weight of my loss hit me at breakfast the next morning. Jilly had made eating and the hour of observation afterwards more bearable for me with her warm camaraderie. Without her presence to give me support and encouragement, I wasn't sure I could eat. I wasn't even sure I wanted to. I was still too upset about her this morning to care about food, as the knot churning deep in the pit my stomach attested.

I moved the scrambled eggs and sausage around the plate with my fork, toying with the idea of hiding the sausage beneath the burnt toast. The toast was disgusting enough this morning that surely no one would expect me to eat it. If I could just trick the staff into thinking I'd eaten! Unfortunately, it was an idea that would never work. Even if I did trick the nurses, I wouldn't trick the scale the next morning. I had to get out of here, so I raised the fork to my mouth and took a bite.

"Good morning, Belinda!" My mind was a million miles away, and I hadn't even noticed that Dr. Kraft was standing beside me at the table.

"Oh, Dr. Kraft, I'm sorry. I didn't see you there." I pushed the half-eaten plate of food away.

"It looks like you're about finished with breakfast, so let's head to your room for our session."

"Sure," I said getting up from the table. Anything was better than the solarium this morning without Jilly – even a session with Dr. Kraft.

"How are you today, Belinda?" Dr. Kraft said pulling up the only hard-backed chair in my room.

"I'm here," I said, choosing to curl up in the comfort of the cushy chair near the window.

"What do I detect in your voice this morning, Belinda – sadness?"

"Maybe."

"Why? What is making you feel sad today?"

I paused for a moment, wondering if I really wanted to tell him the reason why I was sad. Then I remembered that I didn't have to tell him, because it was all written down in my journal. Jumping up from my chair, I reached across the bed and pulled the burgundy journal from beneath my pillow and handed it to him. "It's all in here."

He laid the Sacred Heart prayer card that marked last night's entry to one side and began reading:

Jilly, you don't know how much it broke my heart tonight to look into your eyes and just find a blank stare looking back at me. The thing you feared the most has happened to you. How many times did you say you were afraid of the ECT because you might lose your memo-

ry? And so you have. THEY did this to you! My heart is breaking not just because I will miss you so much but because your family will. I can't even imagine their pain. I am angry, Jilly, really, really angry! I'm angry at the way we are treated in this place. We have no control over our lives. They do whatever they want with us. I am angry with God, too. All my life I have been so deeply devoted to Him, and now all I feel is betrayed. I thought that perhaps when I met you God had sent you as an answer to my prayer because I felt so alone in here. That just maybe He cared about me enough to not want me to be alone in here. But how can that be true when He has so cruelly taken you away now? Why would He give me something only to snatch it back again? I just want to go home. I want to forget this place even exists. I hate everything about it here – everything!

"Belinda, what happened to your friend Jilly? She was the woman that you spent a lot of time with – correct?"

"Yes," I said, nodding. "She had ECT yesterday. I went to see her last night and she didn't even know who I was. From the look on her husband's face when he left her room last night, she didn't know him either."

"I see," Dr. Kraft said, picking his chair up and moving it a little closer to my corner seat. "I hear you are very hurt by the fact she didn't remember you. I understand why that would make you sad. While I don't know your friend or her situation, I do know something about ECT. The memory loss and confusion she is experiencing is very likely only short-term. It is an unfortunate side effect of ECT, but I'm sure her doctor had good reasons for suggesting it as part of her therapy."

"He said she wasn't responding to the medication."

"Yes, and that's a primary reason for using it as part of a patient's therapy plan. But I want to address this anger within you. Let's start with today's journal entry. Would you like to talk about your feelings – your anger in regard to 'this place'? Is any of this anger towards me specifically?"

"Yes," I said, hanging my head, ashamed of my admission.

"If you feel this way, I want you to own it! Express it. I am sitting right here in front of you. Let me have it – all of it!"

I wasn't sure I could 'own' it. Speaking up wasn't something I was familiar or comfortable with. Dad had taught us to keep quiet – to be respectful or there'd be a high price to pay. Fidgeting with the small stuffed pumpkin that rested beside me in the chair, I flashed back to the moment I'd won it in OT just a couple of days before. I could see the smile on Jilly's face just as clearly in my mind's eye as if she was standing in front of me. That memory stung, allowing my tears and my pain to rise to the surface.

"I don't think it's fair!" I blurted out. "I don't think taking away all my privileges is fair. I don't see how this is going to make me well any more than Jilly having shock treatments will make her well! Now she doesn't even remember anyone! She has a little girl. So what happens to her? How is that kid going to feel when her Mommy asks her, 'Do I know you?' How is it you doctors don't see that some of your treatments do more harm than good?"

I had said what was on my mind, but as usual I had left out much of the emotion behind the words. I felt like screaming and raging, but I feared losing all control if I did. Instead, I had expressed my feelings as non-confrontationally as I could.

"I know you're angry. So why don't you say it like you *mean* it? I want to hear the emotion behind those words!" Dr. Kraft's tone was intense. As if he was egging me on, he continued, his voice rising to a crescendo. "Why don't you let all that pain and anger out so it can be healed?"

"I can't, Dr. Kraft. I can't," I said, crying.

"You need to let these emotions out. They're making you sick. Why can't you?"

"Because I'm afraid of what might happen if I do!"

"Afraid of what?" Dr. Kraft said.

"Afraid I may lose it!"

"So lose it! I can handle it."

"Yeah, you'll handle it with more pills!" I screamed at him.

"What if I promise not to do that?" Dr. Kraft said.

I sat silent. I wasn't going to be provoked into a rage, and rage was the form my feelings would take if I were to let them all out. He had no idea at all how ferocious the storm that raged within me was.

"So, you are also very angry at God. Do you want to talk about your feelings towards Him?"

"It's pretty simple really, Dr. Kraft. You think you have a best friend, and they've been your best friend forever. But then you find out it was all a lie. Instead of being your friend and trying to help you, they hurt you or stand back and watch you get hurt when they could have helped you. I feel betrayed. I don't understand why God allows us to suffer so much. He could end our pain instead of letting us wallow in it."

"Belinda, the questions you have about God would best be addressed by your priest. I'll ask again. Do you want him to visit you?"

"No. Not in here."

"I could ask the hospital chaplain to come see you. Would you like that?"

"Thank you, but no."

"Okay, let me or the nurses know if you change your mind. I'm not comfortable answering your questions about God. I do have some news that may cheer you up, though. Your parents are coming to visit tomorrow. You are doing very well with the program and I am lifting the ban on visitors. How does that make you feel?"

"It will be good to see Mom. I've really missed her."

"Good. I hope it gives you something to look forward to. I am pleased with your weight gain so far. Let's work towards a weekend pass out of here and home by Thanksgiving."

"What do I have to do to win that prize?" I asked sarcastically. I wasn't trying to be obnoxious – I just couldn't imagine what they'd want of me to win a trip home.

Ignoring my sarcasm, Dr. Kraft smiled and said, "Let's get you to ninety-five pounds and we'll talk about it then."

I should have been ecstatic at the thought of actually going home and getting back to school, but all I felt was a punch in the gut. Just imagining myself weighing ninety-five pounds sent chills down my spine. Ninety-five pounds was fat! I cringed at the thought, and the fact that I was being forced into weighing so much only added to the anger that simmered beneath the surface. I wondered if Dr. Kraft, for all his trying to understand my feelings, actually understood them at all. How could he not understand why I was angry with him? How would he feel if someone locked him up in this place with bars on the window against his will? And what if they proceeded to humiliate him and take away his dignity by ripping from him every human right, and then topped it all off by telling him that the only way to gain what had been taken from him, the only way to regain a few tattered scraps of whatever was left of him by that point, was to do as he was told?

"Belinda, carry on writing in your journal. Perhaps you can at the very least express the emotions by writing down all the things you don't seem to be able to express verbally. I am sorry about your friend. I hope she gets better soon. Have a good weekend. I'll see you on Monday."

I watched him leave the room and wondered what I would do with the rest of my day. It was still morning and I had the whole day to fill, with no Jilly to help me do that. I didn't want to wander down to the solarium for fear Jilly might be there. I couldn't handle having her look through me as though she'd never met me.

I thought about what Dr. Kraft had said. Was it the anger and pain I had buried so deep down inside for so long that was making me sick? Did I need to let it out before I could get well?

But I didn't want to feel anything. Feeling hurt too much. I didn't want to think. Thinking made me feel, and feeling made me hurt. It was a vicious circle. Today I didn't want to do either, so I curled up on the bed and slept the day away.

Mom called early the next morning to say she would be down to see me before noon. I could sense the excitement in her voice. She seemed as happy about seeing me as I was about seeing her. I didn't want to ruin our visit by telling her I wasn't feeling well today.

It was about eleven when she walked through the door of my hospital room, but she wasn't with Dad. Instead, she had come with a friend, our next-door neighbor Pam.

I leapt from the chair to give them both a hug. It had been four long weeks since Mom and Dad had brought me here, and I had never been away from her for that long in my life. I liked Pam. She was a good friend to both of us, but I was curious as to why Dad wasn't with Mom. "Where's Dad?"

"He had to work today. But he sent something along," Mom said.

"What?" I was curious. Dad was never one for surprises or gifts.

"The nurse should be here with it any minute now," Mom said. I couldn't help but wonder why she was being so mysterious.

The three of us were catching up when a male orderly entered the room carrying a small television. He set it down on top of the dresser, Mom thanked him, and he left.

I looked at her, amazed. "Mom, that's Dad's television from the kitchen. He'd never give that up."

"I thought you'd be surprised! Dr. Kraft said you could have a TV in your room, and Dad offered to let you use this one."

I was speechless. I couldn't believe Dad would do this for me. His televisions were his prized possessions, and this particular TV was the one that he watched the nightly news on every evening during dinner. Dad was as addicted to his TV and the news as much as Peg was to her game shows.

"Tell him I said thank you." I got up to give Mom another hug.

"Belinda, you feel warm to me. Are you feeling okay?

"I don't know. I feel a little sick to my stomach, and I sort of have a headache." I hadn't intended to tell her, but she'd asked, and I wasn't going to lie. That was all it took for Mom to head down to the nurses' station.

When she came back, Nurse Karen was with her.

"I think she's running a fever," Mom said as Nurse Karen came over to take my vitals.

"You could be right, Mrs. Rose. Let's find out for sure." Nurse Karen placed the thermometer beneath my tongue and looked at her watch. Three minutes later she had the results. "101! Belinda, how are you feeling?"

"I don't know. My tummy hurts and I've got a headache."

"Well, we have some stomach flu going around the floor. That's probably what you've got. It is just a twenty-four-hour bug. I'll go get you something for the fever. Be right back."

She returned with a tiny cup of pills. "It's just aspirin," she said. Then, turning to Mom and Pam, she said, "I know how much Belinda was looking forward to seeing you today, Mrs. Rose, but this bug is pretty contagious – and pretty nasty once it gets a hold. So maybe you need to cut this visit short, and come back when she's feeling better."

I didn't want them to go. Why did I have to get sick today of all days? But Nurse Karen was right. I didn't want Mom or Pam to get sick. Pam had a baby at home. I could see the disappointment and worry in Mom's eyes as she and our neighbor said goodbye.

"Call me tonight, sweetheart, let me know how you are feeling. I'll come back just as soon as I can." Flu bug or not, Mom and Pam both hugged me one more time. They were gone, it seemed, just as soon as they'd arrived. But it was for the best, because they had no sooner left than I found myself hunched over the toilet, feeling the full force of the virus's wrath.

For the next twenty-four hours I pretty much lived in the bathroom with Nurse Karen at my shoulder, caring for me just like Mom would have. But neither of us could ever have imagined that this simple stomach virus would be the catalyst that unleashed the full force of my deep-seated rage.

Heavenly Father,
I am surrounded by darkness.
It enfolds me like a cloak.
Within its shadows
Pain is all I know,
Despair is all I feel.
It consumes me like a raging fire;
Surely it will destroy me.
Once upon a time I knew Your gaze.
Your smile filled my heart with love;
Your laughter made my soul leap with joy!
Your light illumined the dark places in my life.
Will the sun ever shine on me again?
Lord, if You are there, I need Your healing touch.
Have mercy on me.
Amen.

CHAPTER 11

AFTERMATH

My friends scorn me:
but mine eye poureth out tears unto God.

Job 16:20

CHILD OF MINE

Child of Mine, don't you know,
I am with you wherever you go?
In your midst I'll always be;
Never shall I abandon thee.
Is your cross is too much to bear?
Come! My arms of love await in prayer.
When you falter ... when You fall;
Trust in Me through it all.
O Child of Mine, if you but knew;
In your darkest moments I carry you.

By Monday morning the virus had passed, but it had left me weak, exhausted and lightheaded. Dr. Kraft had given the nurses orders to let me sleep in, and I had taken advantage of those orders by not rising until 10:30 a.m.

The nurse with the scowling face delivered a breakfast tray

to my room and took charge of my morning weigh-in. She beckoned me towards the scale. I obeyed reluctantly, stepping once more onto the cold steel platform. From the corner of my eye I caught a glimpse of her name tag. It was the first time I recalled her ever wearing one. A closer look revealed her name: *Betty*. So she did have a name.

I watched in anticipation as Nurse Betty balanced the big steel weights with care and precision. Perhaps, as I'd been so sick, I had lost a few pounds! The Voice rejoiced at the mere thought.

"Eighty-six pounds. You've lost three and a half pounds. Dr. Kraft won't like that," she snapped, making a notation on my chart.

No, Dr. Kraft probably wouldn't, but the Voice did! The Voice was ecstatic. Grabbing a spare blanket from the closet, Nurse Betty helped me get comfortable in the cushy window chair. Wheeling the over-bed table and positioning it at the right height for my chair, Nurse Betty set a tray of food in front of me. "Eat your breakfast. Dr. Kraft will be in around noon."

Even though she'd left the room, her presence had left a distinct chill. I couldn't help but wonder what had happened to make her so aloof. Nursing would surely be the last career choice for someone who seemed to dislike people so much.

Because I had been so ill over the previous twenty-four hours, breakfast was light this morning. There was nothing here but soft-boiled eggs, toast and a small dish of fruit. I paused for a moment, reflecting on the three pounds I'd lost before scooping up a spoonful of runny eggs. Losing weight still made me very happy – gleeful, even. But that feeling of glee faded quickly when the realization hit me that losing weight pushed me just that much farther away from my goal of going home. So, like a good girl, I forced myself to eat everything on my plate.

After breakfast I telephoned Mom to let her know I was feeling better. It was wonderful having a phone of my own in my room. Having my phone privileges restored was at least some consolation for the weight Dr. Kraft had coerced me into gaining. Even if I couldn't see her as often as I liked, I could at least talk to her whenever I wanted. Speaking to her – just hearing her voice soothed my homesickness enough to make it bearable.

Mom and I had been chatting on the phone for nearly an hour, making plans for her next visit, when Dr. Kraft walked into the room. He wore a scowl on his face today too, just like Nurse Betty's. I wondered why he was in such a foul mood. Mom and I said our goodbyes. I promised her I'd call later in the day and then I turned my attention to Dr. Kraft.

"Hi, Dr. Kraft," I said, smiling in an attempt to lighten his mood.

His eyes seemed fixed on the chart in his hands. He pulled up his usual straight-backed chair, laid the chart in his lap, looked straight at me and sighed deeply. "Belinda, you've lost nearly four pounds since Friday."

"Yes, Dr. Kraft, I know. I had a stomach virus. I was really sick over the weekend."

"That may well be, but we still have to deal with this weight loss. I'm sorry, but I am going to have to revoke all of the privileges that you've gained. We will just have to start over from the beginning."

I sat there looking at him, momentarily dumbfounded, not sure whether to cry or scream. My opponent had just delivered a hard and unexpected punch to the gut. My first reaction was to cry, and I could sense tears already filling my eyes. But something deeper inside of me was rising up – that anger and rage I had repressed for so long. I'd had enough of people controlling me. *I was sick and tired of it!* Without giving it another thought, I simply gave in to that anger within. Dr. Kraft had finally unlocked that Pandora's box of rage that had been sealed shut for so very long.

Weak or not, I jumped to my feet, screaming, "What do

you mean we are going to start over? I didn't lose this weight because I tried to. I was *sick*, just like three-fourths of the patients on this floor. Sick with a stomach virus. Are they being punished for it? How can you be so unfair? How can you be so hateful and mean?" Even though I was shaking from weakness and fear, I stood my ground. I wasn't going to be intimidated by this devil doctor anymore. My face felt hot and my heart pounded wildly as my anger poured out.

Remaining cool, calm and collected, Dr. Kraft said, "I'm sorry, Belinda. I understand you are upset, but it is just how this program works. You gain weight, you gain privileges. You lose weight and you lose those privileges."

"No, Dr. Kraft, it isn't that black and white! This isn't my fault. Oh, how I HATE this place and ... and ... how much I hate YOU, too! Ever since I got here you've done nothing but humiliate me with your rewards and privileges. I'm DONE! No one should be treated like this! You have no right to treat me like a little kid! I'm going to call my mom and I'm going home."

"No, Belinda, you are not going home. You can't sign yourself out. Only your parents can do that, and they are taking their advice from me." Dr. Kraft continued to remain composed no matter how much I raged at him. Once more, someone else seemed to be holding all the power and control over me.

"You can't do this to me! I'm not a child anymore. I'm a big girl now. Why does everyone think they can do whatever they want to me?" I cried, shaking uncontrollably. Perhaps it was because I was still recovering from the virus, but my knees felt like Jell-O, as if they would buckle at any moment. I felt dizzy, as if I was about to pass out as I stood in front of Dr. Kraft, venting my anger at the injustice of it all. But I wasn't through yet. I was no longer thinking. I was now on autopilot, merely reacting to this latest injustice.

I must have been screaming loud enough to draw attention from the nurses, because there stood Nurse Betty framed in the doorway, and she wore a look of clear astonishment on her face. The look beat her usual scowl, anyway!

I wanted to throw something at this devil doctor. I wanted to hurt him like he'd hurt me. I needed to show him and everyone else that had hurt me so deeply – abused me for so long – what it was like to really hurt, and I needed to tell him and everybody else within earshot that I wasn't going to take it anymore. I just wanted to lash out at my persecutor, so I picked up Dad's precious television from the nightstand and hurled it at him.

Dr. Kraft ducked as the small television flew past him and crashed to the floor. He ordered Nurse Betty, who was still standing in the doorway, to get a tranquilizer.

"Oh, so you can't take my rage, huh? You said you could handle it, but I guess you can't! I told you you'd handle it with drugs. Well, I'm *not* taking your tranquilizer."

Dr. Kraft just stood there watching me react like a wild animal unleashed. Nurse Betty appeared seconds later with a hypodermic needle in hand.

"*No!* You are not sticking me with that thing! You'll have to catch me first," I said, fully prepared to make a run for the door.

Just then Nurse Karen appeared in the doorway. She didn't think twice, and in an effort to defuse the situation she ran towards me and threw her arms around me. "It's okay, Belinda. It's okay. No one is going to hurt you or make you do anything you don't want to do. Hush now. Shh, shh."

As if she had some magic spell over me, I melted into her caring embrace. Her voice was soothing, and somehow I trusted her to put my welfare first. She looked at Dr. Kraft, and Nurse Betty holding the hypodermic needle, and softly said, "Please, Dr. Kraft, don't. I'm not trying to overstep here, but Belinda really was awfully sick over the weekend. I know, because I was with her. Let me stay with her a while and try to settle her down."

Now Dr. Kraft was the one with the dumbfounded look on his face. He seemed amazed by the way I had responded to Nurse Karen. He said nothing, but he seemed to agree with her. But the devil doctor didn't leave the room until he'd directed Nurse Betty to unplug the phone and remove the television. As the scowling nurse did as she was ordered, that old familiar feeling of humiliation rose up once again, and I began sobbing. Nurse Karen held me as if she cared – as if I mattered – just the way I'd always wished my own mom would've held me the night I was raped, or the way I wished she'd held me the day I flew into the house with a bottle of ugly pills clutched tightly in my sweaty nine-year-old palm.

I had nothing to say. I didn't want to speak, and Karen didn't push me by asking questions, scolding me for my behavior or even offering words of sympathy. I just needed to cry it all out, and somehow this wise woman seemed to sense that, so she simply held me like a loving mother would hold her child and let me cry until I was empty and no more tears would come. In that moment, I felt more cared for by a woman I barely knew than perhaps I had in my whole life. How was it that my own parents could never understand what this nurse did – that all I needed was to feel loved?

Dr. Kraft made good on his words. Every privilege I had gained over the course of three weeks was revoked. I had to begin the entire program all over again. The phone and television were history. The OT and RT privileges were repealed. No visitors were allowed. All that rage I had expressed had gotten me absolutely nowhere. This devil doctor could still have his way with me, and I could do nothing about it.

I sulked in my room the rest of the day. My anger had once more retreated to that safe place deep inside. I had seen now that letting it out hadn't helped anything, and probably had only caused more problems for me. Perhaps sealed away was where it belonged after all. Part of me felt terribly ashamed for my behavior that day. Such outbursts were so unlike me. Yes, I had every reason to be angry with Dr. Kraft, but I hadn't planned to explode the way I did. I was sorry for that, but I wouldn't be apologizing to the devil doctor any time soon.

I thought about Mom. I had promised I'd call her back that night. I wondered if Dr. Kraft had called her to tell her what had happened? I wondered what her thoughts were? Was she mad at me? More importantly, was Dad mad at me for throwing his television? Later I found out that I'd only dinged the corner, I hadn't destroyed it completely and it still worked!

With the anger in retreat mode, the depression grew deeper still. It began to feel as if someone was holding my head under water, as if I was gasping for air. I simply couldn't breathe. That all-pervading sense of powerlessness and total lack of control over my life seemed to consume me ... unless ... the Voice had given me an idea! A perfect idea to take back some of that power that rightfully belonged to me. There was only one way out of here, and that was by reverse psychology! I needed to allow Dr. Kraft to think he had won – that he held all the power. I would behave – be good. I knew full well how to be good. I'd been good all my life. I wouldn't resist. As hard as it might be, I'd gain however much weight it took to get released. When I got home my life would be my own again – at least to some extent. I'd lost weight before, and I could certainly lose it all over again.

From my hospital room I peered through the iron bars, recalling how all those years ago, as a little girl after one of Dad's savage whippings, I had created a plan for survival. This was no different. I knew I wasn't going to survive this place much longer without truly going crazy. The feelings of depression and despair were unbelievably heavy. Now I understood why they had bars on the windows here. They tortured you to the point that you wanted to jump to your death. It seemed a fate preferable to being locked up as a prisoner here in this funny farm.

Dr. Kraft insisted I write my feelings down in my journal, but these thoughts and feelings were deeply personal, and I wasn't going to reveal them to him. He had shown his true colors today, and it was obvious he didn't care about my thoughts, my feelings or me. By so cruelly revoking my privileges he had proven to me that he had not one ounce of compassion or understanding as far as I was concerned. Maybe my first impression of him was spot on. I knew from the moment I met him, when he gave me that limp handshake, that I wasn't going to like him. So I'd write in my journal what he wanted to hear. I'd do anything it took to go home.

Pulling the burgundy journal from its place beneath my pillow, I took out the Sacred Heart prayer card. Holding it close to my heart, I recalled all those times I'd met Jesus on that hillside in my imagination as a kid. In my mind's eye I could see His smile, but I couldn't feel it. I couldn't feel the joy in my heart or the light that His smile used to bring me. All I felt was emptiness – a never-ending darkness that was sucking the life from me. I still loved Jesus so much, no matter how many doubts I had or how angry and confused I had become. I wanted to pray. I wanted to close my eyes and meet Him on our hillside. I wanted to be that little girl again playing on the swing that hung beneath that great oak tree. But I was too tired – too depressed. Besides, I told myself, even if I could find that happy place once again in my imagination, what were the chances He'd still be there waiting for me?

Lord, are You there?
I want to pray, but I am too sad –
too exhausted – too empty.
I have no words to offer.
If You still love me – if You are still listening ...
Help me.
I'm begging You, Lord.
Help me hold on one minute at a time.
Amen.

CHAPTER 12

GOING HOME

And now, O Lord, Thou art our Father, and we are clay:
and Thou art our maker,
and we all are the works of Thy hands.

Isaiah 64:8

DIVINE POTTER

O Divine Potter, with great skill
Mold me according to Thy holy will.
Make me a vessel of Your design;
Use my suffering to shape and refine.
Let the sorrow, pain, and adversity
That comes in life with certainty
Be transformed as only Thou could
For the purpose of a higher good
For only the Divine Creator can see
How to mold me into all I can be.
Lord, though mysterious are Thy ways,
I'll trust in Thee for all my days.

*T*hree weeks had passed since the big show-down with Dr. Kraft. Surprisingly, the dust had settled fairly quickly. Although I was worried that Dad would be furious that I had attempted to destroy his television in a fit of anger, there had been no repercussions from Dad because I hadn't seen him. He hadn't made a single attempt to come visit me in the two months I had been there – but I was okay with that. Not having to see him or deal with his icy stares or anger was a definite plus to being here – maybe the only plus.

But on the other hand, I was deeply saddened and hurt by his more-than-obvious absence. I wondered if he cared about me at all. Maybe he just felt guilty for locking me up here, and couldn't face what he'd done. I mean, if he loved me even a little bit, how could he ever have put me in a place like this? But I'd never felt loved by him anyway; why should anything change now? Trying to make sense of my conflicted feelings about him only confused me all the more. Why was it that as much as I hated him, it still hurt that he hadn't come to see me? For the life of me I couldn't understand why I wanted him or needed him to love me at all, given all the anger I felt towards him. It made no sense why I should care about this mean and abusive man who called himself Dad. I was sure it had been his decision to lock me up here in the first place, and I wasn't sure I could ever forgive him for that. Did he have any clue how horrible this place and this experience had been? Perhaps he wasn't even aware of what went on in here, and maybe no one had told him that I'd thrown his precious television across the room in a fit of righteous anger. Mom probably hadn't told him anything about what happened here. If I knew Mom, she would have chosen to stay silent for fear of his reaction.

I gained the three and a half pounds I'd lost to the virus within a couple of days. Nurse Karen told me it was just loss of fluids that had caused the sudden dip in weight – but knowing didn't comfort me in the least, because if Nurse Karen knew that, then surely so did Dr. Kraft. It only made taking away all of my privileges even more cruel and unjustified.

Yet in the three weeks that followed I tried to shrug off the injustice of it all and simply get down to the business of gaining the weight I needed to go home. It had become my sole focus. As difficult as it was, I had succeeded, even though the Voice had gone into panic mode each time the scale jumped up a pound. The only way I'd found to calm the fear every pound brought was to remind myself that this weight was only a temporary thing. It was only being gained as a means to an end – freedom. When I weighed a hefty ninety-five pounds I sensed that the sweet freedom I longed for should be coming very soon!

Although I had slowly regained my privileges and had been cleared to go to OT or take part in RT outings, I chose not to. The depression had become so profound that most days I preferred to stay shut in my room reading, writing in my journal or just sleeping. I had begun to shut myself off from everything and everyone once more. Sitting in my room alone gave me lots of time to think and reflect on everything, including my time here and the people I had met. I knew that for better or worse I'd never forget any of them, for they and this place had left an indelible mark on my naïve and impressionable psyche.

When I brought Father Sam to mind, I remembered his soft, soulful gaze. Since his passing, the general consensus on the floor among the patients was that he had indeed found a way to commit suicide, although the staff would never confirm it. But the truth was we'd never really know for certain how he'd died – heart attack or suicide. I wrestled with the thought that he'd actually taken his own life after seeing the shame in his eyes when he'd spoken about his past suicide attempt just the day before his death. Would he – could he have really done something like that? I could empathize with his inner demons. I knew how hard those inner demons pushed by means of their unrelenting emotional torment to get you to do things that you normally never would. That pain and sadness that could have caused him to end his own life had been reflected in his eyes that day in the solarium; I'd been a witness to it, and it haunted me. I wanted my final memory of him to be something good, such as how much he loved his faith and the priesthood or how many lives had been touched by him – in here alone. But all I could remember was the suffering I'd seen in his eyes, and how tragically his life had ended.

When I brought Peg to mind, my last conversation with her a week ago would be my definitive memory of her. I had taken a walk down the hall late one night to get a magazine because I couldn't sleep. Apparently she couldn't either, because she was standing near the wall of windows in the solarium looking out into the night. When I approached her, she told me that she was being released that morning, and was feeling anxious about living 'in the world' again, as she put it. For the first time she opened up to me and told me her nervous breakdown had been caused by the loss of her only child. He was just twenty-one. He had been out drinking with friends when their car jumped the lane and hit another car head on. His friends had survived, but barely. He was driving and he was killed. She went on to say that they'd had an argument that night before he left. She felt responsible in many ways, because they were both angry and said hateful things to one another before he stormed out that evening. In an instant, he was gone, and the fight they'd had were her final words and memories of him. Although Peg often jokingly called this place the funny farm, it was obvious that she felt safe here, tucked away from the world. Now I understood why Peg had never spoken about what had caused her nervous breakdown. Her grief and pain were just too overwhelming. She used the television we so often found her immersed in as a diversion from that pain. Jilly had often said that TV was Peg's happy place because it was the only place she seemed momentarily to forget her pain. Now I understood.

And then there was my friend, Jilly, who I so missed.

I hadn't seen Jilly since the day of her first ECT treatment, when she'd looked me in the eye as if she'd never known me. That memory still stung. Since that day I'd heard through Nurse Karen that her husband had transferred her to another facility. I missed her. I thought of her so often and now I would probably never know what happened to her. What I did know was that I'd never forget her or the impact she'd made on my stay here. For a short while she had made this place bearable, and I was thankful for that. I'd always think of Jilly as a friend, even if I never saw her again.

"Belinda?" I had been so lost in my thoughts that I hadn't noticed Dr. Kraft come into the room.

"Oh, Dr. Kraft. I'm sorry. I didn't hear you come in. Is it already time for our session?"

"Yes. You looked deep in thought. Anything you want to talk about?"

"No. Nothing important."

"I have good news. I will be releasing you tomorrow morning. Your weight as of today is at ninety-five pounds, which was my target for your release. So, just as we'd hoped for and right in time for Thanksgiving." He gave another of his thin smiles that never quite reached his eyes.

His words were music to my ears! I was elated that I was going home, but I was a bit uneasy about going home for Thanksgiving. The holidays, especially Thanksgiving, were all about food in our house – lots of it! Of course, I loved the idea of not being here, but I hated the idea of being taunted by a table full of food that I had to find some way to avoid. Yes, I had reached his target of ninety-five pounds, but every single half-pound had been an emotional and mental battle, to which Dr. Kraft had been totally oblivious.

"How do you feel about that, Belinda? Are you excited?"

"Sure. You know I want to go home."

"Good. Do you feel ready?"

"Yeah, sure. Does my mom know?"

"Yes. I spoke to her a few minutes ago. She was so excited that she was crying. She asked that you call her after I leave today," Dr. Kraft said, glancing over at the phone that had been replaced on my nightstand. "Well, it sounds like everything is in order then. I will sign your release papers. Your parents will be here to get you in the morning. I want you to make an appointment to see me next week in my office. You will also need to make an appointment with Dr. Giles every two weeks so he can monitor your weight and physical condition. Is there anything else that you feel you need to talk about today? Do you have a journal entry for me to read?"

"No. Not today, Dr. Kraft."

"Belinda, just a reminder. I need you to continue keeping a journal for me. Bring it along with you to our sessions in the office. I know the time you've spent here hasn't been easy for you. I also know that you are deeply depressed, perhaps more so than when you first came to me. That concerns me, so I am increasing your dosage of antidepressants. If you have any new symptoms from the medication increase, please call me immediately. It is that depression that we are going to try to understand as our work together moves forward. We haven't spoken much about that display of anger a few weeks ago, but I believe if we could understand all the reasons why you are so angry, we'd begin to know so much more about what is driving the anorexia. But like I told you in the beginning, we had to get you stabilized physically before we can make any progress psychologically."

I nodded. I didn't have anything more to say to him about my angry outburst or anything else. But he was right about one thing: I was more depressed than ever. Some of it I understood. I knew that gaining the weight had deepened my depression. I knew the things I'd witnessed and my experiences here had compounded this heavy feeling of despair, but I wasn't going to let him be privy to such deep feelings and thoughts, because I didn't feel any rapport with him. I didn't believe he'd ever understand. But for now, my first objective was to get the hell out of here, and then perhaps I could find a way to get him out of my life for good too. My parents could insist all they wanted that I have a shrink – I just didn't want it to be him.

"Okay then, young lady. I will see you in the morning." Dr. Kraft gathered his notes into a neat little pile and placed them into his expensive-looking black leather briefcase. He rose from the straight-backed chair one final time, turned, smiled and said goodbye.

Finally! I was going home.

The next morning I was up, packed and ready to leave by 7:00 a.m. My parents wouldn't be here for at least another hour, so I had some time to kill. I walked down to the solarium to see if I could find Nurse Karen. I hoped she was on duty today so I could say my goodbyes and thank her for all she'd done for me.

I was in luck. As I neared the nurses' station, I spied her on the phone. Seeing me make my approach, she smiled and motioned for me to go eat breakfast. Yeah, it would be great not having everyone forcing me to eat – even if it was only Nurse Karen.

I took a seat at the table, but I was so anxious and so excited that I really wasn't hungry that morning. As soon as Nurse Karen was finished on the phone, she came over and pulled up a chair beside me.

"So, you're going home today. Good for you!" she said, leaning over to give me a hug.

"Nurse Karen, I wanted to say thank you. You have always been so kind to me. That means a lot. You've sort of been like my angel," I said, trying not to cry.

"Nope! No wings on me, just a nurse doing her job. You, my dear, are a very sweet young lady, and I wish you all the luck in the world on your recovery. It has been my pleasure to be your nurse. Take care of yourself, Belinda."

Before I could respond, I saw Mom and Dad walk off the elevator with Dr. Kraft. My heart began racing wildly. This was it! I was out of here.

"They're here!" I said to Nurse Karen, giving her a final goodbye hug. I ran to throw my arms around Mom. She responded with tears.

"Sweetheart, we have to sign some papers for Dr. Kraft and then Dad and I will go to your room and get your stuff."

"Okay, Mom, I'll go to my room and wait for you there."

In my room, I plopped down in the big cushy chair for the last time. It had become very familiar over the past eight weeks. I had shed many tears and prayed many prayers in this chair. Had God heard any of them? Did He care? So much pain and sorrow filled these halls. Did He care about any of the people here who were hurting so much that some of them, like Father Sam, even wanted to give up their very life?

The sunlight streaming through the iron bars grabbed my attention, filling the room with a radiant glow and warmth I'd never noticed before. Perhaps it was just my attitude today. I had something to be very happy about this morning, and it seemed to be making a difference in how I perceived everything. I was regaining control over my life – at least that's how it felt, and that made me very happy. No longer would Dr. Kraft be around to monitor my every move. No longer did I have to sit in front of a nurse after each meal to be watched. No longer did I have to be accompanied to the shower or the bathroom like a prisoner. The humiliation was over – as of today.

Getting up from the chair, I made my way to the window. I peered out through the bars I'd hated so much – the bars that had been a constant reminder of my incarceration. As I looked down to the street below, the city bustled with activity. Cars lined the roadside and people scurried up and down the sidewalk, making their way to work on this lovely late November morning. I had looked out through these bars, watching the people on the street many times over the past eight weeks, but today was different. No longer did I have to look out between the bars and envy them because they were free and I was not. In a matter of minutes, I would be walking freely among them. I didn't know what the future held, but I knew I would fight with every ounce of strength I possessed to never come back to such a place as this again.

Mom, Dad and Dr. Kraft came into the room chatting casually as if they were old friends. I guess everyone was feeling good today.

Dad picked up the suitcase from the bed. "You ready?"

I nodded.

My parents showered Dr. Kraft with praise as if he'd done something special. I suppose they thought that he'd helped me because I had gained this unsightly fat, or that he had somehow taken good care of me. If they thought that, then they were wrong on both counts.

"Belinda, I'll see you next week. Have a good Thanksgiving," Dr. Kraft said, giving me a pat on the back.

Politely, I returned the holiday wishes. "Yeah, happy Thanksgiving to you too, Dr. Kraft."

As we waited for the elevator doors to open, I looked around at the solarium and the patients that filled the room. There was no one I knew there any longer. Jilly, Peg and Father Sam were all gone, one way or another. I recalled the first day I came here and got a glimpse of the patients, so many of them looking spaced out from their meds. I wondered if any of them ever really got well, or did they just take their sorrow and pain along with them when they went home – like I was doing. My heart went out to them. Where was God in all of this? Did He love them or did He forget them? I thought of a sermon I'd once heard at Grams's church about how God was the potter and we were the clay. The preacher had said God molds and shapes us according to His will, using our circumstances. Was God working in the midst of all this suffering to make something good? It was a lovely thought but it didn't feel very likely at this moment. I too lived with such suffering, and I knew now what it was like to live among them – to be one of them. Where was God in my pain?

We stepped into the elevator. As the doors closed I said a silent prayer for those I was leaving behind and for myself:

Lord, comfort us with Your love. Take away our pain, suffering, and sorrow. May Your light shine in our darkness. Wherever Jilly is, help her find her way back to her family. Grant Peg the strength and courage she needs to face each day – be near her in her grief. Grant Father Sam eternal peace in You. Thank You for my very own angel, Nurse Karen. And thank You, Lord, for getting me out of this awful place. Finally, I'm going home!
Amen.

CHAPTER 13

ILL INTENT

Look, and see if there is any sorrow like my sorrow...

Lamentations 1:12

I'll bury the pain deep, deep down
So deep that it can't be found
It will not see the light of day
If it seeks release I'll purge it away
I'll starve the life right out of it
And lull the pain a little bit
I'll beat the pain ... the anger ... fear
Till it – or I – just disappear.

Home felt good. It wasn't perfect – I still had to walk on eggshells to keep my dad's rage from boiling over at any given moment – but at least I was surrounded by my familiar belongings in my own room. I reveled in my freedom to take a warm bubble bath that first day home without the prying eyes of a nurse anywhere in sight. It sounds like such a little thing, but after two months' incarceration I found a whole new appreciation for life's simple things that I'd previously taken for granted. Prior to my captivity, I'd never given a second thought to being able to come and go as I pleased or do as I wanted without restrictions or having someone watching my every move. So perhaps it wasn't so silly after all that something as simple as a bubble bath could make me feel so liberated. This luxurious warm bathtub of bubbles stood as a celebration of my emancipation from the funny farm! I certainly deserved a victory party for managing to survive my imprisonment and the devil doctor's undeniably cruel and humiliating treatment.

Basking in the steaming water, I played like a child with the foamy mountains of lavender-scented bubbles that threatened to spill over the side of the tub. Closing my eyes and resting my head against the sloping porcelain behind me, I allowed my thoughts to wander. I wished that I could just shut out the world and stay here in the warm comfort of these heavenly-scented suds forever. But would it really help me so much? Wherever I was, wherever I went I took the pain, the emotions and the memories with me in spite of the fact that I was doing an excellent job of repressing them. If I could only shut off my feelings like a light switch, this quiet solitude would be exquisite perfection. But I could do neither of those things.

My memories of the psych ward were still fresh, and spun around and around in my head like a hamster on a wheel. Father Sam's sad eyes, Jilly's blank expression after her first ECT or Peg's anguished admission regarding her son's tragic death; all these things would haunt me for the rest of my life. The deep humiliation I'd experienced on that first day there as Nurse Betty sealed up my bathroom door with duct tape following Dr. Kraft's orders still hurt. Every one of these memories was like an arrow piercing my heart, allowing that all-pervading feeling of profound sorrow to rush in and sweep over me. Not even a million tiny bubbles could bring enough momentary joy to vanquish such painful memories.

"Honey! You okay in there? Just checking," Mom said softly, knocking on the bathroom door. "You've been in there almost thirty minutes."

"Yeah, Mom. I'm good. Just enjoying the bubbles."

"Dad and I are going out to do some shopping. Anything you need?"

"No. But thanks anyway."

"Okay then. We should be back in a couple of hours."

The skin on my fingers was beginning to pucker anyway, so perhaps it was time to come out of the water. I stayed in the tub long enough to hear the garage door close. In our tiny four-room house you could just about see or hear everything from any room you were in. Now that I was finally alone, I had some time to do whatever I wished. Freedom felt so good!

I dried off, dressed and made my way to the kitchen. If my parents were going to be gone for two hours I had time to make pancakes. I hadn't had a pancake in months. In a matter of minutes, I had whipped up a large stack of one of my childhood favorites – buttermilk pancakes. With glee, I slathered them with my favorite toppings – butter and grape jelly. Then I dove in. I hadn't binged in weeks.

I devoured that first stack of six pancakes in minutes, and made my way to the bathroom. Bending over the toilet, I expelled them with even more fervor than I'd eaten them. Gagging myself to purge was never required; all I need do was bend over the toilet bowl. It seemed to come so easily to me, like second nature. Then I made my way back to the kitchen to do it all over again.

It had been the first time in a long while that I'd felt in control of my eating. In the midst of bingeing and purging, I wasn't re-living hurtful memories and I wasn't lost in painful thoughts or emotions. In the moment, the pain was anesthetized; nothing mattered but the food – shoveling it in or chucking it up. As long as I was busy bingeing or purging, I was in a space where there were no emotions, and the numbness welcomed me like an old friend.

I had the kitchen cleaned up long before Mom and Dad got home. I was always exhausted after a bingeing and purging session, and I desperately needed a nap. But napping at this moment wasn't what the Voice had in mind.

"You probably gained a pound or two from all those pancakes," the Voice chided. *"You freakin' pig! Oink! Oink! Go weigh yourself, little piggy, and see. And for goodness sake make sure you purged every last piece before you sleep. Sleeping isn't going to burn many calories so you'd better be sure you haven't added to the daily total."*

Guilt and shame overwhelmed me. I agreed wholeheartedly with the Voice. I was a pig, and I had probably gained a pound from eating just like one. I stripped down, tossing my clothes into a pile on the bathroom floor. The clothes had to come off because they too might add an ounce to the readout on the scale. Cold and naked, I stepped gingerly onto the scale, almost afraid of the outcome. It was even worse than I'd suspected! My heart sank as I read the bold, black numerals: ninety-six pounds! I felt so huge – so fat! I turned from side to side to inspect the size and shape of my bare stomach from every possible angle in the bathroom mirror. I wouldn't be content unless it was washboard flat, especially after that pile of pancakes. Perhaps the mirror could bring me the reassurance I needed that I had purged everything and that my stomach was empty. But what I saw reflected in the mirror was nothing short of repulsive – a stomach that bulged and protruded, making me look as if I was pregnant! Everything I'd worked so hard to achieve before my hospital stay had been for nothing. In tears, I collapsed in a heap onto the floor. Oh, how I loathed myself! How could I have let this happen?

I remembered that at seventy-seven pounds I could count every rib like the rungs of a ladder. I remembered how proud I had been of myself. As each rib became more prominent, I had felt as if I'd reached a new milestone towards my goal of the perfect svelte body. But now, a despicable and disgusting padding of fat covered my ribs!

"Look at how fat you've gotten," the Voice scolded. *"Look at what you let that devil doctor do to you! Get off the floor and*

stop crying like a baby! Stop feeling sorry for yourself. You're so pitiful! Damn it, stop it right now! Take control! Get up and do something about it!"

Of course the Voice was right again. Crying wasn't going to solve my problem one little bit. Panicked, I grabbed a glass of water from the bathroom sink and gulped it down, then I bent over the toilet to purge any last vestige of pancake that might have remained. Nothing came back except the water. I did it again and again and again until only yellow stomach fluids dribbled into the toilet bowl. Then I stepped back onto the scale: Ninety-five and a half. Now I was making some progress! Finally, reassured there was no food left in my stomach, I could take the nap my body was begging for. But wait – there was one more thing I needed to do before I could rest.

From beneath my bed, I pulled out an old, ragged boot box. I had hoped while I was away that no one had become privy to my secret little stash. Stuffed deep within the toes of each boot were the tools I'd now need to lose the extra weight Dr. Kraft had forced on me. One way or the other, this pregnant belly just had to go, and the sooner the better. I breathed a sigh of relief when I saw that everything was still there: the diuretics, weight loss pills and laxatives. Closing the lid, I slid the box back underneath the bed into its hiding place and slipped beneath the covers. Still upset by the reading on the scale, I tried to calm down by telling myself to stop worrying. If I'd lost the weight once, I could do it again. I still had all the tools I needed right under my bed to make it happen, and in record time. Pulling the plush pink blanket over my head, I curled up into fetal position and closed my eyes. I just needed to stop thinking and sleep. I tried to focus on the positives. I was home and in my own bed; I was free, and I was back in control.

Christmas had come and gone, and I was looking forward to going back to college right after New Year's. Over my long absence, I had kept in touch with my friend, Cindy. She had called every now and then to see how I was doing. She was the sole person I had entrusted with knowledge of my hospitalization and subsequent stay in Fairhaven. But if I thought I could trust her with that information and that she understood, I thought wrong.

On my first morning back at school, I arrived an hour early. I was hoping to take some time to check in with some of my friends that I'd not seen for so long now. I figured everyone would be congregating in the student lounge, so I headed there first. A group of the girls were huddled together in one corner of the room, and Cindy was among them. I entered unnoticed. They seemed intent on whatever it was they were giggling about, and then I heard Cindy mention my name to them.

"Did you guys know that Belinda's been locked up in a mental ward with the rest of the crazies?" Cindy said.

The small circle of girls shook their heads, their eyes fixed on Cindy and the startling revelation she had just made.

"Yeah, I guess that makes her crazy too, huh?" Cindy said, giggling.

My heart stopped. I couldn't believe these words had just come from the mouth of someone I thought was a friend – someone I thought I could trust. I didn't stay to watch the reactions of the others – I turned and fled.

Bursting into Mrs. Clay's office sobbing, I stood shaking in front of her desk. I had come prepared to quit school – then and there.

"What's wrong, Belinda?" she said. Rising from her chair,

she ran over to put her arm around my shoulder. "Sit down. Try to tell me what's wrong."

I was crying so hard I could barely sputter out what I had just overheard or how betrayed I felt. That word "crazy" could have come from the mouth of any other girl in that room – but not Cindy. I thought she was my friend.

I had expected Mrs. Clay would understand why I was hurt, and I expected her to be supportive, but she wasn't.

"Belinda, you need to grow a backbone and quit caring what people say and think about you. You'll never make it in the business world if you are this sensitive. You need to learn that people really don't care. They gossip. When they say, 'Good morning, and how are you today?' they don't want to hear your life story – so you lie, if need be. Even if you are hurting, even if you're having the worst day of your life – you lie. You say, 'Fine!'"

I looked at her, dumbfounded. What did any of this have to do with what had just happened? How were these words of wisdom going to help me in any way?

"I quit!" I said through the sobs. "I can't face those girls ever again!"

Without giving Mrs. Clay a chance to respond, I ran out of her office and the building and made my way to my car. All I could think about was going home and getting far, far away from these hateful girls I'd thought were my friends. I was never going back to this school again.

Dad was angry that I had just "up and quit", as he put it. Mom, as usual, hardly said a word. It was as if she didn't want to take sides. But my mind had been made up. I knew I had disappointed Dad in the worst possible way, and that only fed the Voice all the more.

All the guilt I felt – all the insecurity and lack of confidence served to feed the beast that lived inside of me. The Voice used things like this to force me to do its bidding.

"So, you quit. You let Dad down again, didn't you, Little Miss Perfect? Only you're not so perfect – are you? I know you're hurting. Do what I tell you. It can be better. I can make it better."

I listened to the Voice. It was the only thing that heard my pain. Mom and Dad were watching me – closely – but that was okay. I'd up my game and become even more cunning, more secretive and more resourceful. Full-on binges were only allowed when I had the house to myself for a few hours, and the only time that happened was on the weekend when they went out to do their shopping. Such opportunities were too infrequent, so I'd need to use laxatives, diuretics and weight loss pills from my stash to take up the slack. I exercised quietly in my bedroom in the wee hours of the night when my family was fast asleep. I skipped any meals that I could put aside without my parents noticing. But there were troublesome family meals at which I was required to sit down and eat with everyone, and it was these meals that proved to be my biggest challenge. Without exception, such meals had to be purged. But making that trip to the bathroom immediately after a meal was becoming more difficult because Dad had grown suspicious.

He never said a word. With Dad, words were never really needed to instill fear, because his piercing icy stares said it all each time I exited the bathroom. It was a look that said, "I'm watching you. I know what you're up to." Yet as watchful as he seemed to be, and as fearful as I'd always been, I wasn't going to allow that fear of him to stop me – not this time. He still held unquestionable power over me, but somehow that power was shifting, because this illness was now vying to be my master, striving to hold all the power and control over me.

Although Mom and Dad hadn't mentioned my rapid weight loss, Dr. Kraft had noticed it during our last session. He'd set up an appointment immediately with our family doctor, Dr. Giles. While Dr. Giles seemed concerned that my weight had dropped from ninety-five to eighty-five pounds so rapidly, it was the results from the blood work that truly alarmed him. My electrolytes were again showing signs that I was putting myself in physical danger.

"Belinda, I'm prescribing liquid potassium for you," Dr. Giles said, scribbling his signature onto the prescription pad. "I know we'd all like you to avoid another hospital stay so we will do it this way on a trial basis. But I want you in here in a week's time for a follow-up. I'm concerned about your weight. Eat! A strong wind will blow you away. Let's see if you can gain a few pounds before I see you next week."

Not likely, Dr. Giles, I said to myself. No, I didn't want to go back to the hospital, but nothing was going to stand in my way of losing weight – not even Dr. Giles's subtle threats of being hospitalized again. The Voice had grown stronger, more defiant and more relentless, but that had only made me feel more in charge. I felt all-powerful. I thought I was the one in control, and that I had finally discovered a way to be perfect, to take charge of my life and my feelings and emotions. Every thought I had and every move I made was now controlled by my obsession to lose weight. It had become my life. Nothing and no one was going to tear this illness away from me. Now six years after it had begun, I realized I simply didn't know who I was without it. No one else understood and – as far as I was concerned no one else needed to – in my mind I needed the eating disorder to survive.

The truth was that like the spider and the fly, the Voice had lured me in with such subtlety, and when I finally began to realize its evil intent and struggle to escape from its web of lies and destruction, it would be much too late.

O Lord,
Have mercy on me.
Grant me peace.
Take away the pain and the heartache.
End this never-ending torment and suffering.
Lift the despair and the hopelessness.
Fill the void within and the emptiness with Your love.
Illumine the darkness with Your light.
O Lord, have mercy on me.
Grant me peace.
Amen.

CHAPTER 14

THE PERFECT STORM

And behold, a great tempest arose in the sea, insomuch that the boat was covered with waves, but He was asleep.

Matthew 8: 24

Abba,
I am afraid
Of the gathering storm.
Wilt Thou allow me to perish?
Arise,
And from Thy slumber awaken
To hear my soul's laments.
I am afraid,
Abba.

*G*etting a good night's rest had once more become impossible. I found myself tossing and turning throughout the night just as I had before when my electrolyte levels were deranged, a term Dr. Giles had often used meaning imbalanced. I had considered telling Mom, but, every time I made up my mind to say something, the Voice stopped me dead in my tracks. For better or worse, the Voice ruled my life. It made all the decisions, and this decision was no different.

"Do you really want someone controlling your life again – making you fat? Keep your mouth shut and follow the plan," was the Voice's sage advice.

But there was a new battle raging inside my head. Up to now I had felt as if the Voice was me – the stronger and more powerful me, and that made it my better half. But now there were fleeting moments when I began to see the Voice as anything but my better half. As poorly as I was feeling, I couldn't help the twinges of remorse I felt for not sharing such important information with Dr. Giles on my last visit.

But the Voice took over once again, playing on my worst fears. *"Do you really want to go to the hospital again? Or what about another stint in the psych ward? How 'bout that! Better yet, what about letting that devil doctor force you to gain a little more weight? He sent you home the last time looking like a little fatso!"*

Game over. My silence had been won through the fear of being fat – a fear the Voice so skillfully manipulated. No, I wasn't surprised that Dr. Giles had found my potassium was low again. The aches, pains and spasms in my legs were all the proof I needed. I'd been religiously taking the potassium he'd prescribed in the hope that it might alleviate some of the painful muscle cramps, but it hadn't. No big surprise there. I realized that my daily intake of laxatives and diuretics, coupled with the purging, had probably cancelled out any positive effects the prescription might have had. Part of me knew

I was in trouble. Yet I was powerless against this inner force – this Voice that drove me to lose another pound, and then another and another. As much as the prospect of another hospitalization terrified me, being fat terrified me even more, so the dieting continued.

I was exhausted all the time, but not even the cocktail of Dr. Kraft's antidepressants and sleeping pills taken at bedtime could help me find the rest my body craved. Even when the pills did knock me out for a few hours, my sleep was fitful, interrupted with nightmarish dreams of vast banquet tables straining beneath the weight of all my favorite foods. I, of course, was sitting smack dab in the center of that table devouring everything in sight like the pudgy little pig the Voice continually told me I was.

I woke from one particular dream drenched in sweat. The clock on my dresser read 2:00 a.m. The medication was still having a powerful effect on me, and as groggy as I was it should have been easy to just roll over and drift back to sleep. But it wasn't. Now that I was awake I became keenly aware of every ache and pain and – and besides that, I realized I was afraid. Afraid the dreams would begin all over again. Afraid I'd oversleep and miss my morning workout.

"Hey, you lazy cow! Get up! It's time to get moving," the Voice nagged. I did as I was told. Fighting the effects of the medication, I threw the covers off and pulled myself out of bed to begin my morning routine with stretches – lots of them, although I certainly didn't want to hurt myself and risk my parents finding out about my early morning workouts. After stretching, I set out towards my goal – two hundred jumping jacks. Most mornings I had no problems getting through my exercise regime, but today was different. It wasn't just that my legs were aching so badly, I was feeling unusually weak and dizzy. I told myself the dizziness was just the effects of the medication I had taken four hours earlier. *"Well, you're certainly not going to let that stop you, are you?"* the Voice interjected.

I had to press on towards my goal – losing another pound. If it had been up to me alone, I might have quit and given in to the aches, the pains, the medication and sheer exhaustion. But it wasn't, because I had the Voice, my own personal drill sergeant, to coach me through my momentary weak-mindedness. *"Come on! You can do this! I know you can. Don't be a quitter like your dad always says you are. Prove him wrong!"* the Voice said, cheering me on.

I am not a quitter! I said defiantly to myself. I ran in place for a good ten minutes until I could run no more. My body ached so badly. I just wanted to go back to bed, but the Voice refused to let me off the hook so easily.

"You have sit-ups to do. You can't quit until you do them. You need some incentive? Think of your dad. Show him you're not a quitter! Now get to it!" the Voice said.

Memories of my little fourth grade self flashed through my mind. Oh, how I had pleaded with Dad for flute lessons. I could still see him in my mind's eye standing over me, bellowing, "No, you'll quit! Your brother quit trumpet. You'll quit too." It had always been the same answer whenever I had wanted to do anything creative. As a child, I had desperately wanted to take flute, violin or even guitar lessons. But his answer was always the same. I was a quitter. Maybe I was. Maybe quitting school had confirmed it. I was a failure, and it was all I'd ever be! Yes, thinking of Dad was all the incentive I needed. I'd show him I wasn't a quitter! I could make quitting school up to him. I could gain his favor again. I wasn't going to fail. Not this time. Losing weight was something I excelled at. I'd show them all.

With renewed enthusiasm, I hit the floor and cranked out one sit-up after another until I had reached the two hundred demanded by the Voice.

Grabbing hold of the bed covers, I slowly pulled myself up off the floor. Huffing and puffing, I fell onto the bed. As worn out as I might have been, the sense of pride and accomplishment I took in seeing my morning workout through was greater.

Relieved that my morning exercises were behind me, I hoped I'd be able to sleep now. I glanced over at my alarm clock, whose bold, red illuminated numerals flashed like a neon sign in the darkness: 2:30 a.m. I needed to rest. But would sleep be possible? Aching all over as I did, probably not. Maybe another sleeping pill would help.

Reaching for the bottle of sleeping pills on my dresser, I popped one more in the hope that it would help me find the sound, dreamless sleep I so desperately needed. It must have done the trick because I slept undisturbed until Mom's wake-up call hours later.

"Belinda, it's eight a.m.," Mom said, gently rubbing my arm. "You need to get up. You have an appointment with Dr. Kraft this morning."

"Yeah. Okay, Mom," I said, trying to get my eyes open and shake off the last traces of the medication.

"I'm fixing waffles for breakfast!" She said it as if I should be excited about it.

"Great!" I mumbled, trying to sound enthusiastic while still half asleep. If she only knew how I really felt; I would have much preferred to skip breakfast altogether. Now I'd have to find a way to purge the waffles she was going to be insisting I eat.

My appointment with Dr. Kraft was for 11:00 a.m. Mom would come with me as usual. Although she and I had always been inseparable, we'd become even closer since I'd come back from my long hospital stay. I could drive and she couldn't, so I was the one who took her everywhere – especially shopping.

We both loved to shop, but she loved bargain shopping in particular. This morning Mom was all excited about her latest find – a pair of expensive designer shoes she'd seen in the morning paper at a ridiculously low sale price.

"Belinda, can we run by the mall and pick them up before your doctor's appointment?"

Seeing Mom's eagerness to claim her newest treasure, I didn't want to spoil her fun by complaining about how poorly I felt. So, I stayed silent about the dizziness, and about how unsure I was about driving today. "Sure, Mom. Whatever you want," I said.

"Honey, you look a little peaked to me. Are you sure you are feeling all right?"

"Yeah. Stop worrying, Mom. I'm good," I said. "Let's get going now, if you want to pick up those shoes."

I was happy to find a parking spot close to the mall entrance. I didn't feel up to walking very far today. I felt odd – lightheaded and shaky. It occurred to me that I should tell Mom, but I kept telling myself to keep quiet; I'd be okay. Besides, she'd promised this trip to the mall would only take a few minutes. Just long enough to pick up that pair of shoes.

I hadn't realized just how much trouble I was in until I started to feel as if the room was spinning as we stood in line at the checkout. My head not only spun, but my hands tingled, I felt nauseous, and then everything went black.

Minutes later I came to with a paramedic leaning over me. "What happened?" I asked him.

"You collapsed. You're in an ambulance on the way to the hospital. Your mom is right here, and I think your dad is meeting you there," the paramedic said, trying to reassure me.

Looking over the medic's shoulder, I saw Mom sitting behind him crying, her face filled with worry. It was that worried look I had tried to avoid by not telling her how I'd been feeling. Only now, she wasn't the only one worrying – so was I.

Tears trickled down my cheek. Oh God, I pleaded silently, let this just be another one of my nightmares! But I was certain this prayer wouldn't be answered in the way I'd hoped. The blare of the siren was too loud – too real. This was my reality. I didn't want to go back to the hospital. I didn't want this to be happening all over again. But it was, and there wasn't one thing I could do about it now.

Once I was in the emergency room the doctors and nurses worked quickly. Within the first half hour an IV had been started and blood pressure, temperature, and EKG readings taken. Numerous vials of blood were drawn from me. The doctor wanted me weighed – stat – so a nurse came in to help steady me as I stood on the scale: seventy-nine pounds.

Through a slit in the curtain that had been drawn around my stretcher, I could see Mom and Dad speaking to one of the doctors. I listened closely as he gave them the grim details.

"I believe your daughter passed out today because her blood pressure fell to dangerously low levels," the doctor began. "Besides that, the blood work shows that her electrolytes are deranged. Her pulse is weak, her temperature is below normal and she is severely dehydrated. Does she have any history of heart problems?"

Through the curtain slit I saw my father shake his head. From the look on his face I could sense how frightened they both were.

"The EKG shows an irregular heartbeat. She is exhibiting

classic and dangerous signs of malnutrition. Her weight is only seventy-nine pounds. Dr. Giles has been notified, and he has notified her psychiatrist, Dr. Kraft. Dr. Giles mentioned that Belinda has been diagnosed with anorexia nervosa and was just recently hospitalized for a lengthy period. It is, of course, up to both of you and her team of doctors, but you may want to consider force-feeding. It is imperative to her recovery that she gets some proper nutrition."

Force-feeding? They wouldn't! They couldn't! They won't! I tried to suppress both my fear and anger long enough to continue listening in on their conversation.

"Mr. and Mrs. Rose, I don't want to alarm you but your daughter is in a very grave condition. Dr. Giles and Dr. Kraft will be here soon and I will consult with them on my findings. If you'd like to go in and see your daughter now, feel free."

The curtain parted and my parents walked towards my stretcher. I couldn't help but notice their somber expressions. They looked as if the doctor had told them I was dying or something. Didn't they realize that dying was the least of my concerns? All I wanted to know is that they wouldn't have me force-fed.

"Mom, I heard that doctor! He said something to you guys about force-feeding me. Tell me you won't do that! Please, I'm begging you! Promise me."

Mom didn't answer. She only cried and looked to Dad. "Belinda," Dad said, "we will do whatever is best for you. Do you want to die?"

"I'd rather die than be force-fed!" I said, nearly hysterical.

"Honey, calm down. Being upset isn't going to do you any good," Mom said, wiping away her tears with a tissue.

"I won't calm down until you both promise me you won't let them do that to me!"

"We won't let you die," Dad said. "I don't know what it is you are doing to yourself, or why, but you're not dying!"

It was no use. No amount of begging or pleading with my

parents was going to make them hear my plea. Why was it that Dad could always do whatever he wanted to me and I had nothing to say about it? Why was it everyone else got to control my life?

By the next morning the decision on force-feeding had been made between my parents and doctors, and no one had even thought to consider how I might have felt about it. Lucky me, I was getting my very own nasogastric feeding tube, whether I wanted one or not! Dr. Giles and Dr. Kraft had made their recommendations to my parents, and yet again they'd gone along with it just like they did in the psych ward. They said it was necessary to save my life. But what if I didn't want my life saved? What if I thought force-feeding was a fate worse than death? What about the fear that now consumed me? How was I supposed to calm the distressed and panic-stricken Voice in my head? No one grasped the power of the Voice or the depth of the fear that drove me to do the things I did. Gaining weight – being fat, in my mind – was the worst thing that could ever happen to me. It was a fate *far* worse than death. To me, being force-fed was no different than throwing someone petrified of water off a ship in the middle of the ocean or pushing some- one afraid of heights out of an airplane at 30,000 feet.

Dr. Kraft came early that morning to oversee the whole fi- asco. It was like a scene from a horror movie – only this movie wasn't make-believe, it was real life.

"Belinda, we are doing this for your own good," Dr. Kraft said. "If we don't, you may die."

No amount of reassurance from Dr. Kraft was going to al- lay my fear. I watched as Dr. Giles and his accomplices – Dr. Kraft and a nurse – assembled the paraphernalia necessary to begin the torture. My eyes were glued to the lengthy tube they were about to insert into my nose and down into my stomach. What was about to take place, what they were about to do to me, was a process I found so terrifying that I was beside myself. I didn't care about the life-or-death scenario everyone kept reiterating. It didn't matter to me. The Voice was screaming inside my head that dying wasn't what I needed to be worried about; getting fat was the concern here. *"Find a way to stop this! NOW! Don't let them take control, don't let them make you FAT! You've worked too hard to get to seventy-nine pounds, and now you're going to let them take it all away!"* the Voice's rant was deafening.

What am I supposed to do? I said, silently pleading to the Voice for direction. *These doctors have all the authority. You saw how angry Dad was last night. I can't defy him so openly. He'll kill me!*

"You're so weak. You're pathetic! Whatever would you do without me? You'll have to work twice as hard to lose this weight they're making you gain all over again."

The closer the time came to begin the procedure, the more anxious I became. My crying became uncontrollable. I heard Dr. Giles quietly tell Dr. Kraft he needed me to be still, to be quiet before he could begin. Dr. Kraft ordered a mild tranquilizer.

His tranquilizer may have been calmed my body, but it wasn't stopping the Voice. Its reprimands played over and over in my head like a broken record. These doctors and my parents, by colluding to save my life, had only increased my mental suffering and anguish. The Voice had been such a powerful force in my life for so long now, but today something had dramatically changed. A shift in power and authority had taken place in my mind, and the Voice had gained control. The Voice was right. I was weak and pathetic. I should have been able to stop this force-feeding plan, but I couldn't. I now realized I needed all the help I could get if I was ever to attain the perfect body of my dreams, if I was ever going to win against such powerful adversaries as these two doctors.

"I love you," the Voice said so comfortingly. *"Who else wants to see you achieve your goals? Who else understands your fear and loathing of gaining weight, food and fat? No one. Only me. Let me do this for you. I love you."*

I'd heard the plea and those protestations of love from the Voice before, but never with such fervor. The Voice was right, because no one else understood my fears, and no one else tried to help me achieve my weight loss goals. The Voice loved me in ways no one else could. Maybe it was my only true friend. Though not a conscious decision on my part, I knew that today's ordeal had given the Voice a new and unstoppable momentum.

Mom came to visit later that day in an attempt to justify what they had done. "Belinda, I know you are mad, but if we don't do what the doctors advise you might die."

"I don't care, Mom. You have no right to make me do this." I wanted to scream those words in her face, but I was afraid I'd gag on the tube that now ran down my nose and throat and into my stomach. It made swallowing and talking uncomfortable.

"Belinda, I want you to know something. I found your dad sitting in his chair last night at three a.m. He was crying."

"Why?"

"What do you mean why? Because he's worried sick about you! Dr. Giles told us that you could die if we didn't do this. You are *that* ill, Belinda. Why can't you get a hold of yourself?" Mom reached into her purse for a tissue to wipe away her tears.

"I don't care, Mom."

"You don't care if you die?"

"No. What have I got to live for anyway? I hate myself and I hate my life."

"Oh, Belinda! Don't say that. You are just a young girl. You have your whole life ahead of you. We love you."

"Do you, Mom? *Do you?* Is this how you show your love? Is locking me up in a psych ward how you show your love? Because it doesn't feel like love to me!"

"What would you have your father and me do? Should we just let you lose weight until you're gone? Do you want to be invisible?"

"Mom, I don't have to lose weight to be invisible to either of you. As far as both of you are concerned, I always have been. All you've ever noticed or worried about is Darryl. How many nights did you yank me out of bed in the middle of the night, only to leave me sitting locked in the car while you and Dad picked him up at juvie hall?"

She looked at me, dumbfounded. I knew I had hurt her feelings. But I didn't care in that moment about her feelings any more than she and Dad had cared about mine – ever. Maybe the truth hurt.

Excusing herself, she got up and left the room. I knew she had left so she wouldn't cry in front of me. I had nothing left to say to her anyway. I had nothing left to say to anyone.

I was beyond angry with my parents, with my doctors and with God. Where was He, anyway, in the midst of all of this? Was Jesus sleeping peacefully in the middle of the storm while I feared for my life just as His disciples had when the waves poured into their small boat? I urgently needed Him to wake up. I needed to hear His strong command to the now out-of-control Voice in my head: "Be still!"

I closed my eyes, trying to calm the panicked Voice down. But my mind was besieged with fear. Perhaps I could pray. I imagined in my mind's eye that I was with Jesus and his disciples on the boat as the storm raged all around them. But in my reverie Jesus wasn't speaking to his disciples, he was talking to me. He was looking into my eyes with such love and compassion, saying, *Why are you so afraid? Have you no faith?*

In my imaginings, I fell to my knees before Him and replied, *No, Lord. It seems as if You have been asleep, and left me alone in this raging storm for so long, that I have lost my faith. Forgive me, but all that's left now is fear.*

Abba
I am afraid
in the midst of the storm.
Will Thou allow me to perish?
Arise,
And from Thy slumber awaken
To hear my soul's laments.
I am afraid,
Abba.

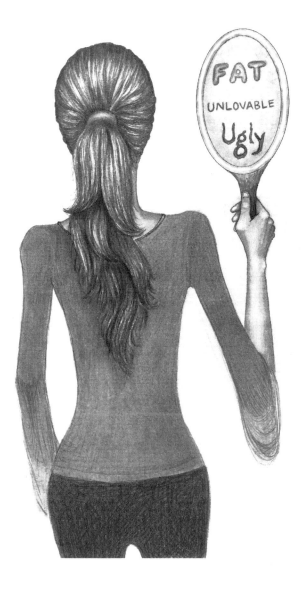

CHAPTER 15

AN EVIL WHISPER

[Jesus prayed:] "I pray not that you would take them from the
world, but that you would keep them from the evil one."

John 17:15

Dear Voice,
I so hate you
For all the lies you tell.
But I can't live without you,
Because
You love me in spite of me.
You won't abandon me.
So, I love you,
Dear Voice.

While Dr. Kraft's re-feeding approach had done much to help stabilize my physical health, it had been devastating to my mental and emotional well-being. The fear, anxiety, and utter panic it had instilled in me were more than I could cope with. The depression had deepened, the tears rarely stopped and the Voice was uncontrollable. To assuage my mental distress Dr. Kraft had prescribed a new antipsychotic drug. However, the Voice had its own agenda about how best to calm the fear – allowing it even more control.

As panicked as I was about being tube-fed and gaining weight, all I wanted was someone or something to help me end the nightmare. I needed reassurance that there was a way out of this, and the Voice stepped up to provide that reassurance and the exit strategy for me.

"I can help you. You know that," the Voice consoled. *"You need me. Yes, they won another battle, but they haven't won the war. You can lose whatever they make you gain. I am stronger than they are. Listen to me."*

And I did listen, giving the Voice free rein to make plans for my return home and then vowing to follow through on those plans. In doing so, I felt a renewed sense of power in the face of being so powerless. The Voice promised that whatever damage the doctors and their forced feeding did could be remedied. *"Just wait until we get home and I'll make it all better,"* the Voice reassured me repeatedly. For better or worse, I trusted it. It been the Voice, after all, that had helped me to get to seventy-six pounds before – my lowest weight to date – so why couldn't I reach that target – or maybe even beyond – again?

Ten days after they rushed me to the emergency room, Dr. Giles removed the feeding tube. The doctors agreed that they wanted to see me eating on my own before going home. Both Dr. Giles and Dr. Kraft were pleased with how rapidly I had bounced back physically. I was still a long way from being well, but my vitals and blood levels had improved dramatically and my weight had climbed to a massive eighty-three and one-half pounds. I was to be released at the weekend as long as everything went as planned.

Dr. Kraft arrived early on the day of my release for a therapy session, and to make one final impassioned plea to send me back to the psych ward for another week of monitoring.

"Belinda, I just feel it would be in your best interest to spend a few more days resting and recuperating. I don't want you having another setback. But I know how difficult the re-feeding was for you emotionally. That is very clear by the deepening of your depression and anxiety. So, I am not pushing this – this time." Then he added with a smile, "Don't make me sorry – okay?"

He may have been smiling, but I knew Dr. Kraft well enough by now to understand he meant business, as evidenced by the look he was giving me. He had a way of peering at me over the top of his hard-rimmed reading glasses that sat firmly on the tip of his long nose. That look said: "Do as I say." But I was no longer intimidated by his stern looks, because I was no longer calling the shots – the Voice was, and *it* wouldn't be intimidated by anyone or anything. All I needed to do was listen to its guidance, and follow through.

"Just be a good girl and agree with him," the Voice instructed.

So I smiled at Dr. Kraft and nodded sweetly.

"Good girl. What he doesn't know won't hurt him," the Voice added.

Dr. Kraft had no idea that even if I had wanted to abide by his advice, I was helpless to do so. The Voice held dominion over my every thought.

"Belinda, we haven't talked much lately about what's really going on in your head. Since you've been hospitalized we've had no journal entries to go over. So I want to ask you to be open and honest with me and tell me what the Gobbler is saying to you. Or perhaps, more precisely, how is it dealing with all that has happened the past couple of weeks?"

"Where did you ever come up with that stupid name? The Gobbler? I hate it," the Voice said, interrupting my train of thought.

Refocusing to answer Dr. Kraft's inquiry, I said with a note of sarcasm, "How do you think, Dr. Kraft? How do you think I'm dealing? Not well."

"That's understandable, Belinda. I realize this has not been an easy thing for you. Now, what does the Gobbler say?"

"You want to know what the Voice says? It says it is the only hope I have of not being fat. It says it is the only thing that cares about me enough to help me achieve my goals."

"What precisely are those goals?"

"To be thin."

"You weigh barely eighty-three pounds. Don't you think you're thin?"

"No! I'm not nearly thin enough. I still feel fat!"

"Watch it. You'd better watch what you say or he's gonna get wise to our plans," the Voice cautioned.

"You are not fat. But I know you don't see that. Belinda, you say that the Gobbler is the only thing that cares enough about you to help you achieve that goal of being thin. Do you believe that?"

"Yes, I do!"

"You can't see that this is the illness speaking?"

"What I see is this is my only chance of being thin. Period."

"I want to know more about these thoughts, Belinda. I want to understand the Gobbler's voice. Is it a voice inside your head or outside? Is it male or female?"

"It's inside my head. I don't know how to describe it. This Voice is stronger and louder than any thoughts I've ever experienced. It sounds more male, or maybe it just feels more male ..."

"How does it feel more male to you?"

"Dr. Kraft, I can't explain the unexplainable. I don't know how to make you understand – it just is. Maybe because it's so dominating and controlling it just seems that way. Now you probably just think I'm crazy, right? I'm hearing voices like a schizophrenic or somebody with multiple personalities."

"No, that is definitely not what I think or believe. What is going on with you is very different than that. Do you feel the male figures in your life are dominating and controlling?

"Yes," I said.

"Hey, big mouth, shut up!" the Voice interrupted. *"You're*

about to let the cat out of the bag. Old devil doctor is about to get wise to your dad's abuse, and you can't have that!"

I listened to the Voice, forgetting that Dr. Tully may have discussed my admission about my father with Dr. Kraft when he handed my care over to him.

"Why do you feel this way?" Dr. Kraft continued. "Can you tell me more about these feelings?"

"No," I lied. "I can't."

"Then can you tell me this: does the voice tell you to do things like starve or exercise or binge and purge?"

"Yes," I said.

"Do you understand this voice is doing you great harm?" Dr. Kraft said.

"I don't know. Sometimes I think it is. Sometimes I think it's just plain evil. But then other times – most of the time – I just think it's a force that I should be grateful for, because it gives me the strength and self-control to do what most people can't."

"What most people can't? What do you mean by that?" Dr. Kraft asked, his eyes peering over the top of his glasses.

"Lose weight – be skinny – not eat. People are always shoveling food into their mouths like they've no self-control. They are disgustingly fat and out of shape. And that Voice gives me the self-control to do what they can't."

"That self-control you believe this voice is giving you could kill you."

"I don't think I'm going to die, Dr. Kraft."

"You've been at death's door several times already."

"Maybe, but being fat is worse than being dead."

"Belinda, I am really concerned about letting you go home today feeling like this. What is the Gobbler telling you about going home?"

"Shut up! Don't tell him our plans," the Voice interjected. *"Are you stupid or what? You're gonna land yourself in that psych ward yet today. Just say there aren't any plans. Play dumb. That shouldn't be too hard for you. End this – NOW!"*

"Nothing, Dr. Kraft. There aren't any plans. I'm just really tired right now."

"Okay, let's stop here for the time being. But I want to see you the first part of next week. I'm going to increase our visits to twice a week for a while. Your parents should be here soon to take you home."

"Okay. Thank you."

"Take care of yourself," Dr. Kraft said, giving me a fatherly pat on the back. "See you in a few days."

"Good job, Belinda. Good job," the Voice said. *"Now let's go home and get started on losing that weight they've put on you."*

I had been honest with Dr. Kraft about a few things in that session anyway. I did sense the Voice as a strong male thought-form, and it did give me the power and self-control I needed to diet in a way many could not. But where I had once felt the Voice was just my inner critic – the sort of voice everyone has – I now wondered if that was the case. As time went on it had gained strength and momentum, and now it was as if it no longer had to be afraid to step out from the shadows and show its true colors. What was I going to do about it now, after it had entrenched itself so firmly within my psyche? Now that the illness was so well established as a part of my identity, the Voice no longer needed to be subtle in its tactics and disguise itself as my own inner critic. Over the years, as it became more deeply rooted in my mind, the Voice had morphed from a persuasive whisper to a loud, shrill and demanding force. In the beginning, it was okay just to stop eating and exercise more, but the Voice had become more demanding over time. Now it was pushing me to extreme limits, commanding me like a tough and unrelenting army drill sergeant to take laxatives, diuretics, diet pills and binge and purge, all the while promising me the pot of gold at the end of the rainbow – the perfect body. When hunger overcame me, it told me to stop worrying about eating just one cookie or one piece of cake, because it would guide my way, and I could have the whole bag of cookies or even the whole cake as long as I purged every last bit. As long as I listened to the Voice and followed its guidance, I would succeed in my pursuit of thinness.

But now I feared it had me in a vise-like grip from which I was never going to be able to free myself, even if I wanted to. Every time I had the smallest desire to be free of the Voice, it played on my fears, saying: *"Without me you will be a fat cow. Do you really want that? You're fat and you're weak. No one else understands your fears like I do. You need me. You know you can't live without me, so don't even try."*

I had been out of the hospital only two days and already I was back to bingeing, purging, laxatives and diuretics. I knew that such behavior would land me back in the hospital yet again, but I couldn't stop. I had no power or control over my destructive behavior. I was physically, mentally, and emotionally exhausted. I lived on autopilot and simply carried out whatever instructions the Voice told me would help me lose yet another pound. I didn't know why being fat paralyzed me with fear. It just did. I didn't know why I did any of the things I did. Was I just going crazy?

After all these years, I was finally beginning to realize that the Voice had me right where it wanted me – trapped in its web of lies and deceit. And I was growing so sick and tired of being sick and tired.

But my awakening didn't matter, because, like a beaten woman who couldn't bring herself to leave her abusive spouse, I couldn't separate myself from the Voice. It was so ingrained into my psyche that I had no idea who I would be without it. I had no sense of autonomy. Love it or hate it, I knew that I was trapped in my relationship with it. I couldn't –I wouldn't leave it, even if it killed me. And kill me it might with its impossible demands. It pushed me to run five miles when I hadn't eaten for two days. I had to purge the water I had just drunk or the scale might show an extra ounce. I had to weigh myself every half hour to make certain the needle on the scale hadn't risen slightly, and if it had, that meant more exercising, more laxatives and diuretics or another skipped meal. When I didn't obey these demands, the Voice rose up, chastising me for my non-compliance, and cast its paralyzing spell of fear all over again.

My mind and my life were totally preoccupied with food, losing weight, weighing myself, exercising, bingeing and purging, calorie counting, abusing laxatives, diuretics and diet pills and then lying to and manipulating everyone around me so they wouldn't find out what I was up to. I was a shadow of the "good girl" I had once been. The morals and values the Voice lived by were in direct conflict with my own. I now did and said things that were contrary to everything I believed in, and to the person I thought myself to be.

Lashing out at my mom became the new norm, and the meaner and nastier the remarks, the better the Voice liked it. Seeing the hurt in her eyes at something I'd said made the remnants that still remained of the real me sad and remorseful. But that didn't matter, because the Voice was calling the shots now – all of them. It was as if that tiny piece of me that was left had been locked away deep inside myself – locked away in a cage. All I could do was look on from between the bars, helpless to do anything to regain my life or my health. Every time I screamed, *Let me out! I just want to be well!* the Voice would mock me and say, *"You can rattle the bars of that cage all you care to. You aren't getting out. Not now – not ever."*

Over the course of the next sixteen months I would find myself hospitalized eleven more times. Each time was a struggle between life and death as my weight plunged to a low of seventy-two pounds and my heart and kidneys showed signs of failure. My electrolytes were stabilized during hospitalizations only to become deranged again within a few short weeks. With the Voice now in charge, I no longer had to concern myself with threats of force-feeding or psych wards. When such ideas were floated, the Voice boldly asserted itself with a firm and forceful, *"No!"* Although I would never have been inclined to throw a full-on temper tantrum myself, the Voice would use anything to have its way. Nothing was off limits. That sweet, quiet, and polite young girl had vanished. The Voice had transformed me into someone even I didn't recognize.

Jesus,
Why did You leave me?
I do recall Your gaze.
For I've a faint recollection,
Sweet Lord,
Of Your most radiant love-light
That illumined the night.
Why did You leave me,
Jesus?

CHAPTER 16

THE VOICE OF DESPAIR

Have mercy on me, LORD, for I am faint. LORD, heal me,
for my bones are troubled. My soul is also in great anguish.
But you, LORD – how long?

Psalm 6:2-3

Despair
Is a black void
Of emptiness and pain
Where you lose all your hope and will
To live.
You pray that God will stop the pain
But the pain never ends
And so you pray
To die.

*B*y my tenth hospitalization, Dr. Kraft had become so frustrated and discouraged by my constant manipulation and repeated hospitalizations that he chose to no longer be my psychiatrist, saying he felt his hands were tied. He had wanted to admit me to a psychiatric hospital for a longer period, and because I had thrown such a fit over the idea my parents had refused. They too seemed intimidated by the temper tantrums and violent outbursts that the Voice so often inspired. It was obvious to me that Dad was angry, but I could sense that beneath that anger he'd simply become so baffled by my behavior and so scared of my frail appearance that he didn't know what to do. He wasn't alone in his confusion. No one else knew what to do with me either. I was as out of control as the eating disorder was.

As a parting shot, Dr. Kraft had told my parents he didn't believe anyone could help me. Mom said Dr. Kraft had told her I would never recover from this illness and would most likely die from it, because I'd been anorexic too long and the illness had become too entrenched.

As much as I'd always disliked the devil doctor, I still felt a twinge of sadness that he was gone – that he'd given up on me. But the joy the Voice expressed about his stepping down overshadowed any sadness that I might have felt.

"Good riddance. With his meddling ways behind us things should be much easier now," the Voice said.

Dr. Giles admitted me for my tenth hospitalization via the emergency room, with my weight at seventy-five pounds. My long hair was now falling out in clumps. The lanugo that had previously been visible only on my arms, was now growing on my chest and back. Dr. Giles had told my parents that this soft, fine white hair was my body's way of insulating itself in an effort to maintain its core temperature as its fat stores were depleted.

With no psychiatrist on my medical team, Dr. Giles worked within his limits as an internist and did the best he

could. He administered the painful potassium IV and stabilized my electrolyte balance yet again. He corrected the de-
hydration. His plan regarding food was to try to get me to eat
light meals on my own while I was in the hospital under the
care of the medical staff. It had been obvious during the time
he had been supervising the tube feeding that he had been
shaken by my somber mood and unstoppable tears. On his
daily rounds, he'd attempted to console me more than once.
Perhaps he wasn't sure how to deal with such behavior this
time around without a psychiatrist on board, so tube feeding
wasn't his go-to solution. Whatever his reasoning, his best efforts were all for nothing because the Voice was a much more
formidable adversary than he'd ever realized.

Some days, I tried to override the Voice and comply by
eating the light meal of soup and Jell-O. There it was again,
that little piece of me rattling the cage and trying to get well.
But such thoughts of wellness and compliance were fleeting
as the Voice came roaring in once more to take dominion over
my thoughts.

*"You know eating like that and all this lying around is go-
ing to make you fat, don't you? Get that fat ass up and out of
that bed and get some exercise. Don't let that IV be your excuse. Please! Take it from the stand and sneak on out of here.
Go find the stairwell. What are a few trips up and down the
steps going to hurt? You might even burn off all those calories
you just consumed like the weak-minded lazy pig that you are.
Now go!"*

Once again that dark and sinister spell had been cast, and
obediently I got up from the bed, took my potassium IV from
its stand, and snuck out of my room to look for the nearest
stairwell. I ran up nearly ten flights before I headed back
down, then I did it over and over again, not giving up until I
began to fear I would pass out if I didn't stop.

"Good work," the Voice said. It was all I needed to hear to
rekindle that sense of pride and achievement that I only felt

when I lost another pound, ran an extra mile or missed or purged a meal. I now lived to please the Voice. It owned me whether I liked it or not.

With Dr. Kraft now out of the picture, the Voice believed it would be much easier to lose weight. But Dr. Kraft wasn't the only doctor the Voice had put on its hit list.

After seven days of hospitalization, Dr. Giles was disheartened and extremely concerned that I had actually lost rather than gained weight. He had of course no clue that I had been sneaking out at the Voice's insistence to do a "cardio workout" twice daily via the hospital stairwell. He had decided that the light meals needed to go and I needed to begin eating full, well-balanced meals that provided much-needed calories.

That evening the attendant brought in a dinner tray that consisted of meatloaf, mashed potatoes and gravy, corn, bread and chocolate ice cream for dessert. I gazed at the plate of food wondering how I was ever going to eat so much. The Voice gasped in horror. *"Don't even think about it! They're just desperate to make you fat. Put the lid back on that plate and push it away. Don't be a pig! If you eat, it'll just mean more stairs after a trip to the bathroom to purge. Is it worth it?"*

I did as the Voice said and pushed it away in disgust. I could refuse to eat. The Voice had said so. But the nursing staff and Dr. Giles had other thoughts about my refusal to eat.

"Ms. Rose," the nurse began, "if you don't eat I will have to report this to Dr. Giles, and he has already mentioned re-feeding."

Bristling at the thought, the Voice spoke through me. "No, I will not eat this tonight and there will be no re-feeding. In fact, I am going home – tonight. Tell Dr. Giles to sign me out."

"You can't do that. You are much too ill."

"I can and I will!" the Voice made me say.

"I'll call Dr. Giles. I'll be back," the nurse said, visibly shaken by my outburst.

"You see, it didn't take much for her to back down," the Voice said to me when the nurse was gone. *"That's how to stand up for yourself!"*

A few minutes later, the nurse returned. Dr. Giles had reluctantly agreed to sign me out, but only if I signed a paper that stated it was against medical advice. I signed the paper. My parents were called to come take me home.

Neither Mom nor Dad was happy that I was coming home so soon, so ill, and against medical advice. Dad hardly spoke on the drive home. I knew he was furious, but he was doing a splendid job holding it all in. Perhaps he was afraid that, in my fragile state, one of his fits of rage would do me in. What else could he do but hold it in? Mom was worried sick, but she too stayed silent. They both tiptoed around me as if they were afraid to speak to me or talk about the illness. But their silence only allowed the Voice to continue to have its way with me, and that could only mean disaster lay ahead.

Our house had always lacked the one thing that made a house a home – love – and being anorexic for roughly six years now had only made its absence that much more obvious. Yes, Dad had been adamant about not letting me die when the doctors insisted I needed to be tube-fed. But his firm stand in that decision didn't feel like love to me; it felt more like him holding power and control over me just like before. He hadn't said "I love you, and that's why I don't want you to die." All he'd said was "I'm your parent and I'm not going to let you die" in an angry tone, as if I'd done something very wrong or he was forbidding me from doing something. Once again, the Voice stepped up in an effort to let me know it was my only real friend.

"If he loved you, he wouldn't sound so angry at you just because you're sick. He'd show a little tenderness. Maybe even say he loved you. You see, I am the one that loves you best," the Voice said.

I couldn't argue with that. Dad seemed angry with me because I was sick. Perhaps his anger stemmed from his inability to control this illness, the situation or me. Dad controlled everything through fear, but maybe the tables had turned. Maybe he was the one afraid now – afraid he'd lost a bit of his power. As this illness spiraled more and more out of control, so did my behavior. At one time, he would have responded to such behavior with a belt, a tree switch or a paddle. But that no longer seemed like a viable option to him in my weakened condition. If he'd relied on his old tactics, he might have broken bones or even killed me. So he had to find a different way to regain the power and control he thought he'd lost – a less confrontational means but one that had always been just as intimidating and forceful nonetheless – and he did: the icy stare.

It was a look that made the tension between us intolerable. He never spoke a word to me – nor I to him. It was as if we were strangers merely living in the same house. But that's pretty much how it had always been. We were an uncommunicative family. There had never been father-daughter conversations or even small talk between us. There had never been a hug or a kiss from him – not a single one that I could recall. There had only been me speaking when spoken to, him ordering me to do something, or him hitting me.

But of all the things that Dad may have been, stupid wasn't one of them. He knew that each time I went into the bathroom and locked the door the odds were good that I was purging. He watched my every move closer than the nurses in the psych ward. Since our home was so small it made it hard for me to be stealthy about purging after a family meal. His eyes followed me everywhere, and I could rest assured that whenever I exited the bathroom Dad would be somewhere nearby, fixing me with one of his angry and hostile stares. They were becoming harder and harder to bear.

His living room recliner sat at an angle from the bathroom so that he had a perfect view of my coming and going. I anticipated he would be looking – watching and waiting – when I walked out of the bathroom and across the hall to my bedroom. His harsh looks were as hurtful emotionally as his belt had been physically when I was a child. I interpreted every piercing look as, "I don't love you, I hate you," and that only fed the eating disorder, deepening that wound that said no one loved me.

Dad's stares overwhelmed me with feelings of worthlessness. I hated myself for being what I was, and yet I felt helpless to change my behavior. I hated myself for being such a disappointment to him. I hated that he was so obviously angry with me for the anorexia. But most of all I hated the fact that he didn't love me. Of all the feelings that his cold, hate-filled glares reinforced, it was the belief that he didn't love me that cut deepest, and I was finding these feelings harder and harder to live with. But I didn't have to suffer alone with my heartache. The Voice was there as my constant companion and friend.

"You know what you need?" the Voice said. *"A bag of cookies and half a gallon of milk to wash them down. That will make you feel better. Now go on. Head to the kitchen and bring them back to your room. Don't worry about gaining weight because you're going to purge every bit of it anyway. What do you think all that milk is for? It will make it so much easier to bring those cookies back up."*

I needed a way to squash this pain that was eating my heart out, and the Voice had given me the only way I knew to do that. As long as I was bingeing and purging I wasn't thinking of how deeply hurt I was or how unloved I felt. So I binged and purged not one but two bags of cookies. I purged until I was physically drained and then I went off to sleep.

While I knew that Dad was privy to the bingeing and purging, Mom was harder to read. For the most part, she acted as if everything was fine, just as she had after the rape. Mom never mentioned if she noticed I was losing weight again. She wasn't saying or doing anything about my frequent bathroom visits. She was simply staying silent, and the Voice was jubilant over her silence. It meant less interference in my pursuit of thinness, and the less interference the better. But with no one at home to step in and say or do something, my mental and physical health was deteriorating at an alarming rate. I was alone with the Voice in control of my every thought and action, even my now dismal prayers.

As the anorexia raged, so did the depression, and the deepening depression brought more and more thoughts of suicide. When I tried to pray through it, I felt nothing but emptiness. Where had Jesus gone? His love had always been my anchor as a child, a place of light and hope where I could retreat in my private reveries. Now there was no light and no hope to be found – not even a glimmer. I felt as if I had been plunged into a darkness from which there was no chance of escaping. I was beginning to believe I had no reason to live. Each day was another battle with food and the Voice, and each night was a struggle to sleep because of the nightmares that never let up and the aches and pains that riddled my body. I had begun to believe that the Voice was more of a demon than a friend, no matter what it said. I was weary from the never-ending battle that raged on in my mind and my body, and now found myself in a place of utter despair. If I couldn't make the Voice stop, then I simply didn't want to go on. Besides, I told myself, no one loved me anyway, and Jesus had long ago left my side. What was there to live for? The suicidal thoughts were now becoming more than just mere thoughts – they were developing into hard and fast plans to end the pain I could simply no longer endure.

Heavenly Father,
Am I loved by anyone?
I ache inside to simply be loved.
Lord, do You love me?
Am I so unlovable that even You've gone away?
I can no longer find You.
Come back, dear Lord.
I miss You.
I need You.
I love You.
Amen.

CHAPTER 17

HOPELESS

Hurry to answer me, LORD. My spirit fails.
Do not hide your face from me, so that I do not
become like those who go down into the pit.

Psalm 143:7

Hopeless.
I want to give up
Because I cannot be fixed
And things will never get better.
No hope
Is there of ever being well
Or stilling the demon's
Roar in my head.
Hopeless.

*H*ere I was again in the pit of despair with no idea how to climb out. I'd been here many times before, but somehow this time was different. Perhaps I'd hit the bottom of the pit and that was why this terrible sense of hopelessness was so much more intense. I couldn't shake it off, I couldn't talk my-self out of it and I couldn't pray it away. I felt hopeless – and with that hopelessness came thoughts of suicide.

Even though my praying had diminished greatly in recent months, I still tried to cast out the suicidal thoughts with prayer. I fought the dark thoughts with all the energy I could muster. I knew that taking my own life was wrong on every level. After all, I was raised a Catholic and I had always be-lieved suicide to be a mortal sin. But even my most valiant efforts seemed fruitless amid the heavy waves that crashed over me like the ocean tide. It was an excruciating sensation of drowning, as if I'd been bound to the ocean floor with a ball and chain around my ankle. I couldn't move, I couldn't breathe, and I was left gasping for every single breath of life-giving oxygen. And along with all of this came feelings of immense despondency. Like a chain reaction, the suicidal thoughts would dance through my head, and the Voice that never missed an opportunity to belittle me would beat me down all the more.

"You're so pathetic! You're weak! You always have been! That's why you need me, and that's why I'm never going away. Go ahead, kill yourself. I'll come with you to the afterlife. I'll see you in hell!"

Was the Voice right? If I ended my life this way would I go to hell and be tormented by its unrelenting demands for all eternity? That would just be my luck. "Stop it!" I screamed out loud. "Why don't you just leave me alone! I just want to be left alone! Go away!" Maybe I was crazy or maybe I was slowly being driven crazy, because for the first time I was talking out loud to a Voice that existed only in my head!

I needed to just stop thinking and shut my mind off. I needed to do something besides mope around in my room all day long feeling sorry for myself. The afternoon sun streaming through my window was so inviting. It was a beautiful autumn afternoon; perhaps a walk outside would help shift my mood.

Stepping out the back door into the yard, I was immediately drawn to my old swing set, which had been one of my favorite childhood toys. It didn't matter to me that I was nearly nineteen now; I still loved to swing. There was something about the swing rising high into the air that had always made me feel free – as if I could fly like the birds, as if one day I'd swing myself up so far and high that I'd never come down; as if I could swing myself to heaven. I had swung on this same small wooden swing since I was five. It was weatherworn and its white paint was chipped and peeling, but as I sat down on it poignant memories of my childhood washed over me – memories of a sad, frightened little girl.

I could vividly recall the six-year-old me that sang nursery rhymes at the top of my lungs, swinging so high that the back legs of the swing's frame jumped off the ground. I smiled at memories of how worried Mom got that the entire swing set would tip over and come crashing to the ground with me on board. She always had worried too much. I could still hear her, voicing her motherly concern as if it were yesterday: "Belinda, you're going too high! The frame's coming off the ground! Stop!" But I paid no attention to her warning and hollered back at her, "I'm okay Mommy. Don't worry!" This was a place where I had no fear. I was flying, and I was free!

By the time I was eight, Mom no longer paid much attention to how high I swung or that I was even in the backyard playing at all. She was working most of the time by then and I was on my own after school, and half of every Saturday. The eight-year-old me was much different from the six-year-old me. She was a sad, lonely and fearful child. No longer did she sing happy nursery rhymes like she used to. Instead she chanted a new and much more somber tune:

Nobody loves me
Everybody hates me!

No one heard that little girl's laments. No one.

At barely seventy-five pounds I still had no problems fitting onto my old swing. As I pumped my legs back and forth, the swing rose higher and higher in the air. I drew in a deep breath of cool, late November air and grinned. Turning my face towards the sun, I basked in its radiance, welcoming each ray that kissed my face with its warmth. My plan to chase away the dark, sinister thoughts must be working, because no longer was I thinking of suicide, but of happier times playing with friends in this very same backyard.

It seemed like only yesterday that my girlfriends and I had taken turns burying each other beneath vast drifts of red, gold and orange leaves from the huge sycamore that towered over our backyard. Even now, nine years later, I could still recall that ten-year-old version of me lying on the ground giggling beneath those piles of leaves, all the while looking up at that immense tree looming like a giant above me. As my friends buried me beneath piles and piles of the sycamore's colorful foliage, I escaped to my own little imaginary world. In my make-believe scenario, the tree overhead wasn't a tree at all, but some made-up creature from outer space. The leaves that covered me were the alien creature's webs cocooning me for dinner, and the tree's massive sprawling branches became alien tentacles that would rip open the cocoon and eat me limb by limb. It was just a little girl's overactive imagination. I was just playing make-believe. It was all in my imagination ... or was it? Monsters and evil creatures weren't real ... or were they? These days it didn't feel as if it was just my imagination that an evil creature had captured me. It might not have been a living, breathing monster, yet it still felt like an evil creature to me, and it had a name – the Gobbler. The Gobbler had long tentacles too – tentacles of lies and deceit. It used them to lure and draw me in and then WHAM! I was ensnared – co-cooned in its web where escape wasn't only a distant dream – not now, not ever. Being devoured bit by bit was my fate. This was no longer child's play, a kid's game where I could merely burst from a pile of leaves and run to safety from the imaginary creature's grasp. Imaginary creature or not, I was in a death match with a very real and formidable foe.

I didn't try to fight or to hold back the tears that now streamed down my cheeks. Dragging my feet in the grass, I brought the swing to a stop and let these tears flow. I had cried so much of late, but these tears were different – they came from a much different place inside. These were tears of grief. I was grieving as much for my childhood friends and those good times that were so few and far between as I was for how horribly wrong my life had gone. I was grieving for the little girl who only wanted to be loved. I was grieving for the young woman who felt so alone and hopeless. I was grieving for the virginity I had lost so brutally. A deep and profound sadness swept over me as I thought of all the events in my life that had brought me to this place: the abuse, the bullies, the rape, and even the trauma of multiple hospitalizations. This time last year I had been in a psych ward under the devil doctor's care, and I'd spent the majority of this year in and out of hospitals, often near death's door. It was all too much to take in and that suffocating wave of hopelessness washed over me once more. Would I, could I, ever be well? No, I didn't believe I could, so my thoughts turned to how I could end this ache that went so deep in my heart that it pierced my soul. No one understood how much pain I was in – no one. But worse than that, no one really seemed to care, especially not my parents. Why didn't they ever talk to me about how I was feeling? The only answer they ever came up with was shrinks, psych wards and medications that made me feel drugged up all the time. Throughout this entire illness not once had either of my parents simply put their arms around me and told me they loved me. Why didn't they love me? Was I so horrible? Was I so unlovable? Maybe I should just end it all now.

It wasn't that I wanted to die. I didn't. I just wanted the pain and torment to end. I just wanted to be well and happy. I wanted to feel loved and cared for. I wanted a normal life like other kids my age had. But most of all, I wanted the Voice to shut up, go away, and leave me alone. It had taken me too long to fully recognize its sinister nature, and now that I had I no longer possessed the strength to fight it. It didn't matter how much I hated the bingeing and purging, starving or being a slave to the Voice's every demand. The Voice had become so enmeshed into every facet of my psyche that I couldn't picture my life without it. The Voice was a trickster that had begun luring me like a wolf in sheep's clothing years ago. That was obvious to me now, and it had begun with that first lie, that first tentacle wrapping around my naïve twelve-year-old mind.

"Just lose a few inches off that stomach, and you will be just as thin, svelte and popular as your best friend Valerie," the Voice had promised. *"It's easy! Just cut out Mom's big breakfast every morning, and eat a pop tart. You'll be thinner in no time!"*

How could I have been so stupid? In my innocence I had believed what the Voice had said because I had thought that Voice was my own. I hadn't realized how deadly its intent was. Naïvely, I'd bought into every word it had uttered – hook, line and sinker. I'd taken the bait, thinking it wouldn't do me any harm to diet and lose just a few pounds. How wrong I'd been! As I beat myself up for my ignorance, it suddenly became crystal clear that my so-called pop tart diet had been the definitive moment when this illness began sucking me in. I had unwittingly left the door wide open for a stranger, the Voice of Anorexia, to control my life through my every thought. Now this uninvited guest refused to leave. I knew of no way to kick this vile and evil creature out of my head. It had not only usurped my thoughts and my life, but it now overshadowed the real me. I no longer recognized myself. I loathed the anorexic me even more than the adolescent girl I'd been before the illness. The old me might have been pathetic and weak, as the Voice always said, but at least I was a sweet girl. Now that sweet girl was a distant memory. She had been replaced by an angry and bitter young woman, whose behavior was manipulative, unruly and unpredictable, and I hated everything about her.

I hated how she did anything to get her way, all in the name of thinness. The old me had been honest to a fault, but the anorexic me wouldn't think twice about lying if it meant getting to lose another pound. I could hate myself and want to change till the cows came home, but it wasn't happening. *"Give it up,"* the Voice said, sneering at me. *"Not happening!"*

I felt helpless and hopeless. The Voice that now dictated my every thought and action was a force so commanding, so deceptive, and so cunning that I saw no way out from under its totalitarian control, and with that thought I slid deeper into this endless pit of despair.

The Voice was a cancer, and if I couldn't cut out that cancer, then I had to die because I couldn't go on living with this pain. What was the point? What future did I have? Dr. Kraft had told my parents I would never be well. Maybe he was right. I couldn't bear living like this for decade after decade. Perhaps death was the only way out. Perhaps that's what Father Sam had thought when he made the decision to end his life. I could empathize with him – his pain and suffering. You had to live with this kind of pain to understand it. It pushed you to extreme measures.

If I were to choose Father Sam's path of suicide, it would be by overdose. I would make my selection from the myriad of prescription drugs from Dr. Kraft that still lined the kitchen counter: sleeping pills, antidepressants and antipsychotics. It would be so easy to just down a bottle or two ... or three ... and say goodnight world, and goodbye Voice. But there were two things stopping me dead in my tracks – my love for my mom and God.

I loved them both with all my heart, even if I did feel they'd both abandoned me in very different ways. There had been so many times I had needed Mom's support and love, and she had simply buried her head in the sand and left me on my own to deal with whatever life was throwing at me. She would never even listen to my problems, much less help me deal with them, and that left me feeling hurt, angry, abandoned and betrayed. I had to keep her secrets all the time to keep peace in our home, to keep Dad from exploding. Why did everything have to be at my expense?

I felt those same feelings of abandonment towards Jesus. He seemed to have vanished from my life when I needed Him most. Prayer used to be the easiest thing in the world for me, and many times it was my only place of refuge from the abuse. Finding Jesus in my imagination, feeling His presence draw near, was as natural to me as swinging on this swing in the backyard – but now I felt nothing. In the midst of this depression there was nothing but emptiness, loneliness and a darkness that permeated my being. No one was coming to rescue me – not Mom, not God, and certainly not any doctor. But even so, I wasn't sure I could hurt either one of them as deeply as I knew ending my life would hurt them, and I didn't want to break their hearts. I didn't want to be the cause of their pain. Besides, who would stay close to Mom and protect her from Dad if I was gone? It wasn't going to be my older brother, for sure. He was never around when he lived at home, and now that he'd left it certainly wasn't an option. It was up to me; it was always up to me. But how long could I hold on?

Getting up from the swing, I walked to the back of the yard and sat beneath the sycamore. Resting my head against its massive trunk, I closed my eyes and tried to stop myself from the crying. As the crisp autumn breeze blew softly across my face, images flashed in my mind's eye of the hillside where I'd so often meet Jesus as a child. I tried to envisage the Lord's smiling face there, waiting, just as I used to see it in those reveries of long ago. I would always have a memory of His face that seemed to glow with the most beautiful and radiant light. But that's all it was – a memory. What my soul cried out for was an experience of Him. I desperately needed to feel His presence once more. But it was no use, because the image in my mind vanished as quickly as it had appeared. In the grip of this darkness, there was no light. Oh, how I ached to know the comfort of His presence once again.

Jesus,
I am lost.
Without You I've no hope.
I'm drowning in a sea of despair.
Help me,
The waves crash over my head.
I am drowning in this
Sea of despair,
Jesus.

CHAPTER 18

A FLICKER OF HOPE

Why are you in despair, my soul? Why are you disturbed within me? Hope in God! For I shall still praise him for the saving help of his presence.

Psalm 42:5

Arise!
Rejoice my soul,
The spirit of hope comes.
A bright new dawn is upon thee!
Give thanks,
His life-saving grace comes this day
As the great gift of hope.
Rejoice my soul,
Arise!

*M*y weight went up and down like a yo-yo, and it all had to do with my secret stash underneath the bed. When I laid off the diuretics, laxatives and diet pills, my weight rose. No surprise there. The surprising thing was that I was managing to control the urge to indulge myself in my downward spiral of behavior since I'd been released from my last hospitalization.

It was simple, really – I didn't want to go back there. I'd had enough of the painful potassium IVs, the force-feeding, and the all-eyes-watching-me routine, I just wanted to be left alone. But I guess I was never really alone, because the Voice was always there with me – forever whispering in my head.

"You weigh eighty-five pounds now. Don't you think you need to shed a few of those extra pounds? You're gettin' kind of pudgy right around the middle, don't you think? A few days of laxatives and diuretics would be a really easy way to take off those extra pounds," the Voice said.

Digging deep, trying to muster the courage to defy the Voice's constant demands, I railed against it. In some kind of nonverbal tug-of-war that was in my mind only, I tried hard to stand up for myself against the onslaught. *I don't want to use them. I don't want to go back to the hospital again. I hate it there. I'll find some other way to lose weight.*

That battle with the Voice raged on in my head, day after day. Most of the time I was just too depressed and too tired to carry out its plans of sabotage. Other days, I simply didn't care, and I let the Voice drone on and on. I didn't care about much of anything except spending the long hours of each day shut up in my bedroom, crying, sleeping, or a combination of the two. I didn't think my parents had noticed how deeply depressed I had become, but I was wrong – about one of them, anyway.

Dad had noticed.

Ever since I had made the Fashion Board at Brighton, Dad had been fascinated with the idea of me modeling. I could still recall how proud he had been the day I'd come home from school to announce that I was one of only five chosen from a class of two hundred girls. Yet it still came as a huge surprise when he made the offer to send me to a ritzy modeling agency in the well-to-do part of town, especially after I had dropped out of Brighton only a few months into the program. He told me it was a surprise for the nineteenth birthday I had coming up in a week. It was hands-down the biggest thing I'd ever received from my parents for my birthday.

I knew that I had disappointed and angered him by leaving Brighton. I had been a quitter, just like he'd always said I'd be. It felt like a self-fulfilling prophecy, and I carried a deep sense of guilt and failure for leaving. I also felt badly that he had lost the money I knew he'd worked so hard for by my dropping out. So why was he offering me this new opportunity? We weren't rich by any stretch of the imagination, and I was stunned that he would make such an offer after I'd let him down so badly. Dad didn't do stuff like this. He wasn't a risk taker. It was a too-good-to-be-true offer. But this amazing offer that I couldn't refuse came with a condition.

I hadn't been to a psychiatrist since Dr. Kraft had departed a month or so earlier. He insisted that I resume therapy with someone, so the search for his replacement was on. That search took no time at all, thanks to Dr. Kraft. When he'd resigned from my case, he'd left my parents with a short list of referrals. This time my parents chose a psychoanalyst by the name of Dr. Duprow. The first appointment was promptly made for the next morning.

Dr. Duprow's office was a long drive down to the south side of the city. He had an office on the twelfth floor of a prominent medical highrise adjacent to a major hospital. I didn't want a new head doctor; I didn't particularly see the point. I had no faith in doctors anymore – period. But if it made my parents feel better, and I got to go to modeling school, then it seemed a small price to pay.

A tall, heavy-set, middle-aged man puffing at the stub of a cigar approached Mom and me in the waiting room. "Good afternoon, Mrs. Rose. I'm Dr. Duprow," he said in a deep, husky voice. My eyes followed the stubby cigar as he moved it from his right hand to his left. His enormous paw of a hand reached out to engulf Mom's more petite one. "And this must be Belinda," he said, towering over me. "Are you ready to get started, young lady?"

Did I have a choice? I nodded hesitantly. I couldn't put my finger on it, but something about this guy made me uneasy. We entered his smoke-filled office and my disquiet morphed into plain fear! I watched as he closed two thick wooden doors, one after the other. Never had I seen anyone anywhere with not one, but two, solid sets of doors like this. Even more curious were the six large locks on the inside of the second door that he bolted one by one. I had just watched him seal us inside this small office space as if it were a tomb. Why? Why does he have two doors? Why does anyone have locks on the inside of a door, and why so many? Where was I going to go from twelve floors up – out the window? More importantly, why would I want to run? What did he do in here, anyway?

"Have a seat on the couch, Belinda," Dr. Duprow said, sitting down in the chair directly opposite me. He put the now-finished cigar in an ashtray on the table beside him. Opening a small drawer in the table, he pulled out another cigar, tapped it on the table and lit it. With a look of sheer delight on his face, he sucked on the cigar like a baby on a pacifier. My eyes followed the thick cloud of smoke billowing into the already foul-smelling air.

As I fidgeted in my seat he said, half-laughing, "Relax. Don't be so nervous. I won't bite!"

If that was supposed to put me at ease, it didn't. I wasn't so sure that he didn't bite. There had to be some reason for all the doors and locks. Nervously, I stared at my feet to avoid eye contact with him as he spoke.

"So, Belinda, I want to start by playing a game. It's a game of words called free association. I will say a word and I want you to say the very first thing that pops into your head. Don't think about it, don't censor it; just say it. Understand?"

I nodded, continuing to stare down at the dingy grey tile floor beneath my feet. This strange guy – his cigar, his double doors and their six locks made me wonder what I'd gotten myself into this time.

"Boy," he said, taking another puff of his foul-smelling cigar.

"Girl," I replied, trying not to choke on the smoke.

"Dad," he said.

"Mom," I replied.

"Fat," he said.

"Ugly," I replied.

"Okay, let's talk about that. Why 'ugly'? Why not 'thin'?"

"Because being fat is ugly," I replied, shifting my gaze from my shoes to the dirty smoke-stained window on my left.

"I'm rather fat. Do you think I'm ugly?"

"I didn't say you were ugly. I said 'fat' is ugly – that's all. I don't want to be fat because I think it makes me ugly."

"Okay. Let's go back to our game for a moment, Belinda. Food."

"Fat," I replied.

Dr. Duprow grinned, and took another puff of his cigar before he spoke. "Tell me more about this. Why do you think 'fat' when I say 'food'?"

"It's simple. Food makes you fat!"

"Not if we don't overindulge. We have to eat to live, don't we?"

"Yeah, I suppose. But that still doesn't mean it won't make you fat," I said, standing my ground.

"Too much food makes you fat. Isn't that a truer statement?"

"I guess." I was confused by this word association game

he played. With every response, I kept waiting for him to say, "Gotcha!" Everything about this doctor and this place was weird. I wanted to stop the stupid game, and ask him why were there two doors and why all the locks. But I was much too intimidated and too frightened for that. All I could think of doing was getting out of there into the fresh air and as far away from him as I could.

"How much food is too much, Belinda? How much do you think makes you fat?"

"Watch what you tell this guy. Don't trust him. Keep your guard up," the Voice said.

"I guess that's different for each of us," I said, heeding the Voice's warning.

"Yes, but we are talking about *you* here. What's too much for you?"

Annoyed, I shot back, "Is this a trick question? You already know I'm anorexic and I don't like to eat. I don't like food 'cause it makes me fat, and I don't want to be fat because being fat makes me ugly!"

"I get that. But I want to understand why you think that."

"I don't know why I think that? Maybe 'cause it's true?"

"Come over here to the scale."

"Oh, just great!" the Voice said. *"This one has a scale in his office as well as a foul-smelling cigar, double doors and six locks! Your parents really know how to pick 'em! Now what are you going to do? Well, it doesn't look like you're getting out of this. Go ahead and step on the scale."*

Reluctantly, I rose from the couch and followed him to the large scale that stood waiting for me in the corner of his office. Slipping my tennis shoes off, I obeyed and stepped on.

He slid the steel weights until they balanced perfectly. "Eighty-five pounds."

Grabbing my tennis shoes by the laces, I headed back to my seat on the couch.

"Do you think eighty-five pounds is fat?"

"I don't know."

"Well you are clearly *not* fat. Yet you still seem to see yourself that way. Are you satisfied with your current weight?"

"Less would be better."

"Earth to Stupid, shut up!" the Voice screamed in my head.

"Less might mean that you die. Is that what you want?"

"Sometimes."

"Sometimes you want to die, Belinda? Are you thinking of suicide?"

No way I was answering this one truthfully. "No, I am not thinking of suicide," I fibbed. "Sometimes I just want to die because I don't think I can get well. I just don't want to live like this anymore. It's too hard."

"I see," Dr. Duprow began, "and by 'like this' you mean anorexic?"

I nodded again.

"I understand from your medical records that you have been ill for quite a few years now. I'd like to try a different treatment approach with different medications. Are you all right with that?"

I shrugged. I knew by the way he kept looking at me – like a stern father – that he wanted, maybe even expected, a more definitive answer than that. "Sure, Dr. Duprow." But I wasn't sure at all. I hated the side effects of the medications these shrinks doled out like candy.

"I'm writing you some new prescriptions. I'll give these to your mom along with instructions to move you from your old medications to these. I'd like to see you twice a week for now."

Twice a week! I didn't want to see this guy ever again. But I had no choice – not if I wanted to go to modeling school. So I agreed, reluctant and a little fearful. Nothing was going to stop me from the appointment my parents had scheduled for this coming Saturday morning to meet with the director of the modeling agency. Not even this eccentric and rather scary shrink.

"Your daughter is very pretty," the agency director said, shaking my dad's hand. "It's good to meet you, Mr. Rose. I'm Scott."

Scott was a tall, lanky and attractive young man – maybe somewhere in his mid-thirties. He asked the three of us to take a seat in his posh and very upscale office. Mom and Dad complied, but I was much too excited to sit still. Mesmerized by the glamorous images of gorgeous models that adorned his office walls, I strolled about his office, unable to take my eyes off them, pausing to take each one in, one by one.

"Some of those girls got their start right here, Belinda. They've done quite well for themselves in New York and Paris," Scott said with a sense of paternal pride. "So, Belinda," he continued, "have you ever modeled before?"

"Yes. A little. I was on the Fashion Board at Brighton Career College. We modeled for local department stores, mostly on weekends."

"Ever done any runway modeling?" he said.

"No, I haven't."

"Well, with your height, and those long, slender arms and legs I bet you'd be a natural. Strutting your stuff on the catwalk is one of the things we will teach you here. We also teach our girls the ins and outs of photographic modeling, and making the camera fall in love with you! I love your image. Love that short hairstyle! Very becoming. I think you will fit in really well here."

"Thank you," I said, blushing and looking away. I thought I was dreaming. I couldn't believe he thought I had a wonderful look – and he told me I was pretty!

Scott and my parents talked about the cost of the school, and then I watched speechless as Dad pulled a large envelope from the inside pocket of his coat that was chock-full of cash. He handed it across the desk to Scott, paying him in full.

"Come, Belinda. I want you to meet our photographer, Matt. You will be working with him to shoot your portfolio. Let's take your parents along for a tour of the agency."

I was breathless. I couldn't ever recall having been so excited in my life. There was a large room with a long runway where Scott explained the girls were taught to walk that special walk. There were rooms full of rack after rack of clothing, with makeup mirrors lining the walls. These rooms, he told us, were used to teach the girls the art of applying makeup. Adjoining the makeup room was another huge room that was set up with floor-to-ceiling white backdrops, lights and expensive-looking photographic equipment. In the corner of the room, a young man stood behind a camera, and he was snapping pictures of a pretty twenty-something brunette.

"That's Matt, our photographer," Scott said.

It felt like a dream, and if it was I never wanted to wake up! I looked on as the young photographer and the model seemed to work seamlessly in unison. When they'd finished, Scott led us over to meet him.

"Matt, I want you to meet Belinda. She is our newest girl. These are her parents, Mr. and Mrs. Rose."

Matt shook Dad's hand and greeted Mom before turning his attention to me. "Hi Belinda! It's great to meet you," he said, reaching out to clasp my hand in his.

Matt was a handsome young man who could have been a model himself. He looked to be in his late twenties. He wore his long, dark brown hair in a neat ponytail that fell to midway down his back.

"It's great to meet you too, Matt!" I said, getting lost in his dreamy deep brown eyes.

"Let's get you on the calendar for some time next week to start shooting your portfolio. I'll be helping you get comfortable in front of the lens."

Reaching into his briefcase on the floor, he pulled a small black notebook out. "So, next Thursday afternoon work for you? Say ... one thirty?"

"Yeah, it sounds perfect!"

"Great. See you then. I look forward to working with you," he said, flashing a smile that made his dimples look all the more enticing.

"Your first class is this Monday evening, Belinda," Scott said, turning to lead us back to his office. "I'll give you the full schedule on your way out."

After giving us the schedule, he shook Dad's hand again and we said our goodbyes. I floated out the agency door, my head still in the clouds all the way to the elevator.

As my parents and I stood beneath the large crystal chandeliers that illumined the long hallway and waited for the elevator doors to open, I turned to Mom and whispered, "Pinch me, Mom."

"Why?" she said, laughing softly.

"Because this just has to be a dream. Nothing this wonderful ever happens to me! Not ever."

"You see," the Voice said as the elevator doors closed. *"I told you to stick with me and I'd make your dreams come true."*

Yeah, so you did, I replied. *So you did.*

I couldn't sleep, but tonight my tossing and turning wasn't due to throbbing legs or visions of suicide. I was just too excited to sleep. It reminded me of Christmas Eve when I was eight. I had begged Mom and Dad for an organ that Christmas. I already knew I was getting it because my girlfriend Deanne and I had peeked and found it hidden away at the back of the attic. I could still remember the anticipation I'd felt that Christmas Eve, knowing that in a few short hours my dream present would be all mine! This was a little like that – that same heightened anticipation had taken control of my emotions. It was a really good feeling compared to the despair and hopelessness I had become so used to of late. At last I had something positive to look forward to – a future that I never dreamt possible. Me? A model? It didn't seem real. Yet it was happening, and it had come from nowhere. There was now at least a glimmer of hope that tomorrow would be better. Dad had made this happen, and I was so thankful. I had something to hold on to, and that made me very, very happy indeed. Could it be that God had been there all along, and He'd worked through my dad? Perhaps He hadn't abandoned me. Perhaps He'd heard my prayers after all, and this was His answer.

O Lord,
Tonight I rejoice.
The despair lifted.
Hope for tomorrow has come to raise me up.
You reached down into the depths of darkness.
You pulled me out of the pit.
You've given me a flicker of hope.
I'm beyond thankful,
O Lord.

CHAPTER 19

THE DARKEST NIGHT

*For the enemy pursues my soul. He has struck my life down
to the ground. He has made me live in dark places, as those
who have been long dead.*

Psalm 143:3

*Seconds
exist between
hopelessness and despair
and your reason to live stolen.
Seconds
for life to sucker-punch you hard
in the gut and destroy
your will to live.
Seconds.*

*A*lthough wild fantasies of gracing the cover of some illustrious fashion magazine lifted my mood temporarily, the battle with the Voice still raged on in my inner world. The Voice knew how to take advantage of any given situation to have its way, and my new modeling gig was its dream personified.

Modeling meant being skinny – really skinny – the Voice told me all too frequently. Every pound lost was a victory won and a point scored towards that dream life I had conjured up in my head as a glamorous fashion model, or so the Voice told me. But the Voice had a much broader agenda than merely driving me to being skinnier. It also had a true knack for wielding words that were meant to sting, bruise and further wound my already frail self-esteem. *"Don't screw this up like you did Brighton. You're such a loser – such a disappointment to your parents. For whatever reason, Dad's given you another chance, so let's try not to blow it, huh? Do you even think it's possible for you to make him proud? Ever? Sorry to say it, sweetie pie, but I don't have much faith in you. But I'll tell you one thing: if you wanna be a model you can't ever be too skinny. So how about you rise to the occasion, lose a few more inches, a couple more pounds, and show everyone you're not a loser?"* the Voice said.

I got it. I did feel like a loser. I always had. Perhaps it was that feeling of being a perpetual loser that drove my desire for perfection. I knew I wasn't perfect, but that wasn't going to keep me from trying to be. I had tried to be perfect in my parents' eyes in so many ways growing up. I tried for perfect grades, and although my grades weren't always straight A's, I always made the honor roll. I tried to win their love and approval by becoming a do-gooder and rarely – if ever – getting into trouble; that too never seemed to be enough. I tried taking on numerous duties at home and cooking and cleaning my way into their hearts, and that didn't bring the desired results either. This time had to be different. It just *had* to be.

If I could win their approval, perhaps I'd win the one thing I coveted more than life itself – the one thing I always fell short of finding – their love and affection.

But the path to perfection and the road to success seemed fraught with obstacles I couldn't overcome. I was fighting a battle I couldn't win as I struggled moment by moment against the Voice's nonstop chatter, and now the medication that Dr. Duprow had prescribed was causing side effects that were debilitating, uncontrollable, and eroding what little quality of life I still had left.

Dr. Kraft had prescribed psychotropic medications, and they often made me feel drugged up or a bit dazed. But this was very different. First of all, I was dizzy most of the time and this wasn't just from low blood pressure. But the dizziness was the least of the problems – it was the tremors and agitation that were making me crazy – if I wasn't crazy enough already.

The tremors made my hands shake uncontrollably, and that was something Mom noticed. But trying to explain what the agitation felt like to her was much more difficult. It was a feeling that never let me sit still for two seconds. I felt as if I always had to be doing something, and I could never do that something fast enough. It was an awful, indescribable feeling that refused to subside no matter what I did or how fast I did it, and quite frankly I wasn't sure I could stand to live with it much longer. It needed to be the first topic of conversation on my next visit to Dr. Duprow.

"Dr. Duprow," I began, "I don't want to be on this medication you have me on anymore. I can't stop shaking. Here, just look at my hands," I said, trying to steady them as I held them mid-air. "The agitation and restlessness is indescribable, but trust me, it's horrible and it's driving me completely batty. Besides that, I'm dizzy constantly, and that concerns me with my driving."

"I can prescribe another medication that may counteract the side effects," Dr. Duprow said, puffing away contentedly on his disgusting chubby cigar. "I'll write you a new script before you leave today."

"Right now I'll try anything," I said, hoping I wasn't just grasping at straws. I walked out of his office that day with a new prescription that I prayed would put an end to the nearly incapacitating restlessness and tremors. But instead of relief from my symptoms, what it would bring me was another unwelcome trip to the hospital emergency room.

The following morning, I had exciting plans to go over some of the proofs from my first modeling shoot with Matt at the agency. Matt had called to say he'd gotten some really good shots for my portfolio, and I was eager to see them for myself. Not wanting this sense of restlessness and the tremors to ruin my day, I decided to take the first dose of the new medication Dr. Duprow had prescribed. It proved to be a huge mistake.

I was in the kitchen talking to Mom when I began feeling very peculiar. Grabbing hold of the kitchen table to steady myself, I called out to Mom, "Mom! Something's wrong. I feel really weird. The floor is moving! Everything looks so strange. Mom! What's wrong with me?" That was the last thing I said before landing in a heap on the hard kitchen floor.

When I came to a few minutes later I knew I was still disoriented because the room was still moving, but I could swear there were police officers swarming through our kitchen! "Young lady," said the one stooping down next to me, "an ambulance is on the way." I heard what he'd said clearly, but his face was distorted – as if there were two of him! Panicked, I called out for Mom. "Mom! What's going on?"

I could hear one of the officers pressing Mom about the origins of the string of prescription medications that lined the kitchen counter. "They're all prescribed by her doctor," Mom said. Her tone seemed defensive.

A big, burly paramedic suddenly appeared, and picked me up from the kitchen floor to carry me to the living room where a stretcher waited. With the assistance of a second paramedic they put me into the ambulance where my vitals were taken. I had grown so familiar with this routine – and so tired of it. As they tried to find a vein to put the IV in that wouldn't collapse, I began to cry.

"Hey, don't be scared, sweetheart. You're going to be fine. You'll be at the hospital in no time. It sounds like you've had a reaction to your medication," the paramedic reassured me. But what he didn't understand was that my tears weren't about my fear of the hospital or even of what was happening to me in this moment. These tears were falling because I was fearful of failing yet again. I had a very important appointment that morning at the modeling agency, an appointment that might represent the start of a whole new life for me and make my parents very proud, but instead I was headed to the ER – yet again. The agency knew nothing about my illness or my personal life. How was I going to explain this without giving myself away? If they knew the truth, maybe they too would think I was "crazy", as Cindy and the girls at Brighton had. If that happened it would just ruin everything.

"There you go – screwing everything up again! You loser!" the Voice shrieked in my head.

At the ER, Mom handed the nurse a list of the medications Dr. Duprow currently had me on. It took no time to figure out I'd had a horrible reaction to the latest prescription. The new medication had not only caused my sudden collapse, but it had also affected my kidney function. I was no longer able to urinate, a side effect the doctor seemed very concerned about. The plan was to insert a catheter, continue to administer IV fluids in an attempt to flush my system of the drug, and hold me overnight. Their plan worked perfectly, and twenty-four hours later I was released to go home.

Thankfully Mom had covered for me with the modeling agency, making both apologies and an excuse as to why I'd been a no-show the previous day. She'd told them a family emergency had come up. Well, at least she hadn't told them the whole embarrassing truth.

Dr. Duprow had left instructions via phone that I was to reduce the dosage of antipsychotic medication until our next visit. I'd have gladly stopped it altogether if he hadn't constantly warned that it was dangerous to quit such medication abruptly. Lowering the dosage at least reduced the severity of the side effects enough for me to finish up my portfolio at the agency.

Mom accompanied me to all my photoshoots. She was like my security blanket. I felt safe with her near me. Although I had deeply buried any thoughts, feeling or emotion about the rape, its repercussions still found ways of surfacing I had no control over. For instance, being alone with Matt wasn't something I felt comfortable with. I had always been nervous and awkward around the opposite sex, but since the rape men in general made me more nervous and uneasy than ever. Besides, Mom was a people person, and she seemed to enjoy watching the shoots and talking with Matt. All that mattered was that she broke the ice for me, and having her there to give me support in my awkwardness and anxiety was a godsend.

The final proofs for my portfolio were nothing short of amazing! Was that really my face in those big, bold and beautiful glossy black and white photos Matt had sprawled across the floor? I looked so – well, so stunning! But I had never been pretty. I was the little girl with the bottle of ugly pills – the teenager with six toes they called Freak – so how could this possibly be? But it wasn't only me that saw a lovely young girl staring back at her in those photos; both Matt and Scott seemed equally impressed. In fact, Scott was so taken that he made me an offer that was hard to refuse.

"Belinda, I think you have great potential," Scott began. "We are getting together a small group of our girls to send to New York this spring to try out for one of the big agencies there. Matt and I are agreed that we'd like you to be one of them."

I couldn't believe what I was hearing! Me? They were giving me a chance to be a New York model? I could hardly wrap my head around the idea. It seemed way too good to be true.

"Oh Belinda, that's wonderful!" Mom gushed.

Scott chuckled, amused by Mom's reaction. "She really has taken to this work, Mrs. Rose. You should be so proud of her. You don't have to give me an answer now. We don't need you to give us your decision until later in the month. Go home and talk to your dad about it."

I didn't walk out of his office that day – I floated – and I think Mom was floating right beside me. I had made her proud – very, very proud, and that made me feel very, very good.

My head may have been stuck in the clouds as I left the modeling agency that morning, but it only took a visit to Dr. Duprow later that day to bring me back down to earth. Each visit began with a weigh-in. Dr. Duprow kept close track of my weight in order to adjust my medication dosages, and although he never seemed to be too concerned if I lost weight, this week that all changed.

"Seventy-three pounds, Belinda," Dr. Duprow said, as I stepped off the scale. "Have a seat. We need to chat."

Taking my usual seat on the couch, I gave him my full attention.

"I want to change your medication again, and this time I want to increase it. But I want to do this in a hospital setting so I can monitor the outcome and adjust the dosages accordingly. You are very thin right now, and it's important I take control over this situation in case you have another adverse reaction. I'd like to put you in Touch Point Mental Health Institute. How do you feel about that?" he said, reaching for a cigar.

"No! I am not going back in one of those places *ever* again! I'm modeling now. I love it! You aren't ruining it with a hospital stay."

"I was afraid you'd feel that way. I will talk to your parents about it. I feel it's important to your recovery. Your weight is plummeting. Two weeks ago you weighed eighty-five pounds. Would you like to talk about this rapid weight loss?"

"No, I wouldn't. Models need to be skinny! You know that. Look at the cover of the magazines in your own waiting room! You're telling me to be fat, but the models that grace the covers of these magazines aren't fat, are they? I've been given the chance of a lifetime, and you're not taking it away!"

"I'm not trying to take anything away from you, Belinda. But you won't be modeling if you're dead, will you?"

"I'm not planning on dying, Dr. Duprow. My parents have never been happier with me. I can't ruin this – not again!" I said, nearly hysterical.

"Calm down, now. Don't get excited. I'll chat with your parents and give them my professional opinion. We will see what they say, and make a decision from there."

"I'm not a child. I should have some say in this decision. This is *my* life, after all!"

"You will, Belinda. You will have a say, but maybe not the final one."

I had no more to say to him. I was trying too hard to not

come completely unhinged. "Unlock the doors and let me out of here. I'm going home," I said, voicing my defiance.

"As you wish, Belinda," he replied in an almost patronizing tone.

After following me to the waiting room, he asked Mom to come to his office so that he could speak to her in private. I glared at him. I hoped he could see my fury, and how much I hated him in that moment. I hated everything about this creepy doctor – from his stinky cigars to those two doors with all the locks! I hated his weird version of therapy. We never actually discussed anything. All we did was play his dumb free association word game, which never seemed to lead anywhere, and then he talked about medications. I hated the medications most of all. I had never been on so many medications in my life.

By the time Mom returned to the waiting room ten minutes later I was in tears. "Are you all right to drive?" she said.

"Believe me, I'll get us home," I said, digging into my purse for the car keys. "I want as far away from this place as fast as I can get there!"

Mom didn't speak on the long drive home. Neither did I. I could already tell by the somber look on her face that when we did speak it wasn't going to be a pleasant conversation. The minute we got home, though, I turned to her for answers. "Mom, what did that creep Dr. Duprow say to you?"

Her voice began to shake as she said, "That he wants to put you in a mental health facility to increase the medication because you are losing so much weight again. He believes the medication can ease the fears you have about gaining weight."

"Ease my fears? Mom, are you kidding me? He nearly killed me with his damn medication. Do you really think it's smart to let him have total control over me like that? The guy's a whack job! Tell me, who has two doors with multiple locks on the inside? You're just gonna do what he says?"

"I don't know, Belinda. I just want you to be well. If you

keep losing weight you will be back in the emergency room fighting for your life again. The final decision needs to be up to Dad."

"Mom! What about modeling school? I'm doing so well there. Does it all just stop because of this crazy doctor? Don't I get a voice here? This is my life everyone is playing games with!"

She had no more to say. She'd shut down. I stared at her dumbfounded as she got up and left the room in the middle of the conversation.

No more was said between us until Dad came home from work later that evening. I had refused supper and I was lying in my room curled up on the floor crying. After Mom and Dad had talked, she came into my room to give me Dad's verdict.

"Your dad is very upset that you've lost so much weight again. He is in agreement with Dr. Duprow. He wants to let him try it his way to see if he can help you. I'll let the doctor know tomorrow."

"But, Mom," I cried, "what about school? Did you even tell Dad what happened today? What they offered me?"

"No. I didn't. That doesn't seem important tonight." And that was the last thing she said before she walked out, closing the door behind her.

I cried until I was empty. How could she say it wasn't important? I had finally found something in life that was worth living for, something to be happy about, and they had taken it all away. All the dreams – all the hope – dashed in one fell swoop. I had excelled at modeling, and Dad would have been so proud of me! But he didn't even know how well I'd done, because Mom hadn't told him. All he knew about was that I'd lost weight and needed to go into another mental hospital, disappointing him all over again. I was a loser. Why was I always such a failure?

"Because," said the Voice, *"it's who you are. A big, FAT loser!"*

In less than twenty-four hours, my entire world had come

crashing down around my feet. I had gone from being happy and hopeful to sad and suicidal. I knew what I had to do.

I went to the kitchen and grabbed two of every pill on the counter. Pouring a large glass of water, I chugged them all down in one big gulp. I went back to my room to lie on the bed, as I waited for the pills to take effect, putting me out of my misery once and for all. But before they did, I needed to do one more thing– say goodbye to Jesus. So, I took out my burgundy journal and wrote:

Dear Jesus,

I'm sorry. I don't want to take my own life – I don't want to hurt You like this, but I just can't go on this way any longer. I can't live a life that feels perpetually hopeless. One minute it seems as if I have a reason to live and the next moment it is snatched from under me. Besides, I see no chance of ever being well. The Voice hounds me relentlessly. How am I supposed to live with its nonstop chattering – its demeaning tone in my head? One day the anorexia will probably just take me out anyway – my heart will just stop. Jesus, I have no right to ask this of You, but, if I die tonight, will You take my soul ... or am I destined for hell for what I'm about to do? I miss You so, and, in spite of everything, I still love You with all my heart, my Jesus.

CHAPTER 20

HAVE MERCY

God, have mercy on me, a sinner.

Luke 18:13

Abba,
I am sorry.
Forgive me, a sinner.
I beg You have mercy on me.
Abba,
I can't handle life on my own.
Without You in my life
I can't go on,
Abba.

*I*n spite of my attempted overdose, death didn't come that night. I had imagined as I'd shut my eyes the night before the horror of waking up in purgatory or in hell, tormented by the shrill demonic voices of the devil's minions taunting me for eternity. Perhaps my "old comrade" the Voice would even be among them – he had promised to follow me there, after all. It would serve me right if God chose to allow my soul to suffer an eternity with Satan after so blatantly shoving His gift of life back in His face. The best I could hope for was that God would have mercy on me and understand that I had reached my limit and could no longer endure the emotional suffering. But perhaps He already had showered His mercy upon me, because instead of waking to eternal damnation I woke in the comfort of my own bed. The handful of pills hadn't killed me, but they had made me very, very ill.

My head pounded and my stomach hurt. As I rose from my bed and my feet hit the floor, I knew from the way my stomach felt that the first place I needed to get to was the bathroom – and fast. But getting to the bathroom quickly proved a challenge, because I was even dizzier and weaker than usual. Holding onto furniture, doors and anything else solid I could find, I steadied myself until I made it to my destination – the toilet. I couldn't recall being this nauseated since the time I'd had stomach flu in Fairhaven. It had been many hours since I'd taken that handful of pills or eaten anything at all, but still I had this desperate need to vomit, and so, I sat on the floor hugging the toilet bowl. The violent stomach contractions came in strong waves until all that was left were the dry heaves. *"You can't even kill yourself right!"* the Voice taunted. *"If you really wanted to die, you should've taken the whole bottle! You're such a chicken and such a loser!"*

Yes, it was pretty sad that I couldn't even succeed at ending my miserable excuse for a life. The Voice was probably right. I needed to take the whole bottle to die. Instead, I'd only made a half-hearted attempt at doing myself in. Maybe I was a chicken. Maybe I was just afraid to die. Picking myself up slowly from the bathroom floor, I made my way back to the edge of my bed and had just sat down to rest when Mom burst into the room in an unusually cheerful mood.

"Good afternoon, sleepyhead! I didn't think you were ever going to wake up," she said, opening the venetian blinds.

The bright sunlight streaming through the blinds' slats made me recoil like a vampire. "Oh Mom, please. Did you have to do that?"

"What's wrong? Aren't you feeling well today?"

"No, not really," I said, hiding my head beneath my pillow to shut out the light.

Grabbing the pillow away from me, she put her hand on my forehead. "You don't seem to have any fever. What doesn't feel well?"

I wasn't about to tell her I was feeling the repercussions from having made an inept attempt at suicide the night before, so I lied and said, "I don't know. Maybe I have a stomach bug or something."

"You look so peaked to me, honey. Let me fix you some toast and a soft-boiled egg. You need to put something in your tummy."

I felt too sick today to fight her on the food. A weak, "Yeah, okay," was all I could muster. I wondered if her chipper mood today was her way of trying to atone for the spat we'd had yesterday about my parents' intentions to ship me back to the funny farm? I wondered how she'd feel if she knew that I'd made a feeble attempt on my life and that it had been precipitated by her and Dad's decision?

"Why don't you just lie in bed until I get your food ready," she said, pulling the covers over me. She hadn't coddled me like this since I was ten and had tonsillitis.

I snuggled beneath the covers, my stomach still aching and my head still throbbing. The medication had left me feeling lethargic as well. All I really wanted to do was sleep, but my aches and pains and my racing thoughts prevented me from relaxing enough to sleep. I was worried – no, petrified – of going into this mental hospital under the care of Dr. Creepy. I was as disheartened about what the good doctor might have in store for me as I was at the prospect of how this would affect my future with the modeling school. Would we be able to cover up the truth of where I'd been and what was really going on? Or would my parents tell them the whole truth so they'd no longer be interested in me?

Mom came into the bedroom to help me out of bed and to

the kitchen table. She had made a single soft-boiled egg and piece of dry toast.

"Well at least she didn't overdo it," the Voice said, somewhat approvingly.

But my stomach did somersaults just looking at food. Picking up the dry toast, I took a small bite and said, "Mom, when are you guys sending me to the loony bin?"

"Belinda, I wish you wouldn't call it that!"

"Why? That's what it is! You have no idea, Mom. You've never been in one."

"I don't know. I haven't made the call to Dr. Duprow yet."

"Why? I thought you guys were anxious to get me gone again!"

"We aren't trying to 'get you gone', Belinda. We just don't know what to do to help you."

"What about school? What are we telling them?"

"I don't know yet. I guess that's up to Dad."

"Of course it is."

"Let's get you feeling better before we worry about Dr. Duprow," she said. "Besides, the final photos for your portfolio should be back in a few days. Why don't we put off the hospital until you have that wrapped up? I can stall Dad – and the doctor. But you have to promise me you'll eat, Belinda. If you don't, you'll be back in an ambulance and there will be no choice."

"Thank you, Mom," I said, finishing the egg and half of the toast. "But right now, I just want to go back to bed for a while."

As she helped me up from the table, I caught tears in her eyes. "Why are you crying, Mom?"

"Because it breaks my heart to see you this sick," she said, breaking down. "There's nothing to you anymore but skin and bones. I don't understand any of this. Why is this happening?"

From out of the blue, vivid memories of the night I was raped overwhelmed me. It was as if I was in the back seat of David's sports car and he was on top of me all over again. I heard myself screaming and begging him to get off me. I saw myself wildly pounding on his back with my fists. I felt his sweaty palm covering my mouth as he told me not to scream.

"Belinda! You're trembling! Are you all right? Sit down before you pass out," Mom said, sitting me back down at the kitchen table.

This had never happened before. I had barred all thoughts of the rape from my mind since the awful night it had happened over a year prior. Why had I suddenly flashed back to that moment? Then suddenly I knew why: it was that single devastating moment that had set my life on this downward spiral at breakneck speed. The rape was the answer to her question about why this was happening. She may have sworn me to silence and I may have tried for the past year to repress the pain of that night, but this sudden flashback seemed proof positive that I had the answer to her question locked up deep inside, and it was begging to come out into the light.

I knew that although I'd been anorexic prior to the rape, it was being raped that had sent the illness into overdrive. No matter how desperately I sought to forget, cover up or repress that one definitive night in my life, it was still there deep below the surface, eating away at me bit by bit. But it couldn't come out into the light. I had made her a promise – a promise that, for now, I intended to keep.

"I'll be okay, Mom. Just help me get back to bed. I just want to sleep."

A couple of days later, Matt called to say my modeling portfolio was complete. I was feeling well enough for Mom and me to make arrangements to meet with him that same afternoon.

Matt met us in Scott's office. I didn't think I'd ever forget that gorgeous smile or those adorable dimples that reflected his own excitement as he handed the finished portfolio to me. It was one of the proudest moments of my life, and if his smile was any indication, he was proud as well! I felt as though I'd accomplished something – that I'd done something well for a change.

The portfolio itself was a black zippered briefcase containing twenty-five 16 x 9 glossy black and white photos. Some of the shots had been taken outdoors and others in the studio. There was a selection of headshots. To accompany the portfolio I had a stack of one hundred Z-Cards – business cards for models. Each Z-Card was 5 x 7 and had a headshot on the front with information about me as well as the usual name and contact information, such as "pretty hands and legs". This sort of information was useful if an employer wanted to use you as a parts model. The back had photos of three of my best shots, each chosen personally by Matt. These cards were to be handed out at job interviews. But knowing another hospitalization loomed, I wondered if I'd ever have the opportunity to use them at all.

Mom told Matt that I was going away for a few weeks to stay with my Grandma in the country. It was a complete lie. But I was thankful she'd lied, because I couldn't have stood the humiliation of him thinking I was a total nut job.

After our appointment with Matt that day, I had a session with Dr. Duprow. I hadn't seen him since the botched suicide attempt, but I wasn't going to be stupid enough to admit it to him. I knew if I had he'd have me in the hospital on suicide watch faster than he could finish one of his foul cigars. But I did reveal something else to him – the peculiar sensations I'd been experiencing since the night of the attempted suicide.

"Dr. Duprow, I have been having this really strange feeling. I want to share this because I am wondering if it is the medication again or something else."

"Go on," he said, puffing away.

"I'm not sure how to explain this, but I feel this especially when I'm driving – like when I drove here today. It's like I'm afraid the car is going to literally fall apart, and I'm terrified. I know it sounds weird. Believe me, it feels even weirder. Any thoughts?"

"Perhaps it's you that feels as if you're falling apart, and this feeling or sensation is just a manifestation of that."

For the first time, he'd said something that clicked, and made perfect sense to me. I did feel as if I was falling apart. Is this what a nervous breakdown felt like? But the bigger question was what I could do about it, because medication and hospitalization didn't seem to be the answer I was searching for.

As excited as I'd been about the modeling, and as happy as I'd been to see the finished portfolio, my dread of being hospitalized at Touch Point overshadowed any joy I might have felt. Now that my portfolio was complete, I knew Mom would be making the necessary arrangements with Dr. Duprow to admit me very soon. If there were only some way I could get out of this. I could consider suicide again. Maybe this time I could even get it right.

Lying on my bed, I stared at the photos of the pretty girl in the pictures, but I felt no connection to that girl at all. I wasn't that smiley-faced, seemingly happy girl I saw reflected – not in the least. Behind that phony smile was a whole world of pain that had been covered up for most of my life – the pain of physical, emotional and mental abuse, bullying, humiliation and betrayal. Behind that false facade was a sick young girl who was literally dying inside and out, and had been for a very long time. Why couldn't someone help her? All she wanted was to be well – to actually *be* that girl in the photos.

Setting the portfolio aside and rolling over onto my stomach on my bed, I propped my pillows up on the windowsill. It had been an uncharacteristically warm day for early spring – so warm that the windows were open. I closed my eyes for a moment to breathe in the warm evening breeze that blew softly through the window screen.

Suddenly I had a strange feeling that someone was there, watching me. I opened my eyes and looked behind me to see if Mom or Dad had walked into the room, but there was no one there. I turned my attention back to the window, and on the outside of the screen a thick, black fog – almost like a dense mist – had formed! But it wasn't the apparition per se that sent chills down my spine, but the ominous and evil presence it seemed to contain or embody. Terrified, I backed away from the window. It was then that it spoke! No, not in words but as thoughts in my head – telepathically saying, *"Try all you want to fight against us. You won't win. You're growing weak. We'll get you eventually."* It was as if whatever it was had come to deliver a message, because once it had said what it wanted to say it vanished right before my eyes.

Was I going stark raving mad? Maybe I belonged in the loony bin! Was what I'd just experienced real, the medication, my mind playing tricks, or was it truly some sort of evil? Gathering the courage to approach the window, I slammed it down and locked it. Grabbing my Bible, I thumbed nervously through the pages until I found my Sacred Heart prayer card tucked inside – the same one that had given me so much comfort as a child. Holding it close to my wildly beating heart, I fell to my knees beside my bed and prayed one of the most fervent prayers of my life:

Lord, I beg You to have mercy on me. I am sorry for trying to take my life. I don't want to die. I just don't want to live in this pain. I'm tired of being sick. Life has no joy. I hurt inside so much. I just can't go on like this.

Forgive me for what I tried to do. I don't know what I just saw at my window or if it was even real, but it sure felt real. It felt evil and hateful and it even threatened me! I don't know what that means, Lord, but I'm scared. Really, really scared. I pray for Your divine protection, Jesus. Place Your shield of divine light around me – keep the darkness at bay. Jesus, have mercy on me. I love You. In the name of the Father, Son and Holy Spirit. Amen.

I was scared, and my next impulse was to run and tell Mom. But would that be wise? Would she believe me, or would she shrug it off, saying it was all just my overactive imagination, or perhaps even a hallucination brought on by the medications? Well, I didn't believe either of those explanations for one moment. Somehow I just knew what I'd been a witness to was something very real – and very evil.

I was too afraid that night to sleep with the lights out, so I slept with them on. I was too afraid to sleep without my prayer card close by, so I tucked it beneath my pillow. Clutching my rosary in my hand, I recited the Jesus Prayer over and over again. I repeated it until I eventually found the deep sense of peace, security and comfort I needed to drift off to sleep: *"Lord Jesus Christ, Son of God, have mercy on me, a sinner."*

CHAPTER 21

FEAR NO EVIL

I will fear no evil: for Thou art with me.

Psalm 23:4

I will fear no evil
It has no hold on me
For by the blood of Jesus
I have been set free.
All the pain and suffering
That my soul endures
Will glorify the Father
In Him victory's assured.

My parents admitted me to the Touch Point Psychiatric Hospital on a Sunday afternoon. I kicked and screamed the whole way there. In the back seat of our crimson '63 Chevrolet Impala I'd cried uncontrollably for the whole twenty-mile trip. By the time we pulled into the hospital's underground garage, Dad's anger had reached boiling point, and although he hadn't hit me or even so much as raised his voice, his furrowed eyebrows and flushed face told me he was dangerously nearing the point at which he was capable of doing either – or both. Any other time I would have been petrified that his rage had reached this dangerous stage of imminent explosion – but not today. Today was all about saving myself.

Any person with half a brain could have understood my vehement protests, especially after I'd spent the past sixteen months in and out of hospitals. So why couldn't Mom and Dad? But the repeated hospitalizations of the past year weren't the only reason – or even the biggest reason – that I had dug my heels in so hard. Call it intuition if you will, but my gut feeling was that Touch Point Psychiatric Hospital signified the beginning of certain disaster for me in every imaginable way. I understood full well that my parents didn't know what to do with me, and because they had no idea how to help me, they listened to everything the doctors told them to do. It was the old "doctor knows best" mentality, but what they didn't understand was that just maybe the doctor in this case didn't know best. Everything Dr. Duprow had suggested so far had seemed to be trial and error – at my expense. What sort of doctor puts a seventy-three-pound patient on heavy dosages of antipsychotics when they are already having severe side effects? It made no sense to me. But instead of listening to my laments, my parents had given in to their frustration and worry and were all too ready and willing to throw me into the fiery furnace of another psychiatric hospital. So if they wouldn't save me from Dr. Creepy and this looming hospitalization, I was going to have to try to save myself.

In a last-ditch effort to avoid the unavoidable, I decided to get down on my hands and knees and resort to begging Dad not to do this horrible thing, despite the certain humiliation such a stunt might bring. As he stood discussing the insurance arrangements with the nurses in admittance, I decided to give it my last and best shot.

Falling to my knees before him, I grabbed hold of his gray work pants at the knee, and began tearfully begging to be spared. "Please Dad, don't do this! Don't leave me here like this! Please, I'm begging you! Don't leave me here!"

But mercy isn't what I received. Instead, he looked down at me with one of the coldest, iciest stares I'd ever seen from him. He gave me a look that would be forever etched in my memory – a look that spoke of his utter disgust for me, a look that said how despicable he thought I was, a look that said "get your sorry butt up off the floor or else." Seeing he wasn't going to budge, I picked myself up off the floor and turned to Mom, throwing myself into her arms. Perhaps she'd feel sorry enough for me that she'd try to get through to Dad. I obviously already had her pity; I could see it in the steady stream of tears that fell from her eyes. But Dad wasn't buying it. Her tears had only made him all the more infuriated, thus sealing my fate.

Dad finished the paperwork and left the room in a huff to head for the car without even so much as saying goodbye. I clung to Mom like a frightened child for what seemed like the longest five minutes of my life before I heard her softly say, "Belinda, I've got to go. Dad is waiting, and I don't want to make him any madder than he already is."

I understood. I knew what was waiting for her when she got into the car to make the journey home. She'd have to deal with the aftermath of Dad's anger, but at least she knew her fate. I, on the other hand, had no idea what lay ahead for me in the days to come.

"I'll come back when I can, Belinda. If I can get someone to drive me here."

If she could drive I knew she'd come more often to be with me, and I wouldn't be so alone here. But Dad held the power over her there as well. She had renewed her driver's permit monthly for as many years as I could remember, but could never make it past that point to actually get her license. Dad had always refused to help her towards that goal. He refused to pay for driving lessons, and teaching her to drive himself wasn't an option, given he wouldn't allow her or anyone else to drive his car. So Mom simply had no way of learning and progressing to her driving test. It was just another way for Dad to keep her powerless and under his thumb.

I was too distraught to speak as the realization began to hit me there was no getting out of this. I hung my tear-stained face in defeat and nodded. A nurse picked up my small suitcase and offered to show me to my room, but I refused to budge. I couldn't take my eyes off Mom, who was now walking away. How could they do this to me – again? I felt so betrayed. Over the past months, I had shared with Mom some of the details of Fairhaven. She knew, even if Dad didn't, how horrible that experience had been for me, and yet now she had turned and walked away! What kind of mother did that? With my tears still falling and my heart shattered, I watched as my last hope of saving myself from a fate I believed worse than death disappeared from view. I didn't take my eyes off her in the hope that she'd come to her senses, turn around and come back to get me. But she didn't turn around – not once. I carried on watching her until she rounded the corner and vanished from sight.

The differences between Touch Point and Fairhaven were significant. For one thing, my small room had a television and a telephone, and I didn't have to earn them through a reward-and-punishment behavioral program. In fact, I had no restrictions here at all like I'd had in Fairhaven. While there were bars on the windows, Dr. Duprow had made it clear they weren't holding me inside. He told me I was even free to go outside for walks on the premises. I wasn't being watched or monitored as to what I ate – or if I ate at all – which made this hospitalization also much different from the outset, and there were other distinctions as well.

Fairhaven had a large solarium where patients congregated, but Touch Point was drab and lifeless – to the point that I wasn't even sure if there were other patients. By my third day there I hadn't seen one other patient – only staff. That seemed very odd indeed, and curious enough to jump-start my overactive imagination into overdrive. What if the other patients, the ones that were supposedly behind all those closed doors, were simply too drugged up to leave their rooms? Perhaps that's why Dr. Duprow had said the bars on the windows weren't holding me inside. He already knew that soon enough I'd be too loopy from the dope he peddled to even notice or care about the bars on the windows! No, the bars weren't going to be holding me inside, because the drugs would be the invisible prison bars that did.

While I still had some semblance of a mind and my senses intact, I decided to take a walk beyond the hospital doors and get some fresh air. It was a warm spring day – a good day for exploring.

Although the hospital itself was drab and depressing, the grounds were lovely, with beautiful flowers and large trees everywhere. In the middle of the cobblestone walkway sat a huge bubbling fountain where I paused to watch a pair of sparrows splashing about taking a bath. There was statuary throughout the garden as well. I found the familiarity of St. Francis of Assisi, the angels and Jesus especially comforting. Any other time I would have enjoyed sitting quietly in such a lovely garden among these divine images. It would have been a great spot to read or even just bask in the warm sunshine, but the slow increase of the medications was already having ill effects, and I was much too fidgety and restless to sit still. So I kept moving and exploring.

Next to Touch Point there was another prominent area hospital. Spying a stairway that led up to its roof, I decided to be daring and see how much or how little I was really being watched. I looked around to see if any of the hospital staff were watching, crossed the street and headed for the stairs. Besides, as the Voice reminded me, *"You haven't had any exercise today. Get to it, Fatso!"*

By the tenth flight of stairs my legs were ready to give out, but my drill sergeant coach, the Voice, refused to let me stop for even one second to catch my breath.

"Move it! Let's go! You can do this! Don't want to be a pig, do you?" the Voice said, egging me on.

Once on the roof I felt exhilarated, as if the climb to the top was some kind of Olympian feat, and I suppose for my frail seventy-four pounds it was a feat of sorts. Leaning cautiously against the railing that ran all the way around the roof, I looked to the street below and thought how liberating it might be to simply tumble over it.

"You could end it all – here and now. This time there'd probably be no second chances. A fall that far down would probably do it. One big splat, and no more pain! Just think – no more of my voice in your head! No more dieting. No more starving or bingeing and purging. No more medication. No more depression. No more icy stares from Dad. No more feeling unloved and unwanted," the Voice said.

"Lord, make the Voice go away! Make it shut up! I'm so sick of listening to it," I silently prayed as my eyes searched out the garden statue of Jesus from my rooftop vantage point.

No, I shouted in my head at the Voice. *I promised Jesus I wouldn't do that. Go away! Shut up and leave me alone!*

Heading back down the steps, I figured I'd better make my way back to Touch Point before they sent out a search party. If they found me on the roof of all places, no telling what they'd do!

As I drew near the nurses' station, I spotted a familiar figure. I drew closer. I looked harder. Oh, my goodness, it was Dr. Tully! I was almost upon him when he turned and said,

"Belinda! I was looking for you." His arms opened wide to greet me.

"Dr. Tully! It is so good to see you," I said, snuggling deep in his hug. "What in the world are you doing here?"

"Your mom called and said you were here. I wanted to come spend some time with you, and see how you're doing for myself. Can we walk outside and talk? Perhaps the garden?"

"Sure. Let's go," I said, as we turned to head back down the long hospital corridor to the doors. I felt such rapport with him. Oh, how I wished he were still my therapist instead of Dr. Creepy.

In the garden, we chose a seat on a stone ledge that surrounded the rose garden, where Dr. Tully began the conversation. "I could see from your face that you were pretty surprised to see me."

"Yeah, stunned is more like it! But happily stunned."

"So, what's it like here? What are they doing treatment-wise?"

"They aren't doing anything but giving me more and more medication."

"There's no talk therapy?"

"No. Not so far anyway. I haven't even seen Dr. Duprow in the three days I've been here. He wanted me here so he could increase the antipsychotics, thinking if I have a bad reaction again I'll be where I can get immediate help."

"What do you mean by 'bad reaction'?"

"I had a serious reaction a while back that landed me in the hospital. I spent twenty-four hours in the ER. So I guess this time he's playing it safe."

"I see, and how are you doing on the medication now?"

"Truth told, I hate it. It makes me feel horrible. There's the dizziness, the agitation, the tremors, and that continual doped-up feeling. Now I'm even noticing my thoughts becoming confused. I don't see how it's going to help me recover from anorexia if I can't think clearly. I really feel as if I am just a guinea pig again, just like I was for Dr. Kraft."

"Belinda, it's unfortunate, but not too many doctors know how to effectively treat anorexia nervosa. There are case histories in the medical literature, sure, but so many doctors have a lack of experience dealing with it first-hand. I bet you're Dr. Duprow's first anorexia diagnosis, just like you were mine."

"You're probably right, Dr. Tully. Not to change the subject, but I want to tell you something that's on my heart," I said, looking away.

"Sure, but look at me when you say it."

Turning to look at him, I caught his warm chestnut eyes smiling back at me, only making what I needed to tell him all the more difficult.

"Go ahead, Belinda. You don't need to be shy or afraid to talk to me."

"Yeah, I know. I just sort of feel stupid saying this. I just want you to know you're the only therapist I've ever genuinely liked. You're caring and compassionate – so unlike the others."

"Thank you, Belinda. That's very kind of you. I try to treat my patients as I'd like to be treated. I wish I could have continued to treat you, but there were medical issues concerning your care that I'm not qualified to help with. From what your mom says you've had quite a time of it the last year."

"Yeah, you could say that. I've spent more time in hospitals this year than out. And I'm no closer to being well than when it all started."

"When you were seeing me, I always knew you were holding back. The pain and anger you refused to speak of were palpable. Do you realize that the pent-up emotions are aiding and abetting the depression and the illness? Unleashing that, Belinda, is the beginning of your path to wholeness. Have you ever been able to open up and do that?"

"No, not really. Look, Dr. Tully, I always wanted to tell you more than I did, but I made a promise to Mom – and then there's Dad. If I let the cat out of the bag and tell people who he really is – what he does – and if someone confronted him about it – well, that could be very bad for Mom and me."

"Belinda, I already know your dad abused you. You told me that much. If you need to talk – as someone who truly cares what happens to you, I will listen. I won't judge or tell a soul. But you need to get this out. Look what holding in all that pain is doing to you. Belinda, you are so thin. It's time to stop worrying about your mom. She's a big girl now. Worry about getting yourself well."

He was right. Everything he said made perfect sense. I had kept so many secrets: secrets for Mom, secrets for the family, secrets about me and secrets about Dad. Keeping so many secrets, trying to repress so much pain and trauma, was destroying me. I didn't want to betray Mom by speaking up about the rape, but maybe I wasn't. She had warned me not to tell Dad, but never had she said don't tell Dr. Tully. Just this once I had to do something for myself. Besides, if I couldn't tell someone as kind and trustworthy as Dr. Tully, then who could I tell? As a therapist he was a treasure, and I saw that clearly now after my recent escapades with Dr. Kraft and Dr. Duprow. If only I would have realized that when I was his patient. No matter how much courage it took, this one thing – that I'd been raped – I had to speak out loud. Tears were already pooling in my eyes as I took a deep breath and released those three words that had altered my life forever. "I was raped."

I knew I had told the right someone when he reached over to put his arm around my shoulder like a loving father would have done, and said, "Oh, Belinda, I'm so, so sorry that happened to you."

His kindness overwhelmed me. Even my own mother had not reacted with such kindness. My tears fell softly onto his shoulder.

"Go ahead and cry. You have every right to those tears. Let it go. Just – let – it – go."

I did let it go. I wept on his shoulder until I was empty. He seemed in no hurry to leave, and I sensed how much he still, after all this time, really wanted to help me. I'd never understood why, but I'd always felt safe with him, as if he had my best interests at heart. Why hadn't I told him this and so much more when he was my therapist?

"How long ago did this happen?"

"It's been a little over a year now. It happened when I was seeing you."

"So that explains the sudden downward spiral."

"Yeah. If I could have told you then, perhaps the last year would have never happened. I might have avoided the horrible potassium IV's, the tube feeding, the debilitating medications, the stint in Fairhaven, and even the stupid suicide attempt."

"What suicide attempt?"

"Oops! I shouldn't have said that. Please don't tell Dr. Duprow. I shouldn't have let that slip."

"But you did. What suicide attempt?"

"I tried to overdose on my medication a week or so ago. Please don't say anything. Mom doesn't even know."

"What happened? Did you go to the hospital?"

"No, surprisingly. It just made me really sick."

"Thank God! You must have someone up there watching over you. You're lucky that's all that happened," he said, with his arm still around my shoulder. "Belinda, what made you do that?"

"The short version: I couldn't take it anymore. I just wanted the pain to stop. I felt hopeless. My parents had said they were sending me back to one of these gosh-awful places so Dr. Duprow could have his way and drug me up a little more. I guess I just snapped in the moment."

"Would you ever consider trying such a thing again?" He paused for a moment and added, "Be honest with me."

"No ... I don't think so, anyway. Maybe I shouldn't tell you this, but I was up on that roof leaning against that rail right before you came," I said, pointing up to the place I'd been only a short time before his arrival. "And no, I didn't go up there intending to jump, but I won't lie that the thought didn't occur to me. But then my eyes were drawn to that statue of Jesus – the one right over there, and I knew I couldn't do that to Jesus. I promised Him I wouldn't after the last time."

"Are you religious?"

"I don't know if you'd call it religious. I was raised a Catholic, but I've been sick for so long I don't go to church much anymore. Let's just say I'm someone that's always been head over heels in love with Jesus. Without that relationship I'm sure I wouldn't have made it as far as I have. He's always been pretty much my everything."

"Belinda, you've been through so much for such a young girl. But listen to me, young lady, when I say this: suicide is never the answer. You promised God you'd never try it again, and now I want you to look me right in the eyes and promise me too."

I hung my head, staring at the cracks in the stone walkway between my feet. I was too ashamed to look him in the eye. I still felt guilty for making that attempt on my life, and I was equally embarrassed that Dr. Tully now knew I'd done so. With his index finger placed gently beneath my chin, he lifted my head until we'd made eye contact. Then he repeated, "Look me in the eyes and promise me, Belinda."

"I promise."

"Good. I'm holding you to that," he said, smiling and giving me yet another hug. "I probably need to get going because I have patients later, but if you need me, call. You gonna be okay?"

"Yeah, I'm okay. Dr. Tully, can I ask you something before you go?"

"Sure."

"Why do you think Mom called and told you I was here?"

"She sounded heartbroken on the phone that you're in this place. I got the sense she is worried sick and wanted someone to look out for you."

"Thanks for telling me that. I'm glad she picked you to call."

Dr. Tully smiled and said, "Yeah, me too, kiddo. I'll come back to see how you're doing really soon. All right?"

"Yeah, I'd like that."

After he left I couldn't help but feel a huge sense of relief – as if a vast weight had been lifted from my shoulders. Perhaps it was finally letting the words "I was raped" outside of myself and realizing the sky hadn't fallen. Perhaps it was just feeling that someone in this world really cared if I lived or died – that someone sincerely wanted to help me. I suddenly found my eyes once more drawn to the statue of Jesus that was only a few footsteps away. Sitting on the stone bench before it, I bowed my head and spoke silently to my dearest Friend in the world:

"Jesus, I believe You had something to do with Dr. Tully showing up here today. Thank You. But I'm still scared, Lord. I don't know what is going to happen to me in here any more than I know what the apparition at my window was. But something deep inside says it isn't anything good – that it's evil. You have told us to fear no evil for Your presence is with us. Today, Lord, I truly felt Your presence with me. I believe with all my heart that evil can have no hold on me if Your presence is surrounding me, Your light is shining on me, and Your love is embracing me. Thank You for reminding me today that I am not alone. Jesus, I love You forever. In the name of the Father, the Son, and the Holy Spirit ... Amen."

CHAPTER 22

BREAKDOWN

As for me, I will call on God. The LORD will save me.

Psalm 55:18

Broken
like shattered glass
shards strewn across the floor
a life scattered in fragments
breakdown

I was discharged from Touch Point on a Saturday morning. Although I knew I'd been there for several weeks, I couldn't have told you exactly how many if my life had depended on it. Was it two weeks or three – or maybe even four – since I'd been admitted? I had no idea, because my memory no longer seemed to function properly. Dr. Duprow had never explained how or why such high dosages of antipsychotics would be of therapeutic value for anorexia nervosa, and my parents had never inquired. Perhaps the good doctor believed that anorexia was just another type of psychosis, like schizophrenia. I did after all admit to hearing a voice in my head that seemed to dictate my extreme behavior, much like a schizophrenic might. But if he thought that medication would successfully mute the voice by chemically handcuffing it and ultimately dragging it off to some drug-induced prison of its own, he would have been wrong. Not even Dr. Duprow's onslaught of chemicals had silenced the Voice. It was still as loud and relentless as ever. The drugs had only served to make everything much worse. Now I not only had anorexia to battle daily, but Dr. Duprow's drug-induced psychosis. The combination of the two had only made the bars of my mental cage that much stronger and more impossible to escape. Reality was blurred, and I found myself confused and disoriented, with huge gaps in my memory. But that was only the start of my mental breakdown. Unable to break out of my mental fog, I began to rely on Mom to fill in the blanks.

"Mom, it's Saturday, right?" I said, nervously pacing back and forth in front of the barred window of my hospital room.

"Yes, sweetie. It's Saturday," she said, neatly packing my pink polka-dot robe in the small blue overnight bag on the bed.

"How long have I been in here?"

"That's an odd question. What do you mean how long have you been in here? Three weeks, you know that."

"No, that's the problem. I *don't* know that." I momentarily interrupted my frenzied need for perpetual motion just long enough to watch her finish zipping the overnight bag.

"What do you mean? Belinda, would you please stop that pacing. You're making me nervous. Come sit down beside me on the bed for a minute."

"I can't sit still. Worse than that, I can't think clearly, Mom," I said, taking a seat on the bed beside her. "My thoughts are so mixed up. I can't remember anything. I can't even recall what I did yesterday."

"It's the medication, Belinda. Tell me, what do you recall? Start at the beginning. What's your first memory since you came here?"

"I don't think I'll ever forget begging Dad not to leave me here, there's that. The rest is only fragments. I remember the nurse coming to my room one morning and giving me an injection that I didn't want to have, and I recall Dr. Tully coming to visit me. But that seems like so long ago now."

"Dr. Tully came to see you? I didn't hear anything about that! Why would he come all the way down here?"

"Uh ... because you asked him to?"

"I didn't ask him to come see you, sweetheart. Why would you say I did?"

"Because he told me you did. I don't think he'd make that up or lie to me."

"Belinda, I don't know where you came up with this idea, but I never called him. I'm sure if Dr. Tully had come to visit you, I would have been told."

"Well, if he didn't, then who was that man I spoke to in the garden that day?" I said, beginning to panic.

"I don't know, sweetie. I just don't know," Mom said, her eyes showing her concern. She put her arm around my shoulder to calm me.

That powerful urge to move brought on by the medication came over me once again. I rose from the bed and began pacing. "But I'm *positive* he was here. There was a nurse standing at the desk that day. He was talking to her when I came in from my walk. Can we see if she's here and ask her?"

"Sure, if it makes you feel better. Dad is still signing insurance papers and he won't be back for a little while, so let's go see if we can find her."

As luck would have it, we passed the nurse in question en route to the nurses' station. "Mom! That's her!"

"Excuse me, Nurse!" Mom said, raising her voice just loud enough to grab the nurse's attention.

The petite blonde nurse stopped, turned and moved toward us. "Yes, ma'am. How can I help you?"

"We have a question for you," Mom said. "Or my daughter does."

"Sure," the nurse said, directing her attention at me.

"Do you recall a while back a young doctor coming to the nurses' station and asking you about me or maybe for my room number? His name was Dr. Tully? He's a psychologist? He's a handsome younger doctor, with longish dark brown hair and brown eyes?" I looked for some recognition of my now long-distant memory.

"No. I'm sorry. I don't know a doctor by that name, and I don't recall anyone like that asking me about you specifically. But we keep track of patient visitors. All visitors sign in. I could check the sign-in sheet for you, if you'd like?"

"Would you do that for us?" Mom said, jumping into the conversation.

"Sure. Follow me up to the nurses' station," the nurse said.

"Thank you," Mom and I said nearly in unison.

It only took the nurse a few moments to pull the record of sign-ins. I watched impatiently as her eyes scanned the page for visitors I'd had in the last few weeks. "No, I don't see a Dr. Tully listed here. I'm sorry."

I stood there frozen. I clearly heard what she had said; I just couldn't believe it. I had been so sure that Dr. Tully had been there. I remembered that hug. I could even feel it all over again when I closed my eyes. I recalled our conversation, and how kind and compassionate he'd been. Now she was saying that none of it ever happened?

"Thank you. I guess my daughter is just confused," Mom said.

"It's okay. I'm sorry I couldn't be more help," the nurse said.

"Come on, Belinda. Let's go back to your room and wait for Dad." Mom's eyes were filling with tears. She was clearly unnerved by the nurse's revelation.

By the time we made it back to my room we were both crying. "Momma," I said, my voice quivering.

"Yes, sweetie."

"I'm scared. I mean I'm really scared. What's happening

to me? What does it mean if I made it all up in my head? Did I dream it? Am I hallucinating? I don't understand. It all seemed so real. Maybe I am just nuts."

"I don't know what it means, but I don't for one minute believe you're nuts, Belinda. It's just the medication. There's no other explanation. Let's not think about that right now. Let's just get you out of here and back home."

But it was all I could think about. Maybe it was the medication or maybe it wasn't. What if I was just plain losing my mind? If the lines between reality and fantasy had merged so that I couldn't tell one from the other, didn't that mean I was going insane?

Being back home hadn't improved my memory, the confusion, the restlessness, the constant dry mouth, the tremors, the horrible nightmares on the nights I could sleep or the all-too-real hallucinations. I had begged Dad not to put me in Touch Point to begin with because of a gut instinct that it would turn out very badly for me – and it had. Anyone on the outside who didn't know that strong antipsychotic drugs were involved would have believed I was just a young girl descending into madness. Although Mom was suspicious that the medication was causing my mental decline, it was no more than that – a suspicion. My mind was a drugged fog, and I was merely the victim. I was rapidly losing my grip on reality, and it terrified me. Because of my hazy memory and my inability to concentrate or keep track of what was happening from one day to the next, I began writing again in my burgundy journal. At least that way I would have some sort of record when I couldn't recall any other way. My decline progressed swiftly. Soon, I wasn't merely having hallucinations, but delusions.

Those brief daily entries soon became the only memories I had of the day before, and when I revisit them all these years later, they are the only hard evidence I have of my break with reality.

That mental breakdown first manifested as confusion, nightmares, and memory loss, as my diary entries clearly illustrate.

Monday

What a horrible day! I had the strangest thing happen this morning. When I woke, I thought it was Sunday and Mom had gone to church and Dad had gone to pick her up. I jumped out of bed to wash up, and when I came out of the bathroom I saw Dad was just getting up and Mom was still sleeping. It was only 6:30 a.m.! Then it occurred to me it wasn't Sunday at all. I'm so confused all the time. I'm falling apart – I can feel it in my bones. I'm fragile like glass, and feel as if I'm about to shatter into a million pieces. I just can't think clearly anymore. How odd. It feels like there's a recording in my head or a wheel that keeps turning. It feels so strange. Dad screamed at me today, "I don't cause you *trouble!" He hates me as much as I hate myself. I'm no good. I cried myself to sleep this afternoon after that. I wish he loved me. I know he thinks I'm just a pain. Now Mom and Dad are arguing again. I'm tired of the fighting.*

Tuesday

I got up at 4:00 am. Did an hour of exercises. The restlessness follows me into my sleep. I toss and turn all night with nightmares. I dreamt about a boy that attacks girls. He has us tied down, and I'm forced to watch, as one by one he rapes, tortures and kills them. I'm the last one.

He comes for me and that's when I wake up. It feels so real. I'm terrified. Sometimes I dream about the devil and God. The devil is asking God for permission to take possession of my soul, and God agrees. God is angry with me. I'm heartbroken I've disappointed Him so. I wake up with the covers drenched in sweat. Why do I have such horrid dreams?

Wednesday

Got up at 5:00 a.m. and did my exercises for an hour. I don't understand what is happening to my mind. I can't remember anything anymore. Mom was asking about my time in Touch Point and I couldn't even recall her and my brother, or my aunt and cousin coming to visit me. It's like that time is wiped clean. How frightening to have no recall. Mom says it's the medicine. She said they gave me injections of it there, and I was too drugged up to remember anything. I only recall one injection and after that nothing. As the days went by, the hallucinations were no longer happy visions, like the first one I'd had of seeing Dr. Tully while in Touch Point. They soon became much more sinister and frightening.

Thursday

The devil follows me everywhere. Lord, please help me, I'm scared. Today when I went to the doctor's office, he was in the car behind me. I saw him in my rear-view mirror. He looked like a normal guy but he had pointed ears. When I parked, he parked next to me and followed me to the waiting room. He sat there and waited for me to come out of my appointment. I didn't tell Mom because she wouldn't have believed me anyway. Then on the way home he was in the back seat. I kept telling my-

self he wasn't there and that I'm only imagining it. But he seems so real. He laughs at me and says, "You can't get away from me. I'm going to get you. God doesn't care about you."

Soon after that, the paranoid delusions began.

Friday

Now I feel like I'm being watched in my bedroom. I was reading and just had this strange feeling I was being watched. So, I pulled down the blind, shut the window, and even drew the drapes. I told Mom I thought someone was watching me and she said, "What do you mean?" I said, "I'm afraid someone wants to kill me." She laughed at me, and said that was a ridiculous idea. Then she opened the drapes, pulled up the blind and opened the window. I was too afraid to stay in my room so I sat in the living room and watched television with Dad. I guess if I told her I thought that someone watching me was the devil she'd laugh and say that was ridiculous too. Am I crazy, or is it just the drugs, like she keeps saying? It's strange but sometimes I feel like I can hear my own thoughts being spoken aloud. I guess I'm just imagining things again. I don't know what's real anymore.

Saturday

I feel as though Mom wants to get rid of me. She denies it of course, but I don't believe her. I think she wants me dead. I think she might poison me. I'm not letting her cook for me anymore. I won't eat her food – only what I make. She hates me. Maybe the devil is putting her up to it.

Sunday

*Mom and I went out this evening, and it felt as if every-
one was watching me. I even felt like there was someone
watching me from the parked cars. I'm so afraid all the
time that someone wants to hurt me, or someone is after
me. I even feel as if the walls in my room have eyes sometimes and there is some evil lurking there that wants to
do me harm.*

Not only was I having hallucinations and delusions, but my
behavior had also become out of control.

Monday

*I got up at 4:30 a.m. and exercised as usual. I threw up
all my meals today. I'm tired of fighting with the Voice
so I just gave in today. I've been so down in the dumps.
I hate my life and myself more each passing day. I see
no place where I belong. Life seems like a waste – so
hopeless. Only death can liberate me from this dread. I
go to sleep late because I can't sleep and wake up early
because I'm always restless. The restlessness even follows me into my sleep. I toss and turn and have bad
dreams. This afternoon I was so fed up with feeling like
this that I grabbed a butcher knife and threatened to
plunge it into my heart in front of Mom. My heart aches
so that I think perhaps cutting it out is the only way
to stop the pain once and for all. Who am I fooling?
I'm too much of a coward for that. Mom didn't respond.
She just walked out the back door. She didn't try to stop
me. Maybe she just doesn't care, maybe she's fed up too,
or maybe she just thinks I'm bluffing. She doesn't know
about the time I took the extra pills and tried to kill
myself. Nor does she know how I often take extra pills*

before bed, hoping I won't wake up the next morning.
Why am I so preoccupied with dying – either from the
anorexia or by my own hand? Why have I always been
so miserable and unhappy, even as a little girl? No one
ever paid attention or cared about what happened to
me. They don't love me. They never have. They never
will. I'm just a problem to them. Why would they care if
I left the planet? They probably wouldn't.

At that point in my life I had never opened up to anyone apart from Mom about the rape, and it was destroying me. While the medications had pushed me over the edge to a place where reality and imagination merged, perhaps they also freed my mind to express the trauma of the rape in whole new ways.

I believed that my psyche was trying to tell me that it would be safe to open up to Dr. Tully, and that is why I'd had that powerful vision, that dream or hallucination or whatever it was of doing so. When I found out it was only a figment of my imagination, I snapped and was simply unable to carry the burden of this "secret" any longer.

The nightmares I had of a boy attacking girls or about God and the devil deciding my fate all seemed to center around the rape – the terror, the trauma and the shame. I carried so much shame inside, just like so many rape victims do. I worried that perhaps I could have done more to stop David or that I had been in some way responsible. I felt I had let Jesus down. I had been the young girl who had vowed to stay a virgin – to be pure and chaste out of devotion for Him, no less. My moral values were strong and perhaps more rigid than those of any of my girlfriends, but they were true to who I was at my core. I'd clung to my virginity until one night when it was brutally snatched away. Unable to accept that, I began to feel as if God was angry at me about it, and that I had been a bad girl – a dirty girl – a sinner not worthy of redemption or forgiveness.

That sin meant I had to be punished, so my hallucinations and delusions became the haunting images of the devil coming to exact my just punishment.

I was having delusions of a mom who I thought hated me, and who even wanted to poison me. Perhaps somewhere deep in my subconscious I felt she did hate me by forcing me to keep secret something that was threatening my very life – something that had plunged the eating disorder into the abyss. The secrets she had made me pledge to keep over the years were as poisonous as arsenic or strychnine.

Now it had all culminated in a mental breakdown that would threaten to see me committed for life.

PART THREE

THOU ART WITH ME

*Yea though I walk through the valley of the shadow of death,
I will fear no evil, for Thou art with me.*

Psalm 23:4

CHAPTER 23

SAYONARA

God is faithful, who will not allow you to be tempted above what you are able, but will with the temptation also make the way of escape, that you may be able to endure it.

1 Corinthians 10:13

There once was a young girl whose mind
Was so drugged that it soon declined.
Her doc had no brain
When he called her insane,
Insisting she should be confined.

Over the course of the next few months my health deteriorated at breakneck speed. After battling the eating disorder for roughly eight years now, my physical health was in ruins. Low blood pressure, below normal body temperature, hair loss, cessation of menstrual cycles, kidney infections and heart arrhythmia were just a small part of the devastating toll the eating disorder had taken on my physical health. My weight swung between a low of seventy pounds and a high of eighty-nine – the latter due to edema caused by the medications and chronic health conditions.

The restlessness, a drug side effect known as akathisia, was perhaps the worst of all the physical side effects I experienced from the medications. That sense of perpetual restless agitation was maddening. It was an indescribably edgy feeling, a sense of disquietude. I couldn't locate the source of this pain, and I could think of no other release from my inescapable inner torment except suicide. The suicidal thoughts had multiplied tenfold, largely due to the agonizing restlessness that I could no longer endure.

The drugs had proved entirely ineffective in helping me recover from the eating disorder. They hadn't stilled the Voice or quelled my fears of being fat one iota, and perhaps because of the akathisia I was more hyperactive than ever. I exercised more, not less, because I couldn't sit still for one second, and had even taken to running laps in the backyard again in an effort to satiate that unyielding inner drive to move. Nor had the drugs done anything to change my eating behaviors; the bingeing-purging and starvation remained a seemingly unstoppable force.

I had long since passed the point of envisioning a life free from the eating disorder. Divorcing my faithful companion, the Voice, and living my life free from its tyranny seemed like a pipe dream, because a funny thing had happened over those past eight years, in some sort of twisted way: the Voice had become me and I had become it – like two people intertwined in a doomed relationship. The eating disorder had become such a powerful and real force in my life that it seemed as if a bona fide living, breathing entity had taken root within me. But how and when did this happen? I had never invited it in, and I had never consciously set out to "become" anorexic. It was the 1970s, and anorexia nervosa was something that I – along with most other people – had never heard of, and yet this mysterious illness was sucking the life out of me. While I didn't know how it had happened, I did at least have a clue as to when.

I had been a naïve child desperately seeking a way to find acceptance and love, and I had somehow illogically associated losing weight with the path to finding the love and acceptance I craved. Enter the Voice. It wooed me – subtly at first, gaining my trust.

It was a voice that initially couldn't be distinguished from my own.

"I'm just losing a few pounds so I'll be prettier, more likable, more acceptable, loved," that naïve child had told herself.

"*Exactly,*" the Voice replied. *"Just a few pounds. What's the harm?"* And with that the trap was set, and the unsuspecting child that I was had no clue as to the direction that Voice would take me in. So that child followed the Voice in thoughts that she believed to be her own as it continued leading her down the Yellow Brick Road, all the while reassuring her that the pot of gold was just up ahead – that ultimate svelte body. This was perfection – the rainbow's end of thinness that screamed love, acceptance – maybe even a hint of adoration. Out of desperation, that innocent wounded soul took the bait and followed the Voice with pure and childlike trust. By the time she began experiencing dire health consequences, it was too late for her to go back and alter her path. She had become dependent on the Voice. On one hand, she loved it because it made her feel powerful and in control; on the other hand she hated it because it made her so sick. But whether she loved or hated it was immaterial, because she was convinced she was nothing without it – that she needed it, and that was the Voice's trump card. The illness owned her now, and every hope, dream or fantasy she'd ever had of ever being loved or accepted subconsciously rested with being thin.

But I didn't know just losing a few pounds would mean all of this suffering! the girl protested to the Voice.

To which the Voice replied, *"I never said it would be easy. You should be so proud of yourself, though. Look how much self-control you exercised to lose this much weight. Bravo!"*

The anorexia had latched onto her with its invisible iron

jaws – making her mind its new home. Now that it had merged with her psyche, she clung to the anorexia like a battered wife might cling to her abusive spouse, and the anorexia could now show its true colors more freely. No amount of abuse was off-limits, because she needed it and no longer believed she had the strength or power to abandon it even if she'd wanted to.

Now that I was under the influence of so many psychotropic medications, the Voice had become louder and stronger as I became weaker mentally. I had little strength left to do more than just get through another day. I had no presence of mind to question the Voice as I'd often done in the past, and what little will or fight I had left had now been chemically gagged.

That combination of antipsychotics, antidepressants and sleeping pills was a poisonous concoction for my frail body, and my mental health had reached a breaking point. With a little help from the drugs, I'd had a complete mental breakdown. These poisons had turned me into a zombie. I walked and I breathed, but I had no recollection of doing so. It was as if I was sleepwalking through life with little or no awareness of what I was doing from one moment to the next. The hallucinations continued as the delusions grew progressively worse, to the point at which I lived in constant terror that some evil entity was pursuing me because I had been a "bad girl" and needed to be punished. Disordered thoughts and a whole new bizarre and horrifying perception of reality became my new norm.

But perhaps far more obvious to my parents were the behavioral changes and loss of memory I experienced. I went about my day-to-day activities devoid of any presence of mind, experiencing what could only be described as blackouts. I was little more than a shadow of my former self. Perhaps the best way to describe my sense of being is to say: "Belinda didn't live there anymore."

I began to do things that were totally out of character

for me, and against every strong moral value I'd ever had. I combined alcohol with the pharmaceuticals without giving a thought to the repercussions of such behavior. I woke up in the homes of strange men who were twice my age without a clue about how I'd met them or gotten there to begin with. I perhaps would never have even recalled doing so except for the morning that I drove home drunk. The terror that seized me as I struggled to keep the car from swerving off the road that morning was something I'll never forget. Although my heart was beating, essentially I was dead already.

Over a period of months, Mom had grown more and more distraught because of my erratic and unusual behavior. More than anyone in my life, she knew me best. She knew that the shameless way I'd been behaving was not who her daughter was. My out-of-character behavior began causing huge arguments between us, and when the arguments reached crisis point I threatened to move in with one of my male friends. Mom was no longer merely suspicious that the high dosages of medication were causing my disordered thinking and brazen behavior – she was certain. I was so doped up and drugged out of my mind that I was beyond grasping that these medications were putting the finishing touches to my imminent destruction.

Mom wasn't one to argue, but she had reached her own breaking point with me. In the heat of one of our arguments she expressed how afraid she was that I had a death wish or I was on a suicide mission. She adamantly stated that she wasn't going to stand around and watch me kill myself – or worse still, put myself in a situation with one of these men in which I could be killed. She knew that some of the older men I often hung around with had questionable reputations. Many of them drank heavily and partied hard. "These men are using you, Belinda! What's wrong with you? Where did my daughter go?" was her tearful lament.

But in my drugged stupor, and my desperation to be loved and cared for by someone – anyone, I fooled myself into thinking I could at last find that love in the arms of a total stranger. I would defend my behavior by protesting, "They love me, and they accept me for who I am!" Nothing could have been further from the truth, but I was too crazed from the poisonous concoction of medications and alcohol to see that.

Mom made it clear that on my next visit with Dr. Duprow she was going to have a little chat with him about the drugs and how she believed they had were pushing me into a mental breakdown. That turned out to be a visit that she and I would never forget.

Dr. Duprow began the dialogue that day. "Belinda, I know you keep a journal. May I inquire about what you've recorded in it of late?"

"The usual stuff. My thoughts. My feelings. Why?" I said, fidgeting in my seat.

"Because I'd like to see it. That is if you don't mind," he said, pausing to catch my reaction. "I'd like to know more about what you think and feel so I might help you more effectively. You've been coming to me now for months, but it's rare that you open up to me."

Of course I'd never talked to him; I'd never trusted him. I wondered why now suddenly he wanted to talk and try to help me? He'd never seemed too interested before in doing so. I watched in disgust as Dr. Duprow put out his stubby cigar in the ashtray on his desk. I would have so loved to tell him how much I loathed his foul-smelling cigar smoke, and how being shut up in his small, dingy office with its locked doors and closed windows made me want to puke. It was nearly as bad as Dad blowing his foul cigarette smoke in my face at the dinner table every evening. "That's personal," I said in an almost belligerent tone. "I don't feel good about sharing my journal with you."

"Okay. Perhaps you don't feel safe enough with me to share such personal things. Can you tell me why?"

"Feel safe with Dr. Creepy? That's funny!" the Voice said. *"Don't you tell him anything or he'll have you right back in the hospital."*

"Because, Dr. Duprow, you'll just think I'm crazy, if you don't already."

"Why would I think that?"

"Uh, because you *do*. I already know you think the anorexia equals crazy. Isn't that why you put me on all the medications to begin with? Isn't that why you badger me all the time about going back into a psychiatric hospital?"

"Are you angry, Belinda? You sound angry."

"So what if I am? You can ask as many questions as you want, but you won't answer one of mine." Dr. Duprow didn't reply. He looked at me as if he was waiting for some verbal confirmation of my antagonistic feelings towards him. "Don't you think I have a right to be angry? What have you really done to help me besides force me to take a lot of pills and spend time in the hospital?"

"That's what I'm trying to do here – help you. But if you don't trust me – if we can't talk – if you can't share feelings, it makes it a bit difficult for me to do so."

"Don't turn this around on me, Dr. Duprow," I said, swinging my crossed legs nervously. "These medications make me so goofy I can't even make sense of my thoughts and feelings. I can't even sit still anymore. I'm so miserable I'd just as soon be dead. At least if I was dead I wouldn't need to move constantly."

"So, talk to me about the medications. Perhaps we can adjust the dosage or change the prescription. But I'd like to progress here today by having you share just one thought or feeling we can discuss."

"What thought or feeling would that be? Do you want to know the crazy thoughts I have? How about when I see things that everyone says aren't there? How about the fact that I feel afraid all the time because I believe the devil is around every corner watching me? Do you want to talk about the Voice in my head that controls me, the Voice that tells me to starve or binge or puke? How about the fact that I'd just as soon jump out that window than live like this? Is that what you want to know?"

"Belinda, please calm down. I was afraid that these would be some of the things you are experiencing, but I needed validation from you. I'd like to call your mom in from the waiting room to join us. Is that okay?"

"What for?" I said, miffed.

"Because we need to talk about something important together."

"Whatever you want." I was too nervous to stay seated. I got up and stared out the small office window watching the people on the sidewalk below. They looked like ants scurrying to and fro from this vantage. Yes, I was sure a fall out this window would put an end to the restlessness once and for all.

"Mrs. Rose, please take a seat," Dr. Duprow said, entering the room with Mom in tow.

Mom took a seat beside me on the couch. I watched as her big blue eyes grew to the size of small saucers when Dr. Duprow bolted all six locks on his weird double door setup. I gave her a look that said, "I told you so!"

Dr. Duprow didn't take his usual seat behind his desk, but stood in front of it directly before us and got right to the point.

"Mrs. Rose, I've called you in here today to discuss hospitalization again for your daughter. It is my belief that she has had a mental breakdown. I believe her condition is much worse than merely an eating disorder. It is my opinion that she is suffering from paranoid schizophrenia. It is my recommendation that she be immediately admitted to the state mental hospital for treatment."

Mom and I gasped in chorus. It was as if the rest of the air had been sucked from the already stuffy room. We looked at one another in shock and horror, a look that said, "Did he really just say what I thought he said?" As I sat there dazed my usually mild-mannered Mom flew at him in a rage.

"How *dare* you!" Mom said, jumping up from the couch and getting right up in his face. "My daughter is no more a paranoid schizophrenic than you or I! Yes, she's had a mental collapse, but you *caused* that with your drugs! Ever since you put her in Touch Point the first time her father and I have stood by and watched her slowly disintegrate. Every hallucination, every delusion was brought on by the crap you put her on! How *dare* you say she belongs in the state mental hospital! What kind of a doctor are you, anyway? These medications aren't helping her. They're destroying her! They've destroyed what little quality of life she had left. They've turned her into someone I hardly even recognize. Any doctor that would do something this heinous to a young girl should lose his license! You, Dr. Duprow, are a charlatan!"

I had only seen my mom this mad one other time in my life when I was five and had refused to take a nap with her that day. In a fit of rage, she'd jumped off the bed and beat a hole in the wall with the heel of her shoe.

"Mrs. Rose, I am very sorry that you feel that way, but that is my diagnosis." Dr. Duprow was trying to defuse the situation calmly and defend his position, but Mom wasn't done expressing herself yet.

"Sorry? No, I don't think you are sorry. Your *diagnosis*, is that what you call it? We brought her to you in good faith that you would help her. But all she has done under your watch is get progressively worse, and I've no doubt that is because of the strong medications you've put her on. So, here's what we are going to do, *doctor*. Belinda is now no longer your patient. This is the last time we will come down here to see you. What you *are* going to do, though, is finally do something that will help her. You are going to wean her off every single damn drug you have her on. If you can't at least do that, then I am reporting you!"

"Fine, Mrs. Rose. She is your daughter. As you wish."

Watching their confrontation, I had to pinch myself to make sure I wasn't imagining things again, and this wasn't just another wild hallucination. I was in awe of how my generally easygoing and physically unimposing mom had just stood up to this big, burly man like a ferocious mama bear protecting her cub.

"Come on, Belinda. Let's go home," Mom said, turning to me. "Doctor, would you please unbolt those doors?"

As we entered the hall, Mom turned to Dr. Duprow, standing in the doorway, to say one final thing. "I will call you this afternoon so you can give me instructions on how to get her off this crap you've put her on."

"Fine. I'll speak to you later today, Mrs. Rose."

Dr. Duprow had the strangest and most bewildered look on his face. I'm sure he wasn't at all expecting the explosive reaction he'd received from this small, unassuming woman.

Goodbye, Dr. Duprow. Sayonara, I thought, smiling to myself as we stepped into the elevator. It was a feeling of relief. Never again did I have to return to Dr. Duprow's smelly, smoke-filled office, and it was a feeling of great satisfaction that Mom had stood up to him. But even more satisfying was the realization that she had taken charge of her own fear for once in her life and stood up for me. I was so darn proud of her in that moment, because I knew in my gut the courage it had taken for her to do that.

CHAPTER 24

DISGRACED

For man does not see as God sees, for man looks at the outward appearance, but the LORD looks at the heart.

1 Samuel 16:7

Disgraced,
I hang my head
in unspeakable shame;
oh Abba, cleanse my tainted soul,
wash me,
whiter than the new-fallen snow.
set me free by Your grace
from the shame that
binds me.

eaning myself off the mind-altering anti-psychotic drugs was the first thing on the agenda if I wanted to find my way back to reality. Dr. Duprow warned me not to quit the medications abruptly, but to proceed slowly to prevent further adverse side effects. So, to oversee this process he'd advised Mom to find a new psychiatrist as soon as possible. Although I wasn't thrilled about the idea of yet another psychiatrist so soon, I desperately wanted off these medications

to alleviate not only the psychosis they'd induced but the maddening restlessness. So within days a new doctor had been found and an appointment had been made. Her name was Dr. Fleming.

My first impression of Dr. Fleming was that she was very pretty. But even more impressive than her flawless olive complexion, shiny jet-black hair and sparkling smile was her infectious personality. She was totally charming. I had never before met a psychiatrist with such a marvelous sense of humor – a shrink who laughed and even cracked jokes like this one did. She immediately made me feel at ease in her presence. I liked her. The truth was she would have been hard not to like. But the big question wasn't whether I liked her or not, but if I would trust her enough to confide in her.

Dr. Fleming met with my mom and me on that initial visit. It was the first time Mom had ever met with one of my therapists to check them out, so to speak. But after the recent fiasco with Dr. Duprow, Mom had decided that the next psychiatrist would need her seal of approval from the very beginning.

Dr. Fleming was happy to meet with both of us, but she wanted to hear my story directly from me. So I told her about the previous doctors and the hospitalizations and my long battle with anorexia nervosa. Her warm brown eyes reflected genuine compassion as she listened to my struggles. She was upfront, and told us that she had never treated a patient with an eating disorder before. But Dr. Fleming believed she could help me, and to do that we'd need to start by getting me off the antipsychotics. She outlined a plan to wean me from the medications, making it clear that I needed to come off slowly and that she would want me to remain on the antidepressants. Although the antidepressants had side effects of their own, they hadn't been nearly as debilitating as the antipsychotics. Mom and I both felt comfortable with Dr. Fleming and her plan for my rehabilitation, and so it was agreed that I would begin therapy with her immediately.

Over the course of the next few weeks I began to feel more

like my old self once again. The hallucinations and delusions subsided and the extreme restlessness eased. I could think clearly once more. I was returning to the land of the living, and as I did, bits and pieces of the past eight months flashed into my mind like faded dreams, and with these memory flashes came deep shame, guilt and sorrow.

I simply could not believe I had done some of the things it appeared I had done while under the influence of the antipsychotics. I had to wonder if the things I thought I'd done were actually real, or whether I had conjured them up somehow, because they were so out of character for me. My recollections of that period were cloudy at best, but it was the huge gaps in my memory that proved most troublesome for me. Because my recall was so sketchy, I couldn't form a complete or clear enough picture of what I had or hadn't done in that period, and the not knowing scared me to death. I tried to make sense out of the few memories I had and what they suggested I'd done by referring to my journal entries of that time. What I found there was chilling. Had I really mixed vodka and margaritas with my medication? How could I have done anything so stupid? It wasn't just dumb, it was dangerous. Besides that, I didn't drink! I avoided every party even my closest girlfriends in high school had ever invited me to simply because of the alcohol and feeling so uncomfortable in such a situation. This wasn't anything I could see myself *ever* doing. It was both heartbreaking and surreal to read these journal entries. It was as if some other entity had taken over my body. But there it was in my own handwriting. On one hand, I wanted every blank filled in – I had this desperate need to know every sordid detail. But on the other, I just didn't want to go there. Knowing too much of the terrible truth might be more than my delicate mind could take at this moment. I questioned what I had written. As the medications had messed with my head, I wondered if all the things I'd written about had in fact really happened. Maybe, I tried to console myself, these men were just a figment of my drugged-up imagination! But no matter how hard I tried, I couldn't escape the fact that the phone kept ringing and the men kept calling. It brought the hard-to-swallow fact these men were real into crystal clear focus. Even more horrifying to me was that I hadn't a clue what their last names were, much less what I had done with them or where I'd met them.

Shamed and humiliated, I immediately cut off all ties to them. I refused every phone call; I asked Mom to tell them not to call me anymore. Somehow I had to find a way to deal with the disgrace and the remorse that was overwhelming, so I turned back to Jesus.

My tears flowed in buckets as I begged Him for forgiveness, pleading for release from the guilt that consumed me. I wasn't sure if He could ever forgive me, or if I even deserved forgiveness, no matter how much I begged Him for it. I had been so far out of my mind that I couldn't recall exactly what I had done. I couldn't move past the sinking feeling that I had turned my back on Jesus through such despicable actions, whether I was fully responsible for them or not. But perhaps the even bigger question was – could I ever forgive myself?

Because I liked Dr. Fleming, I decided to make an attempt to open up to her about my time on the antipsychotics and my unusual behavior. I needed to make sense of it and make my own peace with it. It was all that was on my mind in our next session.

"Dr. Fleming, I do have something I need to talk about today."

She pulled her chair closer to mine, and as she smiled that

beautiful smile of hers that was so full of warmth, I found the courage to begin opening up.

"Now that I'm off the drugs Dr. Duprow prescribed, and I'm no longer having the hallucinations or seeing the devil everywhere, I'm trying to piece together what I've been doing over the last eight months. My memory of that time isn't very clear. It kind of comes back in flashes – bits and pieces here and there. I kept a journal and that's sort of helped. But what I'm recalling and what I've read just isn't me. It's like I'm recalling and reading someone else's life."

"How do you mean, Belinda?"

"The things I did – the people I hung with are not people I would ever have cared to know." I could already feel the shame rising within me, and as desperately as I wanted to get this out in the open to find some small snippet of redemption, I wasn't sure I could move past the embarrassment of opening up, and as the emotion welled up inside, the tears began to fall.

Dr. Fleming passed the box of tissues from her desk to me and said, "You don't need to feel afraid or embarrassed to speak in this room. What you say to me stays with me. It's safe here."

"It's not safe anywhere," the Voice said.

But just this once I needed to ignore the Voice and not listen to what my head was telling me to do. So, I listened to my heart and followed its lead.

"My journal entries say that I was drinking hard alcohol along with the medications. They speak about three particular men who are all near forty years old. I don't even know their last names! I don't know how I met them or why I was with them. I do recall driving home drunk one morning and barely making it home. In fact, I was so drunk that when I parked in front of my house I hit the streetlight and busted my headlight. Dr. Fleming, I'm so ashamed of myself!" Snatching a clean tissue from the box I hid my face in it and hung my head.

"Belinda, why are you being so hard on yourself?" Dr. Fleming said. "You reacted very strongly and quite adversely to the medications you were given. The dosages were much too high for you to begin with. I doubt you knew or were in control of pretty much anything you were doing a lot of the time. It's not that much different from someone who's drunk or high on drugs and acts differently than when they're straight and sober. Do you understand?"

I nodded. I got what she said, but the shame still cut deep.

"Mom and I fought a lot during that time. She said my behavior was dangerous. She thought I had a death wish or something."

"Did you?"

"What? Have a death wish? I don't know – maybe," I said.

"I think that is what we need to explore here. Sometimes the less someone values their life, the more high-risk their behavior becomes. It's often a subconscious choice, mind you. You could say that the eating disorder is high-risk behavior too. Do you agree with that?"

"I've never thought of it that way – but yeah. I guess so."

"So, you put yourself into dangerous situations and flirt with death because why? You don't care if you die? You want to die?"

"More like because I want the pain to stop."

"The pain. Tell me about the pain, Belinda."

"Oh, Dr. Fleming, I can't. Not now. It's too much."

"Okay. So, let's go back to the shame you said you feel so deeply. Can we do that?"

I nodded.

"Good, because I'd like to take a bit of the burden of that shame you're bearing away today by having you leave here with a new understanding. That understanding is that the medications you were on are some of the strongest antipsychotics available. Did you know that? I never prescribe them.

Those medications not only could have created the psychosis you experienced, but they also would have definitely influenced your behavior. Not everyone does well on a given medication, as you have seen for yourself. I believe you told me that you even had to be rushed to the hospital once because of an allergic reaction to a medication. It's important for you to realize that these psychiatric medications can have seriously dangerous side effects, which is why doctors monitor their patients so closely while they're on them. Sometimes the risks and side effects they produce outweigh any benefit. Sometimes they even make the patient worse, which is what's happened to you. Do you understand?"

"Yes. I see what you mean."

"Good. I want you to leave here this afternoon and release some of that shame. Come on, young lady! Put those shoulders back and smile for me!"

Her demeanor was so cheerful and friendly. I couldn't help but do as she asked. I sat up in my chair and smiled back at her.

"That's better. Wear that pretty smile of yours, Belinda! You have no reason to be ashamed. We can talk more about this next week. Do you feel a little better?"

"Yeah. Thanks, Dr. Fleming," I said trying to convince myself. But the truth was it still hurt. I still felt dirty, used and violated. I still felt embarrassed and humiliated. I still felt like a "bad girl", as if I'd let my parents down. But worst of all – and what cut the deepest – was I believed that I'd let Jesus down.

Admitting to another living soul what I'd done or even what I thought I might have done had been embarrassing, and I made the decision after that session with Dr. Fleming that it wouldn't happen again. Yes, she'd seemed to understand, but I just didn't want to talk or even think about it anymore. I would repress my feelings, pretend the emotions that welled up from those out-of-focus memories that pricked my heart like thorns weren't there. When they tried to rear their nasty heads, I would binge and purge them back into submission. It had always been my go-to behavior, after all, when the emotional pain was too much to handle. Sadly, no one had ever told me that by continually repressing and denying my feelings I would be forever stuck without any hope of being truly well. No one had ever told me I had to go *through* that pain to find healing from it and freedom from the Voice. Nor had anyone ever said that these bottled-up feelings and emotions would only fester and become even more poisonous as time went on, until they came to infect every area of my life. But even if someone had said that recovery began with facing my trauma, would I have been able to muster the courage to face it? I knew little about courage; I had never had a role model to show me what it meant to be brave. I looked to Mom for such things, and although she was a good-hearted person and I adored her, courage wasn't anything she taught me through her actions. Instead, she'd unwittingly shown me what it was to be a victim, and how to live my life quietly and in fear.

Fear, shame, and humiliation were the emotions I knew best. I still carried enormous shame that I'd been born with an extra toe, and that kids in school called me Freak because of it. I carried shame and guilt that I'd been raped. Perhaps none of those things were my fault, and perhaps they were things I shouldn't have felt ashamed of – any more than my actions or unusual behavior while under the influence of Dr. Duprow's mind-bending drugs – but that didn't change my feelings. The depth of my shame made me feel hideous inside and out. I may have been nineteen now, but in my heart and soul I was still connected to the wounded little girl I'd once been – the little girl who ran home crying to Mommy with a bottle of Ugly Pills clutched tight in her hand on her ninth birthday. I still felt her pain, her shame and her ugliness, because I lived with it every day. Now I had one more thing to be ashamed of and to bury deep inside – so deep it would never see the light of day – the despicable things I thought I'd done with these men who were old enough to be my dad. This seemingly insurmountable disgrace caused me to view myself in utter disgust, and only served to fan the flames of depression and give the Voice an unshakeable stranglehold. Maybe from the beginning the eating disorder was merely a subconscious death wish, just as Dr. Fleming had suggested. I had already proven I was too much of a coward to actually take my life outright, but I was still killing myself with the eating disorder just as surely as if I'd slashed my wrists and was bleeding out on the floor. If I couldn't live with the pain, and I couldn't talk about the pain, maybe I'd subconsciously believed all along that dying was the only option left. I had promised God I wouldn't try to harm myself again, at least not intentionally, and I wouldn't go back on that promise. But I was downright mortified by my behavior – behavior that I was positive had hurt and disappointed Jesus. To many that may sound peculiar or strange, but I still loved Him more than anyone or anything. He was real to me – as real as anyone else in my life had ever been. I recalled as a child how I'd wanted to be good and pure for Him, so imagining the fallen look on His face as I was mixing booze with drugs or making out with older men broke my heart. I could only imagine how deeply saddened He must have been by my recent behavior and all I felt was sorry – sorry and ashamed. I hoped He could forgive me, and somehow I hoped He could help me with the even harder task of forgiving myself.

Jesus,
I am sorry.
Forgive me.
Help me to forgive myself.
Take this sin, I pray,
Wash it all away.
Make me pure again.
Amen.

CHAPTER 25

IN SUNSHINE OR IN SHADOW

Love is patient and is kind; love doesn't envy.
Love doesn't brag, is not proud, doesn't behave itself
inappropriately, doesn't seek its own way, is not provoked,
takes no account of evil.

1 Corinthians 13:4-5

Do you
really love me
in sunshine or shadow
in life's trials and its triumphs
do you
still love me as you promised to
before God and family
or did you lie,
my love?

*M*y rehabilitation had gone well. Dr. Fleming had worked hard at getting me off the antipsychotics without further complications. Finally free of the medications and their debilitating side effects, I felt like a new person both mentally and physically. My life had taken an unexpected and most welcome upward turn, and looked nothing like it had just six months previously.

Besides the marked improvement in my health, I had a new boyfriend. I'd reconnected with a young man I'd known from my high school journalism class. We had been friends in school, sharing common interests in writing and music, but I'd never suspected he'd ever be interested in me in any way other than our casual classroom chitchat. Jon was a nice guy, a decent guy, and I accepted his invitation to go out the evening I bumped into him at a local convenience store. He was comfortable to be with because of our previous friendship in high school, and our budding relationship was a bit like the high school romance I'd never had. My terrible experience with David had made me really wary of male company and the expectations that came with it, but I'd known Jon for so long that I felt safe with him. This relationship seemed normal in the sense that I knew Jon wasn't a predator like David had been. While I never told him I'd been raped, I told him all about the eating disorder. He listened intently, and seemed sympathetic, although I doubt he really understood what anorexia nervosa really was. Still, him knowing that I'd been so ill seemed to keep him from pressuring me for anything sexual – yet, anyway. Instead of taking me to hidden locations to pressure me into sexual encounters as David had so often done, Jon took me to movies and amusement parks for fun. I couldn't recall the last time I'd just laughed, had fun and enjoyed myself. There definitely weren't any alarm bells going off with Jon as there had been with David.

Although the eating disorder was still as much a part of my life as it had ever been, I seemed to be going through a new phase of learning how to live with it. "Learning to live with it" in retrospect implies a degree of acceptance, making my relationship with food and the Voice perhaps an even more dangerous one, especially as it seemed to denote that I'd given up ever being cured. To a great extent that was true. There seemed to be no feasible way to permanently silence the Voice, so I'd have to do the next best thing, which I believed was finding a way to manage it in a way that didn't destroy me. Dr. Fleming and I rarely spoke about the eating disorder, nor did we ever talk about the deep pain and trauma that had created it in the first place – the rape, the abuse or the bullying. What we did talk about was furthering the agenda of my rehabilitation. Dr. Fleming believed I needed to look forward to my future. I had discussed with her at length my time at Brighton and the modeling agency, and how disappointed I had been that the modeling in particular hadn't worked out. It was yet another way in which I felt I'd failed miserably. But this time it wasn't all my fault. The truth was I'd simply been too ill to continue on there, and though I knew Dad was disappointed too, surprisingly he seemed to understand. Dr. Fleming honed in on my negative self-image – how I had labeled myself as sick and identified myself as nothing more than an anorexic. I had been anorexic for so long that it was often difficult for me to see my life beyond the eating disorder. So we had long talks about my dreams and aspirations and we set goals that would put my focus on other things besides the eating disorder. Our work would begin improving my self-image and looking towards the future. I could see how her focus was trying to help me move out of my always negative mindset by giving me something positive to look forward to. This was more than okay with me because it meant I didn't have to talk about my pain, my grief, and my past – a past I just wanted to forget, and bury as deeply as I could.

One of those new points of focus for me was my new boyfriend. Dr. Fleming was encouraged that I had a boyfriend.
She saw it as a step towards normalcy for a young woman of
twenty. But there were other new and exciting things going
on in my life besides just a new relationship that Dr. Fleming also found encouraging. One of the ways I thought might
help me live with the Voice was signing up at a new gym that
had opened in my neighborhood. It was the first of its kind in
the area – a hardcore gym for serious bodybuilders. I'd always
been intrigued by the muscle and fitness magazines I saw on
the newsstands in the grocery store. Now the latest muscle
magazines were proclaiming that a new era in bodybuilding
had begun – one that included women front and center, and
it had caught my attention.

I saw lifting weights as a way to get strong, and that was
a concept I embraced, having grown weary of being so weak
and sickly. Perhaps I was just fooling myself. While I tried to
convince myself my new bodybuilding agenda was all about
becoming stronger and healthier, the Voice saw it as merely
another tool of control, just as the endless calisthenics I had
done in the past had been. Again, I was engaged in a war in
my own mind. Still, I admired the lean, muscular, and strik-
ingly feminine physiques of some of the top female bodybuilders. These women weren't ultra-skinny by any stretch of
the imagination. They had muscles, *and* curves! Besides that,
bodybuilding seemed like a step towards wellness, because it
was about something that was more than just exercise. Bodybuilding demanded a healthy all-around lifestyle, and that
was something I'd not had for as long as I could recall.

Within the first month of working out I was gaining a little weight and growing stronger. I had found a new passion
in life, or maybe it was just a new – albeit healthier – obsession. My weight rose to 105 pounds over the course of several
months of working out. It seemed an amazing achievement
for me. I hadn't weighed this much since I was twelve years

old! I had discovered what I believed was a magic formula – a real win-win for me. With the help of my grueling daily workouts and a little bingeing and purging on the side, I could keep my weight at a steady 105 pounds. With my weight up, perhaps my parents would believe as much I wanted to that I'd turned a corner and was actually getting better. If I could somehow be more discreet about the bingeing and purging, keeping it my "dirty little secret", Mom might even stop worrying so much, and Dad might ease up with the icy stares every time I walked out of the bathroom. Surprisingly, the Voice hadn't been triggered nearly as much as I thought it would be by the weight gain; I managed to convince myself that the weight was muscle bulk and not fat. But in truth, the bodybuilding combined with my weight control strategy of bingeing and purging was clearly just another method the Voice was using as a power play to keep me where it wanted me – entangled in its web of lies and deceit. This was after all a war. Sometimes the Voice seemed so much like a living breathing entity that I couldn't distinguish my own thoughts from those of the eating disorder. If this was true, and if the Voice did have a persona of its own, then it had to know I was tired of it and wanted it gone. But in its cunning, the Voice had devised a new plan and put it into play so it might hang onto its control over me. The new plan involved bodybuilding and bulimia. But in my desperation to be well and be rid of the Voice, I fell for this new plan hook, line and sinker. I didn't give it – or the fact that my lymph nodes were swelling and giving my face a slight chipmunk appearance – a second thought. I assumed that the bulimia, without the use of laxatives and diuretics, wouldn't land me in the hospital again. This was my ill-fated plan to learn to "live" with the eating disorder. It was born of desperation. But for the first time in a long time, I was busier trying to make a life for myself outside of the isolation cell of my bedroom, and I was less consumed by thoughts about the eating disorder. And that was enough to make me happier than I'd been in a very long time. It was this hope for a new and happier life that I was so desperate to hang onto.

Much of that newfound happiness was because of Jon. I couldn't say I was in love with him, but I did care for him deeply. This newly discovered happiness had restored something else – my will to live! My wonderful friendship with Jon was making my life worth living. It wasn't a serious relationship, but it was fun! I was excited about life at last, and my sole focus was to defeat my arch-enemy, the Voice. I finally saw that Voice for the enemy it was, and it was long past time to take my life back – to boot the Voice out of my thoughts – to dig deep and find the inner resolve to get it out of my life forever. In the year that followed, I tried valiantly to put the eating disorder behind me. But even my best efforts weren't enough to boot the Voice entirely out of my thoughts and my life. That Voice was stronger than I was. It always had been.

Jon and I dated for a year before we ended the relationship by mutual consent. He had grown increasingly frustrated with our relationship, and the truth was, I was still a very sick young woman. The weight gain and bodybuilding was just a cover – a way for the Voice to survive my attempt at a life without it. Below the surface it still reigned supreme, right alongside all the trauma of my past. My brokenness was painfully obvious to both of us, and not very attractive. So, I understood, and I was okay with our parting ways. We both moved on, and with the help of a neighbor I got a new job in an office. It wasn't a job I felt particularly excited about, as I'd always found paperwork and office work boring – but perhaps it was no coincidence that this job had landed in my lap, because it was through it that I would meet my future husband.

A co-worker told me of a longtime friend of his that he thought I "just had to meet". There was only one problem – his friend lived hundreds of miles away. But that wasn't about to deter my co-worker and the wannabe office Cupid,

Tim. One evening, Tim had his friend Brian call me long distance. I thought, just as Brian did, that it would be a one-time conversation just to shut Tim up, an awkward exchange of pleasantries that would go no further. But it was anything but awkward, and it turned out to be anything but a one-time thing. Brian and I hit it off from that first conversation – which lasted well over two hours. He called the next night, and the next. Soon we were talking long distance nearly every night, each conversation lasting for hours. We talked openly about everything and anything. I thought I'd finally found the deep, intimate emotional connection to another soul that I'd always been so starved for, and I ate it up. The distance certainly helped make Brian seem less threatening. What was he going to do that was physically threatening hundreds of miles away? Besides, he sounded like a great guy. Through our nightly phone calls we grew closer than I'd felt to anyone since Valerie in grade school, sharing things neither one of us might have dared shared face-to-face. These long conversations were more therapeutic, cleansing and even cathartic than any of my talks with psychiatrists. Three months later, at Christmas, Brian and I made plans to meet face-to-face.

It would have been impossible to calm the butterflies in my stomach as I waited at the gate for Brian to walk off the plane that first Christmas Eve. But those butterflies melted away the instant our eyes met and we embraced for the first time. The first thing I noticed was the beautiful smile that lit up his face as his blue eyes spied me across the room anxiously waiting for him. Brian was taller and lankier than I'd imagined. But his curly brown hair and neatly groomed beard looked just like the pictures he'd sent in the mail with his letters. But what really threw me was the first time he hugged me. I melted as he swallowed me up in his big arms. It was as if we'd known each other forever. It was love at first sight – for both of us.

Brian called me his "movie star". He treated me with more kindness, love and affection than I'd ever known from anybody. He spoiled me with thoughtful words and the kindest of deeds. He took me out shopping and spoiled me in ways no one had ever done before. I finally felt special to someone. I adored him. Everything in my life was nearly perfect. Now I just needed to find a job I truly loved.

With Dr. Fleming's support, I received financial aid to go back to school through a program called Vocational Rehabilitation. After a battery of aptitude tests it was determined I had strengths in all things medical and domestic. This didn't surprise me – I'd always wanted to be a doctor and I loved cooking and helping Mom care for our house.

I pleaded with the Vocational Rehab counselor to send me to nursing school, but he refused, saying it might prove too stressful and cause me to relapse. Instead, he suggested I train to become a medical assistant. I agreed, and began my studies a month later at a small school near my home. I loved everything about it – the instructors, the classes, the students – and I managed to translate that love into amazing grades. I graduated with A Honors. For the first time I could remember, I loved everything about my life.

Soon after graduation I found a job at an upscale senior retirement center. It was a job that I poured every ounce of my energy into with complete enthusiasm. I enjoyed the people and the doctors I found myself working with daily. It was a job I was really good at, and it fulfilled me in ways I'd never experienced before. As clichéd as it was, I believed I was making a difference to the lives of these seniors, and that gave me a purpose. With the help of the doctors I assisted every day, a small group of seniors showed their appreciation for all the little things they said I did for them by throwing a small surprise engagement party for me. Brian and I had been dating long distance for over a year now. He flew up to see me often, but it was expensive, and we hated being away from one another in between those visits. We were just two young kids deeply and madly in love who wanted to be together every moment. We set a date to be married on April nineteenth – six short months away.

Although it was a Protestant wedding rather than the big Catholic wedding I'd dreamt of since childhood, it was still a beautiful church service. Family and friends from all over the country attended our nuptials. Brian came from a long line of Seventh Day Adventists. He had attended Christian schools, and his Christian upbringing was important to me because God was still at the center of my life. Brian even had an uncle who was a minister and who flew across the country to perform the ceremony for us.

After the wedding, we moved into a small rental home not far from where my parents lived. Brian had already quit his job out of state, and had found new employment in my hometown. But his new job didn't pay nearly what the previous one had and our lack of money created stress at home. I was still working to help out, but the strain was showing and after nearly a year and a half of the Voice simmering below the surface, that sleeping beast was awakening. The stress of the job, and the long, exhausting hours I was working proved too much for me.

I began bingeing and purging at work, not just at home. My weight dropped, and that didn't go unnoticed by my new husband. Brian had known before we ever married all about the eating disorder, and because he did he thought it best that I quit my job. He was concerned that it was putting me under too much stress and causing a setback. Quitting, however, only put us in an even bigger financial bind. Desperate to make ends meet, Brian called his old out-of-state employer, who had always liked him and said he'd be thrilled to take him back. But returning to his old job meant that we'd have to move far away from my hometown and a mom that I had become inseparable from.

Nevertheless, we packed up the few possessions we had, told my parents goodbye and made the long journey from the Midwest to our new home in the North. I had never been away from home or away from Mom, and it was something I was ill prepared for. Devastated by homesickness, I cried constantly and fell back into a deep depression, and the eating disorder came back with a vengeance. The Voice once more began to take total control over my life, and I quit eating. Within a few short months I had lost twenty-five pounds, and I now weighed a scant eighty-five. I soon found myself trying to assuage my loneliness for home by bingeing and purging when Brian went to work each day. My family knew something had to be done to stop my downward spiral or I'd be back in the hospital, or worse – I'd die. With the recent and tragic celebrity death of singer Karen Carpenter in the news, anorexia nervosa had taken center stage in terms of recognition, and everyone was now fully aware that people died from this illness. Mom began searching for yet another new therapist back home – one that specialized in eating disorders.

It was a new decade – the eighties. Eating disorders were becoming more widely known. Even my old hometown now boasted its very own eating disorder unit at a local hospital. Mom wanted me to come back home to see if one of these specialists could provide the answers we were seeking. As difficult as it was to leave my new husband, I agreed to go back home for a short time. Brian understood. His only interest was in wanting me to get well. We said a tearful goodbye at the airport and I was on my way home.

Once there, I met with the chief psychiatrist heading the hospital's eating disorder unit. Weighing a frail eighty pounds, I walked into his posh office to share my long history with the illness, and how much I just wanted to finally get well. But because Brian hadn't been at his job very long, our health insurance hadn't kicked in, and to this doctor our lack of money made all the difference. His response shocked and saddened me. "I'm sorry, but I can't help you. You can't afford me," he said, unapologetically walking me to the door.

Dumbfounded by his cold and, heartless attitude, I quietly left his office in tears believing my last great hope of being well had just slipped through my fingers. But Mom stayed determined. By the end of the week she'd found another therapist who was said to be equally qualified in dealing with eating disorders. Dr. Ross was a psychologist, which I viewed as a definite plus, because unlike psychiatrists he was unable to prescribe, which meant here would be no medications to refuse. He'd also agreed to let us pay on a sliding scale. It sounded like a perfect opportunity – that is, until I met him.

From the beginning, I was uneasy in Dr. Ross's presence. All he ever wanted to talk about was sex. He wanted to discuss my sex life with my husband more than the eating disorder or the problems surrounding it, and that made me extremely uncomfortable. A month into my therapy it all came to a head when he backed me up against the wall in his office and attempted to sexually assault me.

I froze, scared and confused. What in the world was this doctor trying to do to me? Memories of the night I'd been raped flashed through my mind like a call to arms. Determined that nothing like that would ever happen to me again, I fought my assailant off. When he attempted to slide his hand down my pants, I pushed him away with every ounce of strength my eighty-pound body could muster. That push was enough for him to lose his balance and topple over his chair. I made my escape, bolting from Dr. Ross's unseemly grip and his office, never to return.

Therapy had once more been a complete failure. Besides

being wary of therapists, I was tired of them. But my family was adamant we needed to devise a new plan of action, even if it meant we try yet another doctor. All I wanted was to go back home to my husband. After what I'd just experienced in Dr. Ross's office I just wanted to feel safe and find sanctuary in Brian's arms. But Mom and Brian were both worried that leaving home again would only worsen the eating disorder. We didn't have many good options to choose from. Brian made what he thought at the time was the best choice for me, deciding to once again leave his well-paid job and move back to my home state, so that I wouldn't have to be so far away from home.

While we worked on selling the new home we'd bought when we'd moved North, we lived temporarily with my parents. Brian found a new job quickly, but it paid little and Dad was crankier and harder than ever to live with, so Brian took a second job, hoping we could save money faster to get our own place again. But despite our best efforts there always seemed to be new and bigger challenges waiting for us, and as if the eating disorder wasn't enough, I found myself faced with a new health challenge.

The eating disorder was further complicated when I developed a mysterious illness that kept me doubled over with stomach cramps and all means of gastrointestinal ailments. My weight plummeted to seventy-four pounds within the space of two weeks. Specialists were called in to run every test imaginable, but not one diagnosis was ever made. It was the sickest I'd ever felt in my life. The strange illness vanished after three months, just as mysteriously as it had begun, but not until it had ravaged what little health I had left, leaving me at seventy pounds, weaker and thinner than I'd ever been.

Whether it was my health challenges or something else, my two-year-old marriage was suffering, unbeknownst to me. One evening Brian and I went to a country music concert where we had a wonderful time. Each of us took turns on the drive home chatting about the songs we loved hearing most. Brian had given me no clue anything was amiss, when from out of the blue he turned to me and said, "I'm not sure if I love you anymore."

Blindsided, it was as if he'd plunged a knife into my heart. It wasn't anything I would have expected to come out of his mouth. There'd been no warning that something was wrong. Choking on my words, I said, "Why? What are you saying? What do you mean?"

"I don't know what I mean. I'm just not sure how I feel ... I'm not sure if I can do this anymore."

My thoughts raced wildly as I felt my heart breaking. I knew I loved him as deeply as I ever had, so what had changed for him? "Are you saying you want a divorce? Is it the eating disorder?" I said, trying to make some sense of it all.

"I don't know. I don't have any answers for you."

In that instant my happiness died. Brian was my life – my happiness. Despite how ill I'd been of late, or what our struggles had been, the past two years had been incredibly happy ones. For once in my life I'd felt totally and completely loved by someone. To be loved was all I'd ever wanted in life. Now all I could think of was that it had all been a lie and he'd never really loved me at all. The Voice came roaring back with a vengeance.

"How could you be so stupid to believe he loved you?" it scolded me. *"I'm the only one you can trust to stick by you. You're an unlovable Freak. Don't you ever forget it."*

I won't. Not ever again, I replied. We drove the rest of the way home that evening in silence. I was crying too hard to have spoken anyway. Staring out the car window, I recalled our wedding day not so long ago. I could see that moment we said our vows in my mind's eye with such clarity. Brian had cried. His voice had been full of emotion – quivering in fact, when he vowed to love me "in sunlight and in shadow – in gain or in loss – in trial or in triumph". Did he mean any of the things he'd promised? Had he ever really loved me? Had he been lying all along, or was I just too hard to love? Everyone left me – or so it seemed. The light from my precious Jesus had gone out long ago, and now the light that Brian had lit up my life with was going out as well?

But that night was only the beginning of our marital problems – problems that would escalate in ways I could have never dreamt of, and ones the Voice would feed from for decades to come.

Jesus,
Why have You gone?
Oh Lord, How I miss You.
For so long You've been silent.
Jesus,
Do You see how much I need You?
But there's only silence.
Just dead silence...
Jesus.

CHAPTER 26

SAVING GRACE

And he said unto me, My grace is sufficient for thee:
for My strength is made perfect in weakness.

2 Corinthians 12:9

Abba,
I see Your Light
How it shines so brightly
In the eyes of my three children.
Abba,
Your presence is revealed
In the miracle of new life.
Your Love's reflected.
Abba.

*O*n the days and weeks that followed Brian's stunning admission, not one more word was spoken about it. Reverting to type, I chose to vent my heartache via the eating disorder. Brian, on the other hand, dealt with his emotions by acting out. Going out drinking with people from work rather than coming home became his coping mechanism – his means of avoiding his feelings or communicating. When he did at last stroll through the front door late in the evening, he came home to a distraught wife. Inevitably, the big confrontation would ensue about where he'd been and why he hadn't called with every excuse that came out of his mouth a lie.

In those first few years after we'd said "I do" we'd each had a rude awakening. Those perfect, pristine images we'd held of one another had been shattered by a reality that told a very different story of who we each really were. Brian had gotten a good hard look beneath the surface at the pretty little blonde girl he'd married. What lived there was still a wounded and broken soul – a little girl crying. Sometimes that little girl's pain – the pain that she had tried so valiantly to hide away in the depths of her psyche – re-emerged. That re-emergence gave way to the Voice, allowing the eating disorder to come out from whatever stone it had been hiding under and rise like a phoenix from the ashes. Although Brian knew everything about my past with the eating disorder, witnessing it first-hand was something else entirely, and not a very pretty picture.

I, on the other hand, had seen Brian as my knight in shining armor. He had ridden into my life on an imaginary white horse, rescuing me from the dungeon of abuse I called home. In so doing he'd captured the damsel in distress's heart. He'd been the strong arms of love I'd dreamt of that held me in a longed-for sanctuary of safety. He'd been the ear that listened as I unloaded a lifetime of pain – and most amazingly of all he'd understood, or so I'd thought. But the truth was he hadn't understood at all. Maybe I was just too lost in my love for him to see that, or too afraid of losing the closest thing I'd ever experienced to love. I should have seen it coming – the blinders should have come off, when a few weeks before our wedding I tearfully confided in him that I'd been raped. His insensitive response to the single most horrific night of my life was, "Well, maybe you did something to egg it on." Wounded by his callousness, I verbally lashed out. But the damage had been done. I'd seen a side of my husband that showed the deep and serious issues he had with not just empathy, but emotional intimacy, the kind of intimacy I sorely needed. Yet, I chose to look the other way in my desperate need to be loved.

When life was good – when I was semi-well – our life together went along fine. But the moment that it didn't, Brian turned and ran in a desperate all-out attempt to avoid conflict, communication and emotions. Those means of avoidance became alcohol, marijuana, fast cars, continual nights out with the boys, and casual flirtations with other women. When Brian was confronted with feelings, he shut down and went dead silent. Rather than communicate, he shut me out.

I had hoped that restoring our privacy by moving out of my parents' home and finding one of our own again would help our troubled relationship – but it hadn't. In fact, our troubles continued to escalate. In an all-out effort to be the doting wife and to compensate for how I felt I'd let him down by relapsing into my eating disorder, I worked diligently, tending to our home and keeping it immaculate. To greet his arrival home each evening, I prepared wonderful meals of all his favorite foods, just as I'd done for my dad so many years before. The only problem was that, more often than not, he didn't come home.

As each hour passed with no word of where he was or who he was with, my anxiety and worry increased. Was he okay? Had he been involved in an accident? Should I call the hospitals? Was he with another woman? Unable to cope with the anxiety, I turned to the cold food on the table for solace, bingeing and purging until I was overcome with exhaustion. Tired and heartbroken, I cried myself to sleep.

Eventually Brian would come home. Sometimes he was drunk, sometimes stoned, but always full of lies. He thought his lies would be convincing enough to smooth things over, but they never worked on me. It was unfortunate for him that I seemed to have a sixth sense for spotting a liar a mile away, and he was the biggest one I'd ever met. In confronting him, I brought out fervent denials, and an all-out war between us ensued. Worst of all, the lies destroyed any trust there had ever been in our relationship.

Those first five years of marriage, which for most couples are their happiest, were anything but happy for us. They were turbulent, and fraught with one argument after another. Our relationship was disintegrating before my eyes, and I was lonelier than I'd ever thought possible. Without the emotional intimacy there was no sexual intimacy. Our marriage seemed doomed. Yet there was never any talk of divorce. To fill my days, I spent each morning working out at the gym, which had now become just another tool the Voice used to assuage my pain and convince me to lose a little more weight. Then I'd come home to take care of an empty house. The loneliness ate at my soul like a cancer slowly eating me alive, and my dear old companion the Voice returned full on to fill the emptiness.

"You see, Belinda, I'm your only friend. I've always been here. I'll never desert you – ever," the Voice said ever so soothingly.

Maybe you are my friend, I agreed.

"I can help take that pain away – for a while, anyway. You know what to do," the Voice said.

I knew exactly what to do. To nurse my loneliness, I drove down to the corner grocery store, picked up two bags of chocolate chip cookies and a gallon of milk and came home to my very own private binge-and-purge party. Sometimes I tried to fight the Voice and the need to binge and purge, and I'd call Mom for support. She had been the only one there to hold my hand through the depths of the eating disorder before. Mom knew how hideous it could be, and although she didn't always understand, she wouldn't run or turn away from me no matter how ugly it got. Not only could I count on her for support with the eating disorder, but she of all people could understand what it meant to be married but lonely. But I needed more than a sympathetic ear to listen as I cried. I needed a way to fix what was broken – not only myself but also my sham of a marriage. Maybe the cold, hard truth I needed to face was that neither was fixable.

A peculiar thing happened the closer to the magic age of thirty rolled around – I began to experience an overwhelming desire to have a child. That was a strange desire indeed, given that I had always abhorred the idea of being pregnant. The Voice would have never allowed me to have a *big, fat, pregnant* belly! But it was a clear and distinct inner call that I could neither push or will away. What would Brian think about my change of mind? We'd always told each other we didn't want kids, and our marriage was certainly not an environment a child would thrive in. It was a ridiculous idea, I told myself. I probably couldn't even get pregnant, given my poor health. But that inner pull to hold my own child in my arms refused to subside, continuing instead to grow stronger. Miraculously, a year later I was holding my precious firstborn son, Theodore Andrew, in my arms.

It had been a challenging pregnancy due to the eating disorder. Even though little Teddy came into the world prematurely, he was healthy. Within three years, we had been blessed with three boys. Eighteen months after Teddy arrived, Baby Todd was born, and seventeen months after that our precious Tyler came into the world. Each pregnancy was high risk. Each baby was born early, with the last two spending time in the neonatal care unit. There was even a significant chance, the doctor warned, that I might not make it through the birth of the third child. In fact, my doctor, my mom, and my mother-in-law were all so concerned I wouldn't survive a third pregnancy, they pleaded with me to have an abortion, which I vehemently refused. Because my low weight had been an issue throughout my third pregnancy, I was sent to the hospital for monitoring and bed rest. Yet, despite only weighing ninety-nine pounds when Tyler was born, and despite experiencing a complicated delivery, in the end all was well. These three beautiful babies gave my life a new meaning and purpose. I didn't just like being a mother – I loved it.

Unfortunately, Brian didn't share my feelings about parenthood. In fact, he seemed to resent everything about it. Part of that resentment stemmed from the responsibility of children. Three new babies cost a lot to care for, and money wasn't something we had much of. We'd been married for thirteen years by this time, and Brian had struggled with employment due to lay-offs and even a company closure. He simply had no luck in finding a well-paid, long-term job. So in an effort to feed our three babies, Brian worked two jobs and I applied for food assistance. With help from our families we scraped by. But the lack of money only added more stresses and strains to our already ailing relationship. Brian was seldom home to spend any time at all with the kids due to the long hours he worked. But even on weekends when he had time off, he often chose to be away from home and off with friends instead of with us. I missed the man I'd married – or thought I'd married. I still loved the guy I'd fallen in love with the first time I'd set eyes on him. I just didn't know where he'd gone. As much as I ached for him, our three baby boys needed him. While he was AWOL, I was free-falling into the deepest depression I'd ever known.

Motherhood agreed with me. I adored my boys. They were the center of my life. But even my tremendous love for them was not enough to still the Voice and what my doctor had diagnosed as postpartum depression. As joyful as motherhood could be, it was also stressful and demanded all of my energy. In the throes of an eating disorder and battling depression that sapped large amounts of my energy, I was running on empty most days. With Brian seldom home to help with the kids and give me a much-needed time out, I often turned to my mom. Although she was happy to take them for an afternoon or evening, the fact was I was very ill and trying to care for three children under the age of five was more than I could physically handle alone. I needed a husband who shared in the child-rearing responsibilities daily, not just whenever he felt like showing up.

I had no clue how to fix my problems. Divorcing Brian didn't seem like an option because deep in my heart I was still very much in love with him no matter how much he'd hurt me. Besides, I had no means of supporting three boys on my own. As ill as I was, I was unable to work. Trapped within an eating disorder with its relentless Voice forever dictating my every thought and action, held in the grip of a deep and suffocating depression and trapped in a marriage that seemed to be little more than in name only, I could think of but one way out – suicide.

It was a Saturday evening, and Brian was home for a change, watching television. It would be as good an evening as any to put my suicide plan into action. First, I needed to look in on the boys one last time. Teddy, now five, and his middle brother Todd, four, were both playing quietly together in their bedroom. Two-year-old Tyler was in his playpen sleeping peacefully.

Walking to the kitchen, I pulled a knife from the drawer. I knew what I had to do but I wasn't at all sure if I could go through with it. Crying, I stood in front of Brian with the knife gripped in my hand. His eyes were glued to the television as if he were in a deep hypnotic trance. To get his attention I stood smack dab between him and the screen.

"What are you doing?" he said, annoyed that I'd blocked his view of the ballgame. "Get out of the way!"

"Brian!" I said, gripping the knife in my sweaty palm. "I need to talk to you."

"What do you want?"

"I can't live like this anymore. I can't be a good mother to our boys like this. I'm not even any good for myself. You're going to have to step up and take care of the kids." Sobbing, I stopped to catch my breath and said, "I'm going to kill myself."

"So, if you're going to do it – just *do it*."

It wasn't the response I'd hoped for or even imagined I'd get. I'd hoped he'd morph into my knight in shining armor again and rescue me from myself. I'd hoped he'd profess his love for me once more and beg me not to do this horrible thing because he and the boys needed me. But he didn't. With his stunning lack of empathy, he'd sealed the deal. Hysterical, I ran to the bathroom, locked myself in and sank to the floor in a puddle of tears, knife in hand. Curled up in a ball on the bathroom floor, I cried even harder, and for the first time in my life I cursed God.

"I hate You, God! Where are You anyway? You deserted me! I loved You so much and yet You abandoned me. I need You so desperately. I don't *want* to do this. I don't *want* to die! But I can't live like this. I see no options. I've battled this depression, and this eating disorder for over twenty years, and where have You been in all of this? The Voice that drives this illness never shuts up! It drives me *crazy*! I can't do this anymore! I'm tired, so tired. I want peace. I just want peace. I *hate* You, God, for abandoning me – for letting me suffer like this for so long. Is this how You treat those who love and adore You? What kind of friend are You anyway?"

With the knife to my wrist I contemplated where to make the cut. Which vein would cause me to bleed out the quickest and end this nightmare? My kids came to mind. Would they be okay without me? Would Brian be capable of caring for them? He hadn't changed one diaper to date! Would Mom step up to help him? They were little yet, so maybe they'd never remember this night.

Startled by a gentle rapping on the bathroom door, I heard Teddy's small voice calling me, "Mommy? Mommy, are you in there? Come out! Come out, Mommy!"

Frozen, I sat there with the point of the knife pressed into my wrist against the biggest, bluest vein I could find, listening as Teddy's earnest pleas found a new way of breaking my heart all over again. In desperation, I cried out once more to a God I was no longer sure existed, "*God, help me!* I love my boys. I don't want to hurt them. Help me! Please! Give me some sign You are near. I'm begging You harder than I've ever begged You for anything in my life. I need to know You are there! Tell me I'm not alone!"

Teddy's knocking grew louder and his frightened pleas more frantic. "Mommy! Mommy! Please come out!" At the same instant I heard the baby crying in the playpen next to

the master bathroom, and a distinct female voice gently said, *"They need you, Belinda. They love you. Go to them."*

The voice startled me. Where had it come from? Who or what it was I had no idea, but I had received the message it brought loud and clear: I *couldn't* leave my boys. I couldn't do this to them. This pitiful excuse for a mother, kneeling on the bathroom floor in tears with a kitchen knife pressed to her wrist, was all they had. No one in this world loved them like I did. I pulled myself up from the floor, hid the knife away in the bathroom drawer, and unlocked the door. Teddy ran into my arms, with his little brother Todd at his heels. "Mommy's here. I'm right here," I whispered tearfully, scooping them into my arms. When they were quieted, I picked my youngest up from his playpen. His crying ceased instantly as his little body melted into mine. I held him close and wept. But these tears weren't from a place of despair, but from a place of gratitude. These six little arms waiting to cocoon me in love were the answer to my fervent prayer. This was God's reply. Through each of these three living miracles God was there – loving me – giving me a purpose and a reason to be alive. In my dismal existence these three beautiful little boys were my one saving grace. God had answered me. Jesus had been with me all the time, and in my inner turmoil I hadn't even realized it.

O Lord,
I'm sorry. I was too lost in myself to see my
blessings amid the pain ...
to feel Your love shared with me through them or to know
Your presence shines in each of their beautiful faces. Thank
you, Lord, for opening my eyes that I might see. Thank You
for the blessing of these children to love and to hold. Help me,
in spite of myself, to be the best Mother I can be. Give me the
strength and courage I need to face tomorrow for them.
Amen.

CHAPTER 27

ON WINGS OF LIGHT

For he shall give his angels charge over thee
to keep thee in all thy ways.

Psalm 91:11

O angel,
my guardian dear
on wings of heaven's light,
a pure indescribable love,
you saved me.

Slumped in the recliner, Brian slept as the television blared. With the baby on my hip and the two older boys at my side, I searched for the remote to shut off the ballgame now in its final innings. I was pretty sure the remote was wedged between my sleeping husband and the chair, so I motioned to my oldest son, Teddy, to take a look. Brian slept, as oblivious to the loud television and our presence as he'd been to my emotional anguish just minutes earlier. He looked so peaceful in his chair, his chest rising and falling steady and smooth with each slow breath. All vestiges of the heartless creature who hadn't seemed to care if the mother of his three children lived or died were gone. The face that had been so full of anger was now relaxed

341

and serene. How could he sleep so peacefully knowing how distressed I'd been? Why hadn't there been a knock on the bathroom door from him, instead of from my children?

Although he'd made his indifference to whether I lived or died blindingly obvious with his hateful words and hurtful inaction, I looked upon his handsome sleeping face and realized, amid all that hurt and anger, how much I still loved him. When had the warm blood that once flowed through his veins been replaced with ice water? Where was the soul of the gentle giant that I'd married?

I thought of Mom and all the unhappy years she'd spent with Dad, and how she was never able to just leave him and walk away no matter how abusive he was to her or us. Was this the dilemma she had faced all this time? Was she like me? Stuck between the memories of a man she'd fallen in love with and the abusive, uncaring man he'd become? I remembered the times I'd begged her to leave Dad, and she'd said she couldn't support us without him. This was now my truth too. I saw her situation with a new clarity, and rather than feel anger towards Mom for being weak and leaving us at Dad's mercy, all I felt was pity; a sense of deep sorrow and compassion for her washed over me. Her acceptance of the abuse wasn't vindicated, but at least I now understood the inner struggle that might have kept her from walking out the front door with my brother and me. I had seen my parents through the eyes of an abused child, and now as a grown woman I appreciated that their situation had been so much more complicated than that hurt child could have ever understood.

"Here it is, Mommy! I found it!" Teddy said in a loud whisper. He waved the remote with a note of triumph in his voice.

"Great job, sweetie," I whispered back. "Will you hit the big red button on top and shut off the TV for Mommy?" I said, smiling at him for a job well done.

Exhausted physically and emotionally, all I could think of was putting an end to this awful day and curling up beneath the covers to sleep. But, before I could even think of rest, there were kids that needed feeding, bathing and putting to bed.

After I'd bathed them, the two older boys picked out a bed-time story. Reading to them was a nightly ritual before they snuggled up in the queen-sized bed beside me. Brian and I had stopped sharing the same bed after he began working all night throwing newspapers several years ago. The boys fell fast asleep in no time, but I tossed and turned as my restless mind struggled to close itself off from the evening's turmoil. As I replayed the night's events over in my head, my tears fell softly. I gazed at the beautiful faces of my three sleeping children, my heart overwhelmed with love for them. But there was also great sadness. These boys needed a daddy who was there for them, as much as I needed a husband. Somehow, I had to stop thinking about the things that broke my heart – I had to stop focusing on the pain. I had to keep my focus on the things that brought me joy, or that tsunami of pain would once again overwhelm me. In that moment, I made a vow to myself that no matter how low the eating disorder dragged me down, or how deep the depression became, I'd always find a way to be here for the boys. I would live and breathe for them alone if that were my sole reason for being here. It would be enough for now – because it simply had to be. The gentle voice I'd heard that had pulled me back from the brink of disaster had been so very right – the boys needed me. My thoughts turned to that soothing voice of salvation once more. It had come from out of the blue. It had come and gone so quickly. But I knew one thing for sure about that voice – it was full of love. As I thought more about that defin-ing moment, I recalled I'd heard that voice from just beside my left ear. I hadn't made this up, of that I was positive. This wasn't the eating disorder talking – it wasn't the Voice, which always left me feeling moody, depressed and hating myself. This voice had cocooned me in warmth – in love. This voice had touched my heart. The feeling was fleeting, lasting only a few incredible moments, but my memory of it would last a lifetime.

I closed my eyes to pray and I thanked God for that voice – whatever or whoever it was. I was thankful I hadn't harmed myself. Perhaps Brian may not have cared, but my demise would have devastated my kids and my mom. Somewhere in the midst of my prayers, my exhaustion gave in to sleep and I began to dream. I found myself standing before a magnificent being who exuded the most dazzling light I had ever seen. Her enormous glowing wings were rendered from pure golden light, as was the hand she was holding out to me. Although awed by her presence, there was no fear in me. Her features weren't discernible because of the brilliance of the golden glow that emanated from her. As she continued to hold out her luminous hand, she spoke to me in a way that seemed telepathic: "Come, Belinda. Come with us." Instantly, I recognized her voice as the one that had reached out to save me earlier that night.

To be in the path of this angel's radiant light was to be embraced by love, and so I placed my hand in hers, unafraid. We floated from the ground, rising high into the air where we were met by six more angels. Each of these divine beings was equally as luminous as the next, and each emanated the same all-embracing love. We flew among the stars, where together these seven angels formed a circle of exquisite rainbow-colored light around me. Each angel appeared to give off a different color: blue, yellow, pink, white, green, red, and purple. No words were spoken, because none were needed. In the midst of this circle of divine radiance, these angelic beings were immersing my spirit in a profound and indescribable feeling of love, peace and contentment unlike anything I could have ever imagined. Was this what being immersed in God's love felt like? If I could have stayed among them forever I would have. But I woke from the dream with a start, bringing with me a deep knowledge that the voice that had pulled me back from self-destruction had been that of my guardian angel. But even more profound was that the despair and hopelessness I'd felt only hours earlier had been replaced by a sense of deep peace. This dream hadn't felt like an ordinary dream at all. It had been too vivid and too real. Then it occurred to me that maybe this had been a visitation dream – a visitation dream from my guardian angel!

In the days and weeks that followed, the angelic dreams continued. For the most part, it was the same dream over and over again. I didn't just believe that these were visitations – I somehow knew it with a deep and inexplicable sense of inner knowing. I told no one about them, because I didn't feel anyone would believe me anyway. Who was I to be visited by angels? Besides, the visitations seemed too personal to share. Soon, however, the benefits of these near nightly visits began to manifest their effects in my life.

Although the eating disorder hung on, there were now large breaks in my depression. The heaviness would lift for days at a time. Instead of feeling like I was always suffocating under a blanket of depression, I could breathe freely once again. There was a renewed sense of joy and purpose in my life as I focused all my energy on being a good and loving mother to the boys. Sometimes I believed I could even sense the presence of an angel beside me, because I would suddenly feel an unexplainable warmth and love wash over me. It was almost as if it was a reminder that I wasn't alone, that I had a divine support system to hang onto when the depression surfaced or the Voice tried to take control. But the changes that were happening weren't just in my inner world, but in other areas of my life as well.

My gynecologist, Dr. Bailey, had become a dear friend. Concerned about my ability to cope with depression, my eating disorder and three young children, he'd often suggested anti-anxiety or antidepressants to help with the postpartum depression. But I'd vehemently refused such chemical help, vowing never to take pills again after the fiasco with Dr. Duprow. Sympathizing with my refusal to take any medications, Dr. Bailey believed he'd found another way to help me cope. As a devout Catholic himself, he just happened to have a dear friend – a nun and a counseling social worker who had agreed to see me in therapy. Because of our family's financial woes, Sister Anne had even agreed to see me without cost.

Grateful for the opportunity, I had to wonder if this door had been opened with a little help from my dear guardian angel. Sister Anne was someone I could confide in about these visitations precisely because she was a nun. And because she was a social worker, I could share my marital and emotional problems as well. Besides that, Brian couldn't object that it was costing us money we didn't have. It was a win-win!

But one more thing was becoming apparent since the visitations began, and perhaps it was the greatest difference of all. I'd noticed that my faith in God was being gradually restored. He had been silent for so very long, and in the darkness and depth of that vast silence I'd often thought He'd deserted me. But I believed that these angelic dream visits and the way I'd been pulled back from the brink of suicide so dramatically proved that He had been there all along. I didn't believe these angels had acted by themselves – God had sent them to help me. At a critical moment, a life and death moment, He'd sent these heavenly messengers to support me, lift me up, and give me the strength to go on. But I couldn't help but ask the obvious questions. Why me? Why now? I'd prayed so long and hard, pleading for Him to make His presence known when I felt abandoned in Fairhaven and when I'd been near death's door so many times since. Why didn't He send help then? I couldn't presume to answer for God or know His grand design for my life, but I surmised that my three babies had something to do with it. My staying alive was about more than just me right now. So much more, because I was responsible for three other lives. It was the only answer I had at that moment, and, if there was another purpose, a bigger and better one, then I'd simply have to trust in Jesus to make it known if it was His will to do so. But for now I was simply content to know that He loved me enough to send help in my darkest hour – that He had listened to my cries and responded. This Jesus – this God that I had felt so connected to as a child – had drawn near to show me He truly cared! My love for Him had been reignited by the presence of His divine angelic messengers. It had set me on a new path – on a search for God. I wanted to draw as close to Him as I could while on earth. I had tasted His love, embraced in the light of the angels, and now my heart hungered, yearned for more of Him. It was this spiritual hunger for the Lord's presence that was to be the new driving force of my life.

Belinda Rose

Jesus,
Thou alone are my sweetness – my sustenance.
Oh, how I hunger for Thy presence, Thy love.
Thy blessed name is like honey on my lips.
Lead me, Lord, to know Thee better.
Lead my journey to seek and find Thee.
For only in Thy presence will my spirit ever know
true peace, true love or true joy.
Amen.

CHAPTER 28

ANGELS UNAWARE

Be not forgetful to entertain strangers:
for thereby some have entertained angels unawares.

Hebrews 13:2

BLESSED

In God's blessings I am showered
More than I can ever name;
Such abundance He has given me,
So much I am ashamed.

I couldn't see those blessings
'Cause I stood in my way;
So in sorrow and self-pity
I fell on bended knee to pray.

God's answer was to love me,
To dry my every tear;
Through the whisper of an angel
He washed away my fear.

*S*ister Anne was a breath of fresh air. She was un-like any nun I'd ever met – not just because she wore ordinary street clothes instead of the tradi-tional habit, but because she was funny. Her gen-uine warmth and quirky sense of humor was refreshing, a far cry from my recollections of Sister Mary Agnes in catechism school. Distant memories of that cantankerous old nun who had chastised me more than once for making the sign of the cross with my dominant left hand made me smile now, but through the eyes of a seven-year-old, the formidable Sister Mary Agnes was someone to be feared. In my two years in catechism school, I hadn't once witnessed Sister Mary Agnes crack a smile or show a hint of the joy that Sister Anne had shown in the first five minutes of our meeting. It was, in fact, the aura of joy and warmth she radiated that immediately drew me to her, breaking down the barriers that had so often kept me from confiding in a therapist. With so many heavy issues weighing on my heart, I was hopeful that I had finally found a therapist I could relate to. Sister Anne's very presence set me at ease, and it seemed that this caring nun had been placed on my path with perfect timing.

Not only was I taken aback by the sister's lovely personali-ty, but also by the convent where she lived and worked. It was an old, immense and architecturally striking building that covered a few acres on the old south side of the city. Because it was a convent, Sister Anne had to escort me from the lobby to her tenth floor office. Stepping off the elevator, we walked down the long corridor to her room.

"Come in and make yourself comfortable," she said, usher-ing me in with a smile.

Her office was lovely, and exactly as I would have pictured the office space of a nun. To the left, spanning the length of the wall, was a bookcase filled with Catholic classics by every Catholic saint imaginable. But I couldn't take my eyes off the breathtaking ornate crucifix that hung on the wall behind her desk. It gave the entire office an atmosphere of utter holiness.

For better or worse, I generally sized up a new therapist within the first five minutes of meeting them. I recalled the limp fish handshake Dr. Kraft had given me that first meeting and smiled to myself. This little nun may have been only five feet tall, but she was unlike any therapist I'd encountered yet, with a magnetic personality that said she cared before she'd even spoken a single word.

I sensed not a shred of pretense about her as she kicked her shoes off, flopping down hard on the red love seat with her right leg curled up beneath her. Grabbing one of the small decorative pillows from the back of the couch, she wrapped her arms around it as if giving it a warm hug. Her settling in felt more like she was preparing for a chat with an old friend than a therapy session with a client.

"Come and sit," she said, smiling. "Make yourself comfortable, Belinda. Before we begin, though, would you mind if we bowed our heads and said a short prayer?"

"No, not at all." This *was* refreshing! We were bringing God into the session right from the get-go.

With our heads bowed, Sister Anne prayed, asking for our time together to be guided by the Holy Spirit. When she'd finished, she made the sign of the cross, looked over at me smiling broadly and said, "How are you today, Belinda? I mean how are you *really*?"

"I'm not sure how to answer that," I replied, my natural caution in the face of a new therapist taking charge for a fleeting second.

But it would take more than that to put Sister Anne off. "Let's begin with what's weighing on your heart today. What brought you here to therapy?"

"Wow! Where do I begin? What has Dr. Bailey already told you about me?"

"He mentioned you were married with small children, and he emphasized the depression you're struggling with, and your long and difficult struggle with anorexia."

"Yes. But I'm not really here today thinking you can help me with the eating disorder."

"Why is that, Belinda?"

"I don't know. I guess over all the years I've just resigned myself to living with it. I've seen more therapists than I care to remember, and not one of them has really understood the eating disorder or has ever been able to help me conquer it. I suppose I've just given up."

"So, you feel defeated by it?"

"Pretty much. Honestly, Sister Anne, I feel defeated by life in general."

"Tell me more about those feelings of defeat," Sister Anne said.

"I want to be as open with you as I can, Sister, and believe me that's saying *a lot* for me! I've never really opened up to therapists very easily in the past. I find it very hard, and I haven't found many therapists who've shown much empathy. But to answer your question, I guess I feel defeated for numerous reasons. The eating disorder obviously is a major one for me. But right now my marriage is pretty much tied with the eating disorder for first place."

"What is happening in your marriage?"

"I don't feel my husband loves me anymore."

"Why don't you feel he loves you?"

"Goodness, where do I begin? Let's just say his actions and behavior say he doesn't."

"How so, Belinda? Give me an example."

"Well, for one thing he chooses not to come home after work. Instead he'd rather be carousing with friends, drinking or smoking pot."

"So he chooses to spend his free time with other people besides his family. He doesn't help with the children?"

"No. He has yet to change one diaper, feed them, read them a bedtime story or put one of them to bed. Except for when my mom watches them, it's all me – all the time. I'm not complaining. I love being a mother. But I also know the kids need a father, and frankly I miss sharing those moments with him. I didn't have three kids just so I could raise them alone. To be fair, he works a lot, but I still don't understand why he prefers to stay out rather than come home to us in the free time he does have."

"I can hear how much this is hurting you, Belinda. Tell me more about that pain."

"The worst part is the loneliness." As the pain of that loneliness overwhelmed me, I began to cry. "I didn't think I could be married and still feel so alone."

Sister Anne scooted the tissue box that sat between us on the couch closer to me and said, "Have you told *him* these things?"

"I've tried, but Brian doesn't listen. He just doesn't talk. When he's upset or when I confront him he goes silent. It's like talking to a wall."

"I see. So he's emotionally unavailable. You aren't alone in that. There are many couples I see that deal with this same issue. I imagine that his inability to communicate and his silence only makes those feelings of not feeling loved all the greater for you?"

"Yes, it does. I want the kids to have a dad that shows them they're loved, as much as I want a husband that loves me."

"So how do you cope with these feelings?"

"Not very well. I fall into depression and then try to binge and purge the pain away. Not very healthy, huh? The loneliness is eating me up, and I'm sure it's one of the main reasons I wanted to commit suicide last week."

"Are you saying you *tried* to kill yourself?"

"Well, sort of."

"What happened?" Sister Anne said.

"I locked myself in the bathroom, planning to slit my wrists. But my oldest son came to the bathroom door begging me to come out at the exact moment I had the knife on my wrist. Then I heard the baby crying in his playpen just outside the door. I just sat there pleading with God to help me – to give me a sign – to help me go on. I'd no more than said those words when I heard this gentle and loving voice – a clearly audible voice – that stopped me in my tracks. That voice reminded me how much my kids loved and needed me. It was so odd how it all came together – Teddy at the door, the baby crying, the voice speaking – all at the same exact moment."

"First, Belinda, I have to ask you, are you still feeling suicidal?"

"No. Honestly I am not. I really didn't want to die. I just wanted the pain to stop. Since that moment of desperation, I've realized I have to be here for the boys."

"Good," Sister Anne said, breathing a sigh of relief. "The way you speak about that voice, it sounds to me as if you just might have had a divine intervention."

"That's really what it felt like," I said.

"And you said you found it odd that you heard that voice at the exact same moment that Teddy knocked on the door and the baby cried? That isn't odd at all – that's God, Belinda! He was working *through* those children to get your attention! And it worked, didn't it?"

"Yes, it really did! But He had to kind of club me over the head!"

Sister Anne laughed. "Indeed! As He must do to all of us now and then! The truth is, Belinda, God knows you better than you know yourself. He knows how much you love your children. He had to get you to snap out of that dark mindset long enough to realize that, to grasp that you do indeed have something bigger than yourself to live for. If God could do that, then He could get you to put that knife down."

I sat, silent tears trickling down my cheeks as I began to grasp the truth of what had really happened and the enormity of that one incredible moment – a defining moment that had altered the course of my life and those of my children forever.

"What are you thinking, Belinda?"

Pulling another tissue from the box, I wiped my tears away and said, "I'm thinking how much I regret what I did and how sorry I am for it."

"You mean the suicide attempt?"

I shook my head. "I promised Jesus many years ago that I'd never try to harm myself again. I tried to overdose on pills once as a teenager. Thankfully, I didn't take nearly enough to kill myself, and all they did was make me ill. But I hated myself for doing it. Just like I hate myself now."

"Why do you hate yourself, Belinda?"

"Because I let Him down! I let Jesus down one more time! I promised, and I broke my promise, again. Yet, He still loved me enough to save me. I don't deserve that."

"None of us do. It called God's grace. And yes, Belinda, He loves *you* that much! This God forgives – always. Besides that, He knows your heart ... all those deep, dark places you try to keep hidden away. He sees them. Jesus knows how much you hurt inside without you ever having to say a word, and even better than that – He *understands* your pain and wants to help, if you will only surrender that pain to Him."

Sister Anne's words registered deep within me. I knew what she'd said was truth. Somewhere inside I'd always known God loved and understood my deepest, darkest moments. It was just that I had been so caught up in the misery – so beaten down by the eating disorder and the stifling depression that all I'd felt was my loneliness. "Sister Anne, do you think maybe the angelic dreams I've been having are sent from God?"

"Tell me about the dreams."

"They're always the same. My guardian angel and six other angels form a circle of rainbow-colored light around me and I feel completely embraced by this indescribable love. I awaken feeling loved and uplifted – and they feel much more vivid and real than any ordinary dream."

"They sound heavenly," Sister Anne said, smiling warmly.

"Yeah, they're pretty wonderful! They've helped me quite a lot too. I've felt less depressed since they began."

"These dreams comfort you?"

"Yes," I nodded.

"If they're having such a positive effect I'd say you need to embrace them! Thank God for them!"

"I do feel very grateful for them."

"Now, I'd like to go back to what brought you to such a place of despair that you wanted to take your life. I feel it's important we talk about those feelings. You mentioned the loneliness, Belinda. Is there anything else? Other emotions or feelings that pushed you to a place of such hopelessness?"

"I don't know. Maybe it's just feeling so unloved. Those feelings of being unloved have been with me nearly all my life. I think my lousy relationship with Brian just triggers them. Is it so horrible to just want to be loved? To want to be special to someone?"

"No, Belinda, it's not horrible. It's normal. Everyone wants to be loved and to feel special to someone. So, did Brian ever make you feel that way?"

"Sure. That's why I fell in love with him. I can't believe things have gotten so bad that I actually told him I wanted a divorce last week."

"How did he respond, Belinda?"

"Not well. He told me if I left him that he'd go so far away that I'd never find him for child support."

"How did that make you feel?"

"Angry. Unloved. Trapped. Hopeless." I said.

"I understand. So, I hear the loneliness, a sense of being unloved, and this feeling of being trapped in your marriage are some of the issues that drove you to feel so hopeless that you wanted to take your own life. Is there anything else?"

"Yes, I can't forget the deafening Voice of the eating disorder that constantly nags me."

"What about this Voice? Can you explain this to me?"

"I can try. I believe the Voice *is* the eating disorder. It's what drives the disorder. It's kind of hard to describe what the Voice is like, but if you've ever been on a diet and you went for that piece of cake that you know shouldn't have, and that little voice in your head pops up screaming, *"No, no, no! You little pig! You know you shouldn't be doing that."* Well, magnify that Voice a million times over, and imagine it as rude, irrational, relentless and demonic as you can. That's the best way I can describe the Voice."

"That must be horrible. I don't know how anyone could live with that."

"Yes, after twenty-plus years of listening to it, it's driving me crazy. I just want to scream at it – to tell it to shut up and get out of my head! But it just goes on and on and on."

"I'm going to be honest here. I've not dealt with an eating disorder before. But I do want to try to help you with this if you're willing."

"Sure. We can't do any worse than the previous therapists."

"Don't be so optimistic," Sister Anne said with a smile and wink. "We can pray about it. I bet those other therapists didn't include God in their therapy sessions, did they? With Him on our side, miracles can happen!"

"I'm sorry, Sister Anne, I know I should be more optimistic. It's just hard after all these years to believe I'll ever be better."

"Never give up. Have faith. Belinda, I do have something I'd like to bring up before our session is over today. I know you've said you're having problems in your marriage. Are you or the children in any danger? Has there been any physical abuse?"

"Brian slapped me one time, and busted my lip open. That was several years ago when I was pregnant with my youngest. I've seen him get pretty rough with my oldest once in a while. That's caused huge fights between us. He's toned it down lately. But he says I'm spoiling them by not disciplining them more. I just don't see hitting them as appropriate discipline. As I said, I've thought about leaving him, but he's not letting me go - at least not easily. Besides, leaving would just be another admission of defeat. I can't take charge of my life. Who am I fooling? I've no clue how I'd ever support the boys while I'm still so ill myself. I can't hold down a job like this, and he's made it clear he won't provide child support. So, what am I supposed to do? Believe it or not Sister Anne, I really *do* love him in spite of everything, and I want my kids to have their father alongside them. I don't want to give up on our marriage. I just wish he'd change and be the man I married thirteen years ago. Right now, I see no answers," I said. The tears were flowing again.

"So, I hear you are feeling very trapped, and not only in the marriage, but by the illness."

I nodded and reached for another tissue.

"I know this is very painful for you, Belinda. Thank you for being so open and allowing me a window into your despair. Perhaps you could speak to your husband about getting counseling or perhaps seek marriage counseling together? Have you considered that?"

"No. It's not that it isn't a good idea. I just doubt Brian would ever go for it."

"Suggest it to him. Just see how he responds."

Shaking my head, I said, "I will. But I'm not holding my breath."

"Well, then, it's one more thing we shall give to the Lord! In the meantime, we will work towards helping *you* get through this very difficult time. Don't give up hope, Belinda. That divine intervention and those lovely dreams are telling you that God's presence is with you in a very big way, and never forget how much you are loved by Him. Do you pray often, Belinda?"

"Yes. I do."

"Wonderful! Ask the Lord to be your strength when you feel you can't go on, and *call me*," Sister Anne said. Reaching into her sweater pocket, she pulled out her business card and handed it to me. "My direct line is on this card. Call me anytime you need to. You aren't alone in this anymore. You have me."

"Thank you," I said. "I appreciate that."

"I hate to stop here, but our time for today is about up," Sister Anne said, rising from the couch.

"Thank you again, Sister Anne," I said, reaching out to give her a hug.

"You are so very welcome, dear Belinda. Now, can we pray together once more before you leave?"

"I'd like that a lot."

We bowed our heads and held hands as Sister Anne prayed:

"Dear Lord, thank You for Your presence here today. Thank You for the blessing of Your angels that minister to us in our times of greatest need. Grant Belinda the courage and strength she needs in each moment. Help her to be strong for her children. Guide her journey, Lord, that she may be led ever closer to You. When her heart aches, I pray You comfort her, Lord, with Your love. In the Name of the Father, Son and Holy Spirit. Amen."

As I began the long drive home I couldn't help but feel blessed. Sister Anne had been a godsend. I had felt an instant rapport with her, and after all the difficulties I'd had relating to past therapists, I felt that was a blessing in and of itself! I was as comfortable with her as if she'd been an old friend I was visiting. That sense of being at ease with her had allowed me to trust and confide in a counselor in a way I'd never been able to before. Perhaps my ability to speak so openly was also due in part to the fact I was a grown woman now. I was no longer a child or an adolescent under my parents' control, I'd been emancipated by adulthood! At long last I was free to share with my therapist what I *chose* to share, and not what my mom told me I could or couldn't share. That gave me just enough encouragement to think that just maybe Sister Anne could help me cope with my situation – or, dare I hope, help me find my way through it. Was I asking for too much? I had been so disappointed in therapists in the past.

Although these positive feelings of hope and gratitude that I was experiencing were a bit foreign to me, they felt really good! I realized that even amid the misery and turmoil of my life, I did have blessings. I just hadn't noticed them before, because I'd been too consumed by myself and my pain. My recent suicide attempt, along with the presence of angels, had opened my eyes to my three greatest blessings of all – those children at home. But the kids weren't the only blessings that God had showered on my life. There was also the blessing of Sister Anne, a therapist I believed I could at last open up to in a way that I never had before. There were the angelic dreams, and the divine intervention that had not only saved me, but had also given me a new perspective on life and God's merciful love. Knowing I had Sister Anne to turn to, my guardian angel by my side and God's loving presence with me, I no longer felt so completely alone in my suffering. Finding a religious therapist like Sister Anne seemed a perfect fit at this point because she could guide me spiritually, and maybe I was more in need of spiritual guidance than anything else just now.

I pulled the car into my driveway, turned off the engine and sat there in the quiet, reflecting on all those things I felt so grateful for. Closing my eyes, I recalled the gentle angelic voice that had brought me to my senses, stopping me from ending my life. I allowed the feeling of gratitude that memory brought with it to wash over me. I imagined being in the midst of one of those divine dreams; instantly, that sensation of love the angels instilled as we circled the heavens filled me all over again. But there was one more blessing I needed to reflect on and thank God for – the real, living, breathing angel God had sent to minister to me, Sister Anne.

Belinda Rose

Heavenly Father,
Thank You.
In the midst of despair You lifted me up.
Suddenly, I feel surrounded by angels.
Some human ... some divine,
but each bringing the same message:
"You are loved."
Oh, how blessed I am.
Amen.

MY CHILD WITHIN

I found my child within today,
So long abandoned and locked away.
I watched her swing rise high in the air;
I heard her poignant song of despair.
"Nobody loves me; everybody hates me," was the refrain.
It was time to come forward to end her pain.
"I love you!" I shouted, with arms open wide.
"Come, darling, I'll wipe every tear you've cried."

She ran to my arms and we hugged so tight.
"You're safe, so release all the fear and fright.
I love you more than you'll ever know.
Darling Child, never more will I let you go!
In my loving embrace you may safely reside,
Together we'll heal all the pain that's inside.
You won't be abandoned – I'm here to stay.
Let my love wash your pain and heartache away.
No longer abandoned ... no longer unloved,
We'll transform our wounds in the light of the beloved!
I've come to reclaim you. Put your sweet hand in mine.
Let's start our hearts' journey to where His love shines!"

From my shoulder she raised up her dear little head;
Tears of happiness fell from her cheeks as she said,
"Thank you for coming and rescuing me.
Today you have finally set us both free!"

CHAPTER 29

MY DARLING CHILD WITHIN

Suffer the little children to come unto me, and forbid them not: for of such is the kingdom of God.

Mark 10:14

*O*n the past, therapy sessions with previous doctors had been weekly or even twice-weekly, but unfortunately that wasn't the case with Sister Anne. I saw her just once a month. The convent where she practiced was nearly forty miles from my home, so frequent visits were difficult. Mom wasn't as readily available to help out with watching the boys as she had been in the past, because Dad's health was declining, and Brian wasn't always an option since he was juggling two jobs. So, when I did have an opportunity to see Sister Anne, I looked forward to it because I always came away from those visits in a better place than when I arrived.

A month after the first session, I found myself beginning my second at exactly the point where the last one had left off – my relationship with Brian.

"Sister Anne, I asked Brian about going to counseling."

"And his response was...?" Sister Anne asked, her voice trailing off.

"He said no. He says he isn't telling a stranger his problems and he works too much to find the time."

"I see. How does that make you feel, Belinda?"

"Hopeless. Trapped. Doomed."

"Let's discuss those feelings," Sister Anne said.

"I feel like our relationship is doomed. If we can't talk about our problems together and work through them, then how is anything ever going to get any better?"

"Unless your husband has a change of heart about wanting to actively do something to improve your relationship, the truth is that things may not get better."

"But that's not the only reason I feel hopeless, trapped and doomed."

"Go on, Belinda."

"Well, there's our financial struggle. You know all about that – it's why you so graciously allow me to see you without charging me one red cent."

"And I'm very happy to do that," Sister Anne interrupted.

"I know you are, Sister Anne, and thank you, but I still wish I could pay you something. I doubt I've told you this, but the only reason we survive is because of my folks helping all the time. It's really getting old. They've been helping us out for years, more so after the boys were born. All three of my boys were in neonatal. Brian was between jobs so we often had no insurance in place. We were left with nearly $100,000 of debt just from medical bills. My parents even put a second mortgage on their home to help us pay it down, but we still owe a bundle."

"That was truly wonderful of them to do that for you," Sister Anne said.

"Yes, it was. They've been really great about helping us when we can't make ends meet, even though they don't have much themselves. But it has caused *so* much animosity between us."

"How so, Belinda?"

"Well, Mom is resentful. She throws it in my face constantly, which only makes the guilt I feel all the more unbearable. And Dad – well, he's so angry that this past Father's Day he wouldn't even open up my card and gift. Instead he spent the afternoon giving me his hateful icy stares. I spent the afternoon on the porch crying because I was so hurt."

"So you feel as if they give you the money, but not willingly?"

"Yes, exactly. I think they do it for the grandkids more than me, and I believe they feel forced into it. I mean, if we lose our home where would we go? Back to them? I *know* Dad doesn't want that, no matter how much he loves my kids."

"What about Brian's family? Can't they help?"

"His mom is a widow. His dad died from cancer when Brian was just eighteen. So no, she hasn't much money either."

"So yet again you feel trapped by your situation?"

"For sure."

"You have so much going on in your life, Belinda. The eating disorder by itself would be enough, but you have much more than that to deal with. How are you coping with all of this?"

"I don't cope well most days. But I'm trying. I really am. That's why I've started writing again ... to at least get some of the feelings out."

"You're a writer?"

"I've loved creative writing since I was six. My teachers always told my parents I'd be a writer when I grew up, but my folks never encouraged creativity. They just weren't creative people. Then I began writing poetry in junior high, and went on to be the feature editor of our high school newspaper. Writing has always been the way I express my deepest emotions the best. For years, when the eating disorder was at its worst, I wrote nothing to speak of. But I've been writing children's stories for my kids and poetry for myself."

"Writing is a wonderful means of expression. I hope you'll keep going with it. What about a journal?"

"Yeah, I've kept journals for years. They've been very helpful, too. I have one in particular that I call my Burgundy Journal – it was my first journal. It dates back to when I spent time in the care of my first psychiatrist and the eating disorder was perhaps at its peak."

"Are you keeping one now?"

"Yes, I am," I said, smiling. "But probably not the kind you're referring to. I'm writing a journal of love letters to Jesus."

"Oh! I *love* that idea!" Sister Anne said, grinning from ear to ear. "This is all so positive! Wonderful! Are you using that as a form of prayer?"

"I hadn't thought of it that way, but I suppose it could be. For a really long time I felt abandoned by God. Then the divine intervention happened and the angel dreams began and changed all of that. I felt His presence in my life again. It's hard to explain, but those experiences changed something deep inside of me."

"You felt His presence. His nearness?"

"Yes, His nearness, but it was more than that. What I feel is like an actual longing for Him. I've always loved Jesus deeply. I've always longed to be in His presence – to belong to Him. As a kid, I felt a profound connection to Him. I used to play a game where I imagined Jesus as my best friend. We'd meet beneath this majestic old tree that was on a hill overlooking a vast meadow. An old wooden swing hung from a branch of that tree. It was our special place, even if it was only in my imagination! Jesus would play with me there, and I felt safe and loved. Perhaps as a kid it was the only place I did feel safe and loved. I don't know if what I feel for the Lord today is deeper or if it's just a more grown-up love."

"That's beautiful, and I understand what you're saying, Belinda. Words can't adequately describe that longing for the soul for God. You know that great St. Augustine quote, don't you? 'Our hearts are restless until they rest in God.' So, you're finding great comfort then in God, and in prayer?"

"Sure. I feel as if my prayer life is deepening ... changing. I've even been doing sacred reading and meditating on the passages."

"Tell me more about the prayer," Sister Anne said.

"I've been reading in my Bible – Psalms and New Testament mostly, and I'm reading St. Teresa of Avila, and Brother Lawrence. I love reading the works of the saints, but I especially feel drawn to St. Teresa. I love what she says about mental prayer, and how we can find the 'King dwelling in the little palace of our soul.' So I've been reflecting and meditating on Bible verses, and then I spend some time alone with God just seeking Him in this way of mental prayer as St. Teresa describes. I have to say, I love it."

"What is it you love about it?"

"The peace and quiet for starters. The Voice tends to quiet down for a few brief minutes. I know that might sound a bit odd. I mean, most people complain that their thoughts grow louder when they try to meditate. But it's the opposite for me. That's why I began meditating years ago in the first place. But now I simply feel drawn to the silence itself. I don't know why, but it's somehow wrapped up in that longing I feel for Him."

"It sounds to me as if you are being called to contemplative prayer."

"I don't know much about contemplative prayer really. Only that some of my favorite saints like St. Teresa were contemplatives. Did you know I wanted to be a nun as a child?"

"No," Sister Anne said with a look of surprise. "So why didn't you pursue it?"

"Because my mom hated the idea, and I believed I had to please her. Looking back, though, I wish I hadn't given up the idea so easily – that I'd prayed about it to see where it might have led. But the eating disorder started when I was twelve or thirteen, and it became my life. So it probably wouldn't have worked out anyway."

"I'm curious, Belinda. Why did you feel called to religious life as a child?"

"I don't know. I suppose because I adored Jesus so much as a little girl. I lived for Him. Like I said earlier, I wanted to belong to Him alone. I never wanted to get into trouble, I was always a good girl. Of course, I had to be good or Dad would have hurt me, but it wasn't difficult to be good because I wanted to please Jesus anyway. The little kid I was thought He'd be sad if I did bad things, and I couldn't stand the thought I'd caused that sad look on Jesus' face! I guess that sounds pretty silly, huh?"

"Not at all, Belinda. It's beautiful. It sounds like you've been in love with Him all of your life."

"Yeah, I have. When I heard in catechism class that nuns were married to Jesus – that He was their spouse – I was overjoyed! I could marry Him and devote my entire life to Jesus. My mom flipped out! Said it was a ridiculous idea. That's pretty much the story."

"Was there a particular order you were drawn to?"

"Maybe the Carmelites. I've always felt a pull towards the Carmelite saints."

"Ah! Now it makes sense why you're so drawn to meditation and mental prayer, Belinda! You do know you don't have to be a nun to follow a path of contemplative spirituality. Just pray about it and see where God leads you. It sounds like you've found two incredible ways of coping with your emotions – writing and prayer. Very good! I'm pleased!" Sister Anne said, smiling with a nod of approval. "Now before we move on, you mentioned a burgundy journal. I wonder if you would mind ... would you feel I'd be invading your privacy if I asked to see it? If it's from the period that the eating disorder was most acute, it just might shed some light on the issues you need to deal with most."

"Sister Anne, I haven't opened that journal for probably fifteen years. It holds so many dark memories and so much pain. Even so, I think I'd feel safe letting you to read it. I'll bring it to our next session."

"Thank you, Belinda. Thank you for trusting me enough to do that. So let's move on. What about the eating disorder? How's that doing?"

"Same as always. For years, it was more at what I call the acute stage. I was constantly in and out of the hospital with it. Now it's more chronic. I think I stay out of the hospital because I've learned to control it to some degree."

"What do you mean by control?"

"If I stay away from the diet pills, laxative abuse, diuretics and excessive vomiting, my electrolytes don't go berserk. For the most part, that's what put me in the hospital so often before."

"I see. Do you still binge and purge, or are you controlling your food intake, Belinda?"

"Both. The eating disorder began with restricting my food intake. That starvation went on for nearly six years, and then I somehow discovered I could binge and purge. The bingeing and purging comes and goes at times of great stress and emotional upheaval. I've really noticed that over the years."

"You sound like you're going through such a time right now. Are you bingeing and purging more because of it? What about your weight?"

"I can't believe I'm honestly telling you all of this, Sister Anne, or that the Voice isn't screaming in my head telling me to shut up. My weight is hovering around ninety pounds. I'd say I restrict my food intake more right now – like I did in the first years of the illness. When I restrict food, I feel in control. I don't know; maybe it's the only part of my life that I'm in control of right now. When I binge and purge, I feel totally out of control, and I loathe that feeling. But the single worst aspect of this illness is that Voice. It still drones on. But I've sort of learned how to live with it, if that makes any sense."

"But wouldn't it be wonderful to be rid of that Voice for good?"

"Sure! But I don't see that happening, Sister Anne. On days that the Voice is at its loudest, I battle not only the eating disorder at its worst, but also the depression. When I don't give in to the Voice's demands, the depression gets worse. Some days I get a slight reprieve and the Voice wanes. But it always comes back. Maybe I've just had this illness so long that I'll never get over it, like one of my past therapists said."

"I hope you didn't buy into that doom and gloom prognosis. I don't believe that, Belinda. I don't want you to believe it either. There's always hope. You've given up hoping for recovery ... is that it?"

"Pretty much. Just don't see it happening."

"Perhaps we should go all the way back to the beginning, the place where the illness began, and talk about your childhood and all the issues that may have helped create this illness in the first place."

"Maybe, Sister Anne. But I'm not sure I can do that right now. I need to keep myself together to some degree for the boys. If I unearth that tidal wave of pain and memories I'm not sure I can deal without the eating disorder coming back full on. Do you understand what I'm saying?"

"I do. I hear you have a lot of stuff that you've never dealt with," she said, smiling warmly. "And I understand that it may be very traumatizing for you to do so. You're afraid you may get so ill again that it may require hospitalization, and you don't want it to affect the children's lives."

"Exactly."

"You need to understand, though, that going *through* that pain is the path to healing it, and just may be the path to silencing the Voice forever. You've repressed the issues that created that Voice in the first place, and doing that will never free you from it. There must be a very sad, hurt, and lonely inner child in there somewhere just waiting for you to rescue her. I wonder ... would you be willing to do a short, guided visualization to meet her? I'm sure she could use some love!"

"Sure. I think I'd like that."

"Good. Put your head back on the couch and get comfy. I'll dim the lights." Sister Anne handed me a light blanket and said, "Throw this over yourself so you don't get a chill."

Settling into the soft, cozy cushions of the couch, I closed my eyes, unsure of what to expect.

"Just listen to my voice, Belinda, as I guide you. Know that you are safe and in control at all times. Now take a few deep cleansing breaths and release all the tension of the day."

With every breath I could feel myself letting go just a little bit more and relaxing.

"Good. That's perfect, Belinda. Now let's go back to a time when you were just a child. I want you to imagine yourself as a little girl. Imagine or visualize that former you," Sister Anne said. "When you have that image in your mind there's no need to speak ... just lift your index finger. Either one will do."

In my mind's eye I saw her. There she was – the little me. I lifted my finger to acknowledge I had her in view.

"Can you describe her, Belinda? What's she wearing? What's she doing? How old is she?"

"She has a ponytail, and she's wearing a pair of blue pedal-pushers and a white top. I think she's about seven or so. She's sitting on her swing with her head down, kicking the grass ... like she's sad. I think she's crying."

"I want you to approach her, Belinda. Ask her why she's crying. Talk to her with all the gentleness and love you speak to your own children with when they're hurt."

"She's says she's crying because nobody loves her."

"Why does she feel that way, Belinda? Ask her."

"Because her daddy's mean. She's crying because he's a monster, and she's afraid of him. He hurts her, and no one – not even her mom – will make it stop. No one loves her enough to make it stop."

"You will, Belinda. Let her know *you* will love her. Tell her she's safe now."

The image of that seven-year-old me seemed so real and alive in that moment – as real and alive as the pain that I was now reliving. It poured over me in powerful waves as if I was still that little girl of so long ago. And as all that pain bubbled up, reminding me of the deep sorrow and grief this precious child felt – I felt – it overwhelmed me. This child's heart was shattered – truly shattered. She believed with every fiber of her being that no one loved her – that she was unlovable. The mother in me just wanted to scoop her up in my arms and make all her pain go away.

"Belinda, you're okay. You're safe, right here in my office. Can you give her a hug? Talk to her, Belinda, and tell her you will care for her, that you love her and will do whatever is needed," Sister Anne said, continuing to lead the visualization.

I opened my arms wide, tears trickling down my face, and the little girl ran into them, hungry for the love I offered her. Wrapping my arms around her, I held this child so tight, just as she'd always dreamt of being held by her parents. In my mind's eye, as I embraced her I whispered into her ear, "I love you. I love you so very much. I'm so, so sorry for all your pain. I'm sorry no one heard or listened. I'm sorry they hurt you, laughed at you, abused you and abandoned you. But you're safe now, and I love you." Sobbing, I struggled to go on with the visualization.

"Before you leave, tell your inner child you'll come back to see her. Reassure her she isn't alone anymore, and then I'm bringing you back into the current time and place," Sister Anne said, and then paused. "Are you ready to come back now, Belinda?"

I lifted my index finger to signal yes.

Sister Anne counted up to five and asked me to open my eyes. It had been one of the most profound therapy sessions I'd ever experienced. I broke down in her arms. I *was* that little girl crying. I still carried deep within every wound she bore – every bit of her pain I owned. That sad, lonely and abused child who needed rescuing had simply grown up to become a sad and lonely woman. No one had ever stepped up to rescue the little girl then, but I could now. Then it dawned on me: "Sister Anne," I sobbed, "I'm still that little girl crying, and I'm *still* waiting for someone to rescue me. I thought that someone was my husband, but it isn't ... it's me. I have to rescue that little girl crying inside so I can rescue the woman I am now. But how on earth do I ever do that?"

"By doing just what I told you earlier in this session – by going *through* the pain. You can't keep it all locked up hidden away in a little box deep inside, hoping it will just disappear one day. You'll never be healed and whole until you find the strength and courage to dust that box off, open it and hold each of those issues up to the light. The trauma has to be dealt with – *all of it* – as painful as that might be for you. We do that one step at a time, Belinda. You've gained more insight from this fifteen-minute visualization today than I could have ever hoped for. I'm thrilled. What do you say, let's bow our heads and pray. Let's give thanks to God."

Still seated beside one another on the couch, we bowed our heads and Sister Anne prayed:

"Lord, we thank You for guiding this session. We feel the power of Your presence in our midst. We are awed, humbled and grateful. Thank You for the gift of Your amazing grace – grace that allowed Belinda to gain such clarity and insight today. Help her now, Lord, to use this wisdom as she walks this path of healing. Grant that her inner child, who still carries deep and painful wounds from a lifetime of pain, may find healing and transformation in the light of Your precious love. May Belinda find the strength, courage and wisdom she'll surely need as she travels this healing path with You always at her side. In the name of the Father, Son and Holy Spirit, Amen."

As I left Sister Anne's office that day I knew that I had experienced something incredibly profound, although I couldn't explain it. I'd had only had two sessions with Sister Anne, yet it seemed this tiny, middle-aged nun had done what all the other therapists hadn't with kindness and compassion – provided a safe place for healing to begin. Not since Dr. Tully had I felt so safe in a therapist's care. Perhaps I'd have gotten farther in therapy with Dr. Tully had I been ready to open up, had I not listened to my mom continually telling me: "Watch what you say." But I was just a scared naïve child then who refused to go against Mom's wishes, and now I was a grown woman.

Sister Anne's suggestion that I needed to go through the

pain to heal wasn't a new concept to me. Dr. Kraft had said much the same thing years before. But I'd never trusted Dr. Kraft, and so going through that pain with him as my guide would have never been an option, no matter what Mom would or wouldn't have said about it.

Sister Anne only confirmed what I'd known all along but refused to admit – that unleashing the torrent of pain that I had kept repressed my entire life was where the healing would begin. It was only by doing so that I could rescue that traumatized little child that was trapped within me so that her crying could finally cease. But where would I ever get the courage to face the abuse, the bullies and the rape all over again? What about the psychiatric hospitalizations and the things I'd witnessed and endured during those confinements? What about the unseemly behavior I'd exhibited during my psychotic breakdown? Could I face all that again – the guilt, the shame and the embarrassment? Yes, it had been caused by psychotropic medications and a doctor's incompetence, but I still felt dirty and humiliated for acting the way I had. All these things had left their mark, damaging my already wounded psyche even more deeply. How could I ever face it all? I wasn't that courageous! So, did I dare go there even beneath the compassionate guidance of Sister Anne? Perhaps my burgundy journal held the key to my redemption.

Jesus,
Guide me, Beloved.
Take my hand and lead me
to the still and quiet place within.
O Lord,
Soothe my wounds with the healing balm
of Your radiant love
that I may know
true peace.

PART FOUR

HE RESTORES MY SOUL

He makes me to lie down in green pastures:
He leads me beside the still waters.
He restores my soul ...

Psalm 23:2-3

CHAPTER 30

REDEMPTION

I have blotted out, as a thick cloud, thy transgressions, and,
as a cloud, thy sins: return unto Me, for I have redeemed thee.

Isaiah 44:22

Today
I face my pain
anger, denial, shame
humiliation, betrayal
O Lord
to look these demons in the eye
grant me strength ... courage
and most of all
Redemption.

*T*he month until my next appointment with Sister Anne passed quickly. I had felt a lot of anxiety in the days leading up to this session, because somehow I just knew it was time to face some of my pain at long last. All those feelings that I had so long repressed – all those dark memories that I'd buried – were about to be exhumed. I wasn't sure if I could bear finally opening that Pandora's box of anger, denial, shame, humiliation and betrayal. But I knew Sister Anne was right. I had to go through this pain to be free of it.

While the burgundy journal made no mention of the abuse I'd received at Dad's hand or the bullying by the kids at school, it did speak to the rape – at least briefly. I told myself that maybe, now that I was a grown woman, it was time to open up about the rape to someone that might be able to help me move past it. But what about the time that I'd spent in Dr. Duprow's care – if care is what you'd call it? I'd been his guinea pig, his experiment. He'd tried me out on pharmaceutical mixtures of his own devising to see what effect they'd have on the eating disorder since he seemed to know of no other way to treat it. Such misery he'd caused in my life with his medications, and all in a misguided attempt at best to control the Voice that drove the illness and the fear. But his experiment had failed miserably, and instead of helping me, the medications had only served to push me to a total breakdown – an unfamiliar and terrifying space of rebellion against everything I'd once held dear. I remembered those lost months patchily at best. It was as if that time had happened to someone else, but of course it hadn't. It had been me, and if I wanted to move past it I'd have to relive it. All of it. What I did remember was that those few months of my life were the ones that brought me the most shame. No matter how patchy my memory was, I knew I had done things that I had never forgiven myself for – shameful things – like sleeping with those older men whose faces I could barely even remember. I had tried to assuage my guilty conscience by telling myself that it was the poisonous combination of five different prescriptions and alcohol working on the seventy-four-pound body of a young woman with anorexia nervosa, causing me to hallucinate and become delusional, and to do things I never would have done in my right mind. But it didn't matter, because every time one of those memories tried to surface it was like a poison arrow piercing my heart. To keep myself safe from the sting of remembering, I shoved it back into its safe compartment in the deepest recesses of my mind where I could forget it had ever happened. Today, I had to face this shame, this pain, these demons once and for all, and who better to do it with than sweet and caring Sister Anne.

Sister Anne was as gracious as always, welcoming me into her warm, cozy office with a hug and a smile. We got comfortable on the red couch and readied ourselves to begin the session. Sister Anne and I joined hands, bowing our heads as she led us in prayer:

> *"O Holy Spirit, enter our hearts, guide and lead this session that Belinda may find the healing she seeks. Be the voice that speaks through me today, that I may help her. In the name of the Father, Son and Holy Spirit. Amen."*

"So Belinda, how are you today?" Sister Anne said, smiling that warm inviting smile that was so full of love.

"I'm okay," I said, pulling the burgundy journal from my handbag. "Here it is, Sister Anne. I'm not going to lie. I'm pretty anxious about this session and about letting you read this."

"Why, Belinda? What does this journal hold that you are so fearful of?" she said, reaching out to take the journal from my hand.

"There are things in here that I am very ashamed of – secrets I've not shared with another living soul. These are things I know I have to face, but I'm scared to death about facing them," I said, feeling the emotion already rising up from deep within.

Sister Anne put her petite hand on mine in a gesture of support and said, "Belinda, today we will face whatever is in here *together*. We are not alone. God is in our midst. He will give you the strength and courage to do this. I am very honored to be the one that you've chosen to help you on this leg of your healing journey. Shall we begin?"

I nodded, and tears began to flow softly down my face in a

steady stream. Sister Anne placed the box of tissues between us on the couch, and opened the journal to read.

I was too ashamed to watch her face for a reaction, so I closed my eyes while she read, silently praying that somehow I could find a way to get through this session without totally falling apart. A few minutes later she was ready to begin the conversation, and her first question floored me.

"Belinda, were you raped?"

I nodded.

"How old were you when this happened?"

"Eighteen," I said.

"Have you ever shared this with anyone?"

"Not really," I said, breaking down.

"You've held the pain of this trauma in for nearly twenty years? Why?" she said, her voice full of compassion.

"Because Mom told me not to tell anyone. She was afraid it would set Dad off."

"Your mom was afraid your father would be angry that something this deplorable had happened to his own child? I don't understand. Didn't she feel he had a right to know? Help me understand this, Belinda."

"Dad has always had a volatile temper. He was abusive. I guess she was just afraid he'd blow up – do something rash in a fit of rage – maybe even go after and hurt the boy that raped me. I'm sure she thought his knowing would upset the status quo in the house, and Mom is always one to avoid conflict."

"So, your mom abandoned you, is what you're telling me? Because that's what happened here."

"Yes, I suppose you could say that."

"Belinda, one of your entries suggests that when you were raped you lost your virginity. Is this correct?"

"Yes, it is." She had touched on one of the deepest wounds I bore – the loss of my virginity. I could no longer hold back the tears and the pain rose up within me like a tsunami. I broke down.

Sister Anne held my hand between hers and said softly,

384

"It's good to cry, sweetheart. It's time to grieve." We sat togeth-er in silence as I cried until I felt no more tears would come, and then she began again.

"Do you feel you can tell me about what happened that night? I would prefer you share whatever you feel you need to get off your chest than have me sit here asking one question after another. Can you do that, Belinda? Are you ready?"

I nodded. I took a deep breath to try to regain my compo-sure, and began. The Pandora's box of secrets that had been carefully locked and guarded for so many years had at last been cracked open for the light to enter. It was now time to open it wide and reveal its dark and ugly contents. I knew full well it was long past time to share this pain with someone, and this particular someone had as much compassion as I was ever going to find in a therapist. I began by telling her about Grams's death and how I'd met David. I told her how much my virginity had meant to me, and how I'd loved Jesus so much as a child that I'd made a vow of chastity – promising never to let a man touch me until I was married. It had been a sacred vow to me – a pact between Jesus and me. David, as an em-bodiment of evil, had violated me that night in the worst way possible, taking away something more precious to me than anything I had in this world – my purity. But even more than that, he'd broken the vow I'd made to Jesus and held so sacred in my heart. I told her how the eating disorder spiraled out of control after that. I moved on to the psychiatrists, the hospi-talizations and the drug-induced mental breakdown. I told Sister Anne how the concoction of medications had induced hallucinations of the devil following me, seeking to punish me. And then I told her the most shameful part of the whole sordid story – how I'd mixed this lethal cocktail of drugs with alcohol, causing blackouts and memory lapses. I told Sister Anne how snippets of that time still came back to me now and then, telling a frightening tale of how my behavior had been totally out of control. I had vague recollections of being with three different men who were twice my age, and those recollections brought with them such shame that I couldn't face it. I didn't want to remember that time. It hurt too much. It was too painful – too shameful – too disgusting. Sister Anne listened with tears in her eyes. When I had emptied the Pandora's box and had no more to say, she spoke.

"Belinda, my heart breaks for you that you've carried this pain for so long. The first thing I want you to know is that none of this is your fault. Do you *hear* me? *None of it.* What happened to you was a tragedy, and I'd like to help you heal and understand your trauma and your reaction to it. First, let's talk about the shame you are carrying regarding those older men. In the first place, you were very ill. Your weight was *extremely* low, making the prescribed medications far too much for you. Then, on top of that, you mixed alcohol with those medications. You're lucky it didn't kill you. The behavior you exhibited during that time tells me that the pain you were holding in was simply more than you could handle. You broke. That's what breakdowns are, Belinda. The psyche can't cope anymore. It's pushed beyond its limits and it breaks down. You were raped. You lost your virginity – something truly precious to you – a sacred vow even – in a most vile way. On top of that, your own mother forced you to keep it all secret – to keep that pain buried. But that pain was too deep, too vast. You couldn't bear all of it – not alone, anyway. It had to come out somehow, and since you wouldn't – or couldn't – allow it any other means of expression, it came out through the eating disorder. Your mom should have known better, and she should have helped you through this difficult time. But for whatever reason she didn't, and you suffered all the more for it. Did you know that it isn't uncommon for rape survivors to act out sexually after they've been raped?"

I shook my head.

"It's true. But these women aren't acting out in this way because they are necessarily bad, immoral or promiscuous. It is the pain, the despair and the grief that often drives them to do these things. You had much to grieve in losing your virginity, and that grief process was denied you. I don't believe for one minute, knowing how deep your devotion is for the Lord or given your strong moral compass, that you'd have allowed any of these men to touch you sexually had you not been under the influence of that heavy dosage of antipsychotic drugs. Add a little alcohol to that mixture, and you've a lethal combination. Stop blaming yourself for something that is not your fault. You aren't a bad woman, and you are certainly not immoral. I've seen how your eyes sparkle when you speak of the love letters you write to Jesus in your prayer journal. That isn't something that a bad or immoral woman would spend her time doing.

"So can you begin to forgive yourself? That's really the question here," Sister Anne continued. "I am sure God has already forgiven you for anything you might *think* you've done wrong here. Can you begin to let go of the shame? These horrible events of your life aren't something that you did, but things that were done *to* you. You are innocent here. Our Jesus sees the heart, Belinda, and yours is a good one." Sister Anne rose from the couch and opened her arms, inviting me into her warm embrace. As she hugged me she softly said, "God loves you. Do you believe that?"

"Yes, I do. I doubted it for a long time, but now I really do believe it."

"Good, because He wants you to heal. So give this pain to Him, and let His love transform it. Can you do that? Will you let me help you?"

"Sister Anne, you already have. It just feels good to just finally get all this outside of myself – to tell someone."

"Are you okay to drive? Our time is up. In fact, we've gone way over today."

"Yes, I'm feeling so much better now." And I was. I had unloaded so much this afternoon, and I felt so much lighter. It felt like a new beginning – a new path to healing had opened up because of this beautiful and charming nun whom I was beginning to adore.

"Let's pray before you leave, shall we?

"Lord Jesus, I ask You to go with Belinda today. Give her courage and strength to continue to face her pain. Draw her near to You. Guide her in Your healing light – enfold her in the comfort of Your love and grant her peace – the peace that only You can give. In Thy name we pray ... Amen."

Although I spoke to Sister Anne several times on the phone after this remarkable healing session, it would prove to be the last time I actually saw her. One of those inevitable curve balls life throws was about to come my way. Still, as I reflect on how this time spent with her fits into the whole picture of my prayer journey and my eventual complete healing from the eating disorder, I see God's hand at work in incredible ways. Though I am sure subsequent sessions with her would have proven valuable, what I needed most was to unload the heavy burden of carrying at least some of the secrets and pain alone, and she allowed me a safe and loving environment in which to do that. It was this pivotal unleashing of the trauma of keeping the rape a closely guarded secret, losing my virginity in such a violent manner and the deep shame I felt concerning my behavior while on Dr. Duprow's vast array of psychotropic medications that turned the key for a new door to be unlocked – a door that would ultimately lead me to contemplative prayer. This new path of prayer had one destination in mind – the everlasting arms of my Divine Father, where by grace I'd be given a miracle and find true and lasting healing in His transforming love.

CHAPTER 31

A TIME TO DIE

To everything there is a season, and a time to every purpose under heaven: A time to be born, and a time to die...

Ecclesiastes 3:1-2

Daddy,
I love you so,
how sad you didn't know
until time came for you to go.
Daddy,
today my spirit's full of woe
for love we didn't show.
how do I let go,
Daddy?

The hospital room was buzzing with a symphony of sounds – from the heart monitor's regular *beep ... beep ... beep* to the rhythmic swoosh of the ventilator that provided the old man with every life-giving breath. My tear-filled eyes rested on the frail figure of the man lying beneath the stark white hospital sheets, kept alive only by the array of machines and tubes that came and went from every conceivable orifice. But the tube that kept grabbing my attention – the one that finally caused my tears to overflow – was the large spiral tracheostomy tube the doctors had inserted in his throat and connected to the ventilator. It was this tube alone that sustained his life.

This frail comatose figure was but a shadow of the man that had been Dad. As I sat beside his hospital bed holding his thin and frail hand, my mind drifted off to a long-distant memory of a terrified five-year-old child and an enraged middle-aged man. The petrified little girl cowered in the furious man's presence because the belt clenched so tightly in his fist meant only one thing to the child – that he meant to do her great harm. Every slap of that belt left more than just stripes on her legs; there were stripes invisible to the naked eye – the stripes left on her spirit, stripes she still carried that said *Unlovable ... Unwanted ... Not enough ... Worthless*. The words now ran through my head to the insistent rhythm of the hospital machines. To this child the furious man with the beet-red face and the volatile temper had ceased being her daddy in that instant, and had had become a genuine monster in every sense of the word.

My deep sobs jolted me from my memories, transporting me back to the current time and place. Squeezing Dad's hand tightly in mine, I whispered to him, "Why, Dad? Why did it have to be that way?"

From between swollen eyelids I saw Brian standing near the door. I knew full well he didn't want to come any closer to me because this entire situation reminded him of losing his own dad to cancer years before. Brian had been just eighteen when his father, still a young man at forty-six, had died. The cancer had ravaged his father's entire body, eventually even attacking his brain. Brian had witnessed his dad – his best friend – die a slow and excruciating death. I understood my husband's distance. I wouldn't have expected more from him, even if I had wanted it. It was comforting just to know he was near.

My dad, now eighty-one, had succumbed to his third stroke. This one had left him in a coma, unable to even breathe on his own. Doctors had told us to prepare for his imminent passing. I recalled how I had so often as a child cursed his very existence, wishing him dead. How I'd hated him! So why was my heart breaking in two at this moment? Why wasn't I rejoicing that the monster had finally been slain, and could no longer cut me down, even with an icy stare? The answer was as easy as it was complicated – I loved him.

A nurse entered the room to check Dad's vitals and record the readings from the machines and monitors that kept him on this side of the veil.

"Is there any change?" I asked the nurse, hoping for a bit of good news.

"He appears to be about the same. But he's stable, and that's definitely a positive," she said, smiling. Picking up the chart she'd placed on the bed, the nurse jotted down the readings she'd taken. "Would you like to leave a message for the doctor to come speak with you?"

"Thank you, but no. He spoke to our family earlier today. My husband and I took the night watch so my mom could go home and get some rest."

"That's good. She seemed exhausted when I spoke to her earlier this evening. If you need to get some shut-eye yourself there is a cozy couch in the waiting room next to the nursing station. If either of you need anything, let us know," the nurse said, turning to leave.

"Thank you," I said. "We appreciate that." Everyone in ICU had been so nice to us, and so caring towards Dad, but a hospital was still one of the last places on earth I wanted to be. Over the years, I'd cultivated a strong dislike for anything associated with them. I'd been the patient once too often, and it was a bit surreal to see Dad lying in the hospital bed and not me. I recalled all the times he'd admitted – or even committed – me to a hospital, and then never came to pay a visit. Fairhaven in particular came to mind. That had been twenty years ago this month, and memories of it were still as vivid as if it'd been yesterday. Dad had never been privy to the things I'd witnessed there, any more than he'd known I'd been raped or that the kids in school called me Freak because of a peculiarity of birth that he had once borne himself. He'd never even known who I was. I had to wonder as I gazed on him in his fragile state, would it have changed the outcome for me if he'd known all these things? Would he have taken charge and brought my rapist to justice? Would he have made a trip to school to vent his rage on the principal or Eddie the bully? Would it have brought him closer to me somehow? Would his knowing have changed the outcome with the eating disorder? I'd never know.

I had so much in my heart – so much I had to say to Dad before he left this world. "Where do I begin, Dad? So many things between us have been left unsaid." I spoke to him softly, as if he wasn't in a coma and could hear my every word. Now that the monster had been defeated – now that he lay chained to a hospital bed by tubes, unable to lash out in any way – now it was safe to be near him, to speak to him.

Positioning myself on the bed as close beside him as I could get without interfering with the hospital apparatus, I laid my head next to his on the pillow. Closing my eyes, I snuggled beside him and let go of all the things I'd always wanted to say to him but had always been afraid to. In that moment, time stood still and age didn't matter, I was simply a little girl pouring her aching heart out to her daddy.

"Dad, I'm so, so sorry for all the times I've failed you," I whispered in his ear. "I'm sorry about all the money you've lost because of me. I know how angry you've been with me over it. I'd never have asked for your help had there been any other way. It killed me seeing the look of disappointment in your eyes. If you'd only realized how I wanted to make you proud of me, just like you were that day that you signed me up with the modeling school. I'll never forget the way your eyes shone or that big smile you gave me as we stepped onto the elevator. How proud you were of me that day! But I failed at that too, didn't I? All because the eating disorder got in the way. Dad, you don't understand this illness. You and Mom have never got what it's like to live each day – each moment – with an eating disorder controlling you. I never really expected you to understand it, but I did expect you to have a little more compassion. Sometimes you'd glare at me with a look of contempt when I came from the bathroom, and I knew you knew I'd been bingeing and purging. But what you didn't know is that I couldn't control it – a Voice in my head was controlling me. It's an illness, Dad, a demonic disease that devours your body, mind and soul. It had me in its grip and I couldn't get free no matter how desperately I tried to claw my way out of its cage. And you hated me for it. You looked at me with that look that said, *You're worthless. You're a loser. A big, fat failure.* And every time you looked at me that way I binged and purged some more, starved and exercised some more to try to forget that look on your face, and to bury the pain of you not loving me. Why did you hit me like you did, Dad? Did you do that because I was so despicable in your eyes? You beat me for no good reason. I was a good kid. I didn't cause trouble. I got great grades. But you flew into your rages and took them out on me. Why couldn't you just love me? All I ever wanted was your love. And do you know the craziest thing of all? As much of a monster as you were in my eyes as a child, I still love you. I've wrestled with those conflicted feelings of loving and hating you all my life. I just didn't ever believe you loved me because all I saw and felt was hatred and contempt from you. You never hugged me – not once. *Not once!* Do you have any idea how desperately I needed that hug? What kind of a dad never hugs his child? You never even said you loved me. Those words never passed your lips. Not *ever*. I've watched you hug and kiss and make a fuss over my babies with such tenderness, and I wondered why you could never love *me* like that. Dad, I'm truly sorry this horrible thing happened to you. I hope somehow you know that. I also hope you know, in spite of everything – all the hurt and anger – how much I truly love you."

"Belinda," Brian said in a near whisper, trying to grab my attention from his position near the door. Raising my head and glancing over at him, it wasn't the tears falling from his face that got my attention, but the look of surprise he wore. "Look! Look at your dad's face!"

Turning to Dad, I was stunned. Tears were streaming down his cheeks! "Oh my gosh, Brian! *He heard me!*"

"I think he did, Belinda. I think he heard *every* word."

Pulling a tissue from the box on his nightstand, I wiped Dad's tears and mine as we cried together. Holding his cold, limp hand against my wet, tear-stained face, I said in a hushed whisper, "Oh Daddy, you *did* hear me! At least you won't leave this world without knowing I love you."

After Dad's latest stroke, the doctors had told us he had at best a few days to live. But Dad was stronger and tougher than they knew, and he fought to live. After nearly a week and a half in ICU, although his coma had deepened his vitals appeared stronger and the ventilator had even been removed. He was once more breathing on his own. The doctors wanted us to find a skilled care facility for him to live out whatever time he had left, so we moved Dad to the skilled care unit connected to the hospital.

Dad never regained consciousness. We spent the next three months watching his life slowly fade away. It was pneumonia that would eventually take his life. Dad passed on January 14, 1997.

His funeral attracted more people to pay their respects than I was aware he even knew. Listening to them tell their stories of my dad wasn't merely entertaining, it was a bit bizarre. I didn't know the man they spoke of as witty, funny and even a bit mischievous. I wished I had known him that way. All my brother, Mom and I knew was the angry, strict authoritarian who ruled over his children as if it were still the Second World War and we were his little soldiers. We fell in line or else. I yearned to know the other side of the man I called Dad.

My grief was deep, inconsolable and unexpected. I never thought I'd grieve for Dad this hard. I cried, and cried and cried some more. My heart ached with a profound physical pain.

The evening before his funeral, I wrote two poems for him and a brief letter to be placed inside a small compartment inside the casket.

The letter read:

Dear Daddy,

I miss you so much already. Wherever your spirit is I pray that you know I love you so very much. A large part of you will forever be in my heart. Whenever it is my turn to come home and walk towards the light and love, please be waiting for me. If there were one thing I could have asked you for before you left it would have been for a giant hug. We never had that chance, so next time I see you, let that be the first thing we do. Rest, Daddy. Be at peace in God's light and love.

Until we meet again ...

All my love,

Belinda Marie

I thought that as soon as I closed that small wooden drawer, leaving a small piece of myself with him forever, the moment we closed the casket would be our final goodbye. But how wrong I was, because my letter was to open the way for a miracle. No, this wasn't the end at all, but the beginning of my healing journey.

CHAPTER 32

SEVENTY TIMES SEVEN

Then Peter came to him and said, "Lord, how often can
my brother sin against me, and I forgive him? Up to seven
times?" Jesus said to him, "I do not tell you up to seven times,
but up to seventy times seven."

Matthew 18:21-22

Jesus,
Deep within my heart
I know what I must do;
"Forgive and be forgiven"
Your words ring loud and true

Seventy times seven
Times seven hundred more
I must forgive another,
Never keeping score

Still I struggle to let go
Of past pain and misery
Keeping me imprisoned
So my spirit may fly free

Forgiveness isn't easy;
Still, I know it can be done.
With Your grace upon me
Sweet freedom can be won.

Three nights after Dad was laid to rest he came to me in a dream – an extraordinary, life-altering dream that would mark the beginning of my healing journey.

In my dream he was standing in the kitchen of our family home, and I was in the doorway. But the Dad that now stood before me was nothing like the one we'd buried only three days beforehand; he had been transformed! No longer was he a broken-down old man of eighty-one, but a vibrant young thirty-something man. His face was the one I'd seen so often in our old family photo albums – the young man I'd always thought so handsome. But it wasn't merely his new-found youthful appearance that astonished me. There was something else about Dad that stood out – something even more incredible – he was wearing a smile that went from ear to ear! Gone was that vicious scowl I'd so feared; gone was the icy stare that had so intimidated me. In fact, the aura of anger and negativity that had always clung to him was absent, and in its place was one of genuine warmth. And then there was that smile – that beautiful smile on his face that radiated such love! I couldn't recall a time that Dad's smile had ever exuded love like this, so for a moment all I could do was gaze at him in stunned silence. The transformed image of Dad that stood before me took my breath away.

Seeming to understand my amazement at his radical transformation, he chuckled as if to say, *Yes Belinda, it's really me!* Then opening his arms wide, he said, "I came to give you that hug!"

It was something I'd waited for all my life – a magical moment that made my heart leap with joy! Just like an excited child running into Daddy's arms, I flew. Time stood still as I snuggled deep in his embrace, eating up the affection I so hungered for. Then he said, "Sweetheart, I love you. I never said those words to you, but I do. I needed you to know."

Overcome with emotion I clung to him, never wanting to let him go. This was the Dad my heart had so longed for, the

Dad that wasn't about whips, hateful words and cold stares. Here was the Dad I didn't fear, the one I could love and be loved by. Nestled in his arms, I broke down and cried like a baby.

But before he left I had something in my heart to say, too. Trying to catch my breath between sobs, I said, "I'm sorry, Dad ... about the money. I'm sorry if I disappointed you. Forgive me."

Still deep in his loving embrace, he whispered in my ear in the gentlest tone I'd ever heard from him: "There's nothing to forgive."

As the hug ended, Dad reached for my hand. I was taken aback by the gentleness of his touch as he folded my hand in his. These hands that now held mine with such tenderness belonged to the same brute who had gripped the belt, the tree switch, the paddle, striking me so cruelly as a child, but now every trace of harshness was gone. Hand in hand we walked into the living room, where he sat down in his old recliner by the window. I sat beside him, and in my dream I sensed that we were about to have that conversation we'd never had, but in that instant the dream faded.

Sobbing, I woke with the full awareness that the experience I'd just had was as real as the tears that soaked my pillow. I didn't doubt for one second Dad had reached out from the other side to pay me a very special visit. This was no different than the dream visitation I'd had from my grandfather several years ago. In that dream, Grandpa was sitting at my maternal grandma's bedside. He turned to me and said, "I'm coming to take her home with me." Three days later Grandma passed away. This dream fit all the same criteria as the one I'd had about my grandparents. It was vivid, with a quality of authenticity that was unlike an ordinary dream. The emotions I experienced were strong. Dad's presence was real and the feeling it left was profound – and it had a message to convey.

The letter I'd written only days before and placed in his

casket immediately came to mind. Maybe it wasn't logical but I couldn't shake this feeling I had – this deep knowing that told me he'd read that letter, and this visit had been his reply. The thought that he'd cared enough to come back in this way to give his little girl the hug he'd never given her in life – to say the words her broken heart had always needed to hear: "I love you" – was beyond comprehension. Not only that, but he'd also released me from the horrible guilt I'd carried over losing the investment he'd made in a failed business that he'd helped Brian and me start years before. That investment was meant to help us get on our feet financially, but I was in the midst of a difficult second pregnancy, in which I was already on medication to stop labor pains by my second trimester. To add to the stress, our then-eighteen-month-old son, Teddy, was wearing a partial body cast due to a freak accident in which he'd broken his leg. I had tried desperately to make the business work, but the stress proved too much, and we lost the business and my parents' investment with it. It was a burden that had weighed heavy on my heart for a long time. Losing that money had only served to make Dad angrier than ever with me, and in turn created an even deeper rift in our relationship.

Dad's visit wasn't just a gift. It was divine grace. It was a miracle. In an instant, I saw him with new eyes. No longer could I simply remember Dad as a cold and heartless beast. He'd shown me another side that was gentle, kind and loving. Yet in some ways this dream visitation had deepened my grief. Now I grieved not only for all the things we'd left unsaid and for the loss of his physical presence, but for the father-daughter relationship we never had. My heart was hurting: I cried inconsolably, waves of grief washing over me as I mourned the loss of the loving Dad who had so tenderly held me close to him, whispering, "I love you."

The deep sorrow I felt over losing Dad lasted well over a year. The tears at times seemed nonstop, and the heavy ache in my heart aggravated a very real physical condition the doctors thought might have a connection to my long-term battle with the eating disorder: mitral valve prolapse with symptoms of dysautonomia. The Voice reared its ugly head once more, wreaking havoc in my life, and the depression was difficult to keep at bay. Struggling to make sense of this seemingly bottomless pit of mourning, I decided to call Sister Anne. Over the course of a fifteen-minute phone conversation she guided me, telling me what I needed to do that might best help me move through my grief.

"Belinda," Sister Anne began, "you experienced nothing but abuse and a complete absence of affection from your dad your entire life, so you've held onto this image of your dad as a monster, and you've no reason to feel guilty about that. That just says you're human. In the dream visitation you were blessed with the opportunity of seeing your dad in an entirely new light. What a gift of divine grace! All the things you wanted him to be, he was. All the things you needed him to say or do, he did. I think your feelings are conflicted between these differing images of your dad, so while one part of you is still hanging onto a deep-seated anger and maybe even some hatred towards him, the other part is feeling equal quantities of love."

"I desperately want to let go of all the ill feelings I feel towards him and just embrace who he was in that dream. I love *that* Dad. It's the other one I can't make peace with. How could he be so radically different in the dream visit?" I said.

"I think you already know the answer to that, Belinda. Because, in the presence of God's love and light, we're made whole again. What you need to do – as hard as it might be for you – is to forgive him. You need to set him free ... let him go ... so you can be set free yourself. It's the only way forward for you – I think you have already said as much. You know the direction you need to go. Pray about it. Ask for the Lord's help with this."

I knew what Sister Anne said was true. I had to find a way to forgive Dad, but I realized I couldn't forgive him on my own; I'd need the Lord's help, so I prayed to be delivered from the past in order to free myself from the misery that was keeping me imprisoned.

Not long after that conversation with Sister Anne, my mom gave me a small tin box of some of Dad's belongings. But this antique candy tin contained more than just an old wallet filled with cherished photos of Dad's army days and an old watch. It contained treasured poetry and several letters he'd written to his beloved sister, my Aunt Genny, while serving in World War II. The letters must have been important to my aunt because she'd held onto them all her life. At her passing, they'd been given to my mom.

Mom handed the little tin box to me, saying that although she didn't know why, she felt strongly I needed to have these things. What she couldn't have known is that the contents of that little tin would forever change my life.

By the time I got to the third letter in the tin box, I was crying so hard I could hardly see to read. What I was discovering was that my dad had been so much more than I'd ever thought. There were reasons why he'd acted as he did. I knew full well how my own life experiences had changed me by creating an eating disorder, and now I began to realize that his life experiences had changed him as well. The third letter read:

July 26, 1942
Fort Lewis, Washington

Dearest Sis,

Just a short line to let you know that our division is to make a move before long. Sis, I was selected to go as a Reconnaissance Scout, which is a very important mission. I was selected along with twenty other fellows out of 9000 men to go on this important mission. You have every reason in the world to feel proud of me. It's a great honor to be selected out of so many fellows. I can't tell you all the details, as it would take more paper than I have! Sis I am sending my pictures and a few personal items home, take care of them for me. If worse comes to worse, if I shouldn't happen to return do with my stuff what you think best. You've been a dear sister, and I shall never forget you. I'm going to try to make you proud you had a brother like me, although I'll probably run into hardships I never knew before. I'll do my best to keep alive, and maybe we'll meet again someday soon. There's no use trying to answer, as I'll probably be on my way by the time you get this. And so with this parting thought "In God be our trust" I'll close and hope to hear from you while I'm over there.

All the love I possess I send to you ...
Your brother,
Bill

I wept, and at first those tears were bitter. I wept for the sweet, kind, sensitive and God-fearing man who had written them and never made it back from the war. Yes, he'd come back physically, but his heart and soul had been crushed on the battlefield. All that was good in him had died somewhere in a dirt trench in the Philippines.

Growing up, I couldn't recall Dad ever speaking much about his wartime experiences. He didn't tell war stories. Now I understood why. It was too painful for him. All I could ever remember him telling me is that he knew Morse code, and would go ahead of his troop to see if the way was safe and radio back to them. I didn't know he'd been a part of such a dangerous mission with the Reconnaissance Scouts. But now all the fragments I did know were coming together to make a complete picture.

I recalled the few things Aunt Gen had shared with Mom. She knew more than anyone about Dad's time in the service because he kept in contact with her, even living with her when he came home from active duty. She'd shared her memories of how deeply disturbed he'd been at that time. How he'd had night terrors, and every little unexpected sound had sent him into hiding. When an airplane went over her house, he hid beneath the bed. When a car backfired going down the street, Dad would hide in the closet or bathtub.

I remembered a story about a young Japanese soldier whom Dad was said to have fought in hand-to-hand combat. The fact that he had been a Recon Scout shed new light on this old war story. He had been on a reconnaissance mission when this tragic incident occurred. As I recalled, the enemy soldier had spotted Dad and they had fought hand-to-hand. Dad couldn't fire his gun or he'd have alerted the nearby enemy troops, so the fight ended with Dad stabbing and killing the young enemy soldier. Dad had wept in his sister's arms over this tragic encounter that had changed him so profoundly. I could only imagine the fear and horror Dad must have experienced in the midst of this life-and-death struggle. I only wished I would have known some of what he'd gone through that I might have comforted him, too.

I recalled the many times as a child when I'd heard Dad say that he was an atheist. I'd never understood why. Now I did. The young man who had gone off to war believing in God – acknowledging God in his letters home – had come back an atheist because the war had made him one. Somewhere out in the Asian jungle on the other side of the globe, where he'd witnessed first-hand young men killing and being killed – and where he himself had killed – he'd lost his faith. Not only had he lost his faith, but he'd also lost himself.

The sensitive young man who had gone off to serve his country with honor, hoping to make his beloved older sister proud of him, had come back suffering from PTSD. But no one knew. No one recognized PTSD for what it was when WWII veterans returned home, and no one treated it. He was like me. No one understood anorexia very well in the 1970s. None had known about the humiliation and bullying at school I endured day after day, or about the rape, or the vicious whippings for no good reason that I kept secret. Dad had held secrets of his own – secrets that had threatened to destroy him in the same way mine almost destroyed me.

Those bitter tears kept falling as my heart broke for my dad. His rage had come from the horrors he'd witnessed – the things he'd been forced to do to stay alive. I got it. It all made such sense now. Those experiences had left an indelible mark on him. It was the war that was responsible for creating the raging beast that abused his family for no good reason. He was a broken man through no fault of his own.

The loving, sensitive man I met in a dream visitation died somewhere on the battlefield surrounded by the stench of death. Gone was the gentle soul who had written such moving letters to his dear sister, and in its place a bitter and angry man had been born. It took death to finally set Dad free from that rage. Sister Anne was correct; his spirit had been made whole once more – transformed in the presence of God's love and light.

Suddenly my bitter tears changed to tears of joy as the realization hit me that these letters had set me free. Although Dad's abusive behavior wasn't right, and although it would never be anything I could condone, I at least understood it now. I understood him in a way I never had before. He hadn't always been the beast with the volatile temper. At one time he'd been a sensitive man, obviously very capable of loving another deeply, as he had loved his sister. But then war broke out and he'd stepped up to do what young men of that era believed to be their duty, and he paid dearly for it. Had it not been for World War II, perhaps he'd have lived his whole life as the wonderful soul I met in a dream visitation, and things might have been very different for all of us.

I realized in that moment that everything I thought and felt for him had shifted. It was as if all the old feelings I'd carried – anger, resentment, even hatred – had been washed away. Not only had I forgiven him for the abuse, but in this new understanding I felt such compassion for him. I pulled out an old photo of him from the tin box. It was of him with one of his army buddies. He was smiling from ear to ear. This was the smile – this was the face of the Dad who had hugged me so tenderly in a dream visitation. This was my dad minus the pain, and anger. This was the Dad I was choosing to remember – to hold close in my heart, because this was who he *really* was. Gazing at the photo with tears falling, I took out my journal and wrote him another letter. Who knows, I thought, perhaps he will read this one too!

Dear Dad,

I'm so sorry for all the pain you carried inside and locked up for all those years. My heart truly aches for you. I know a little bit about keeping feelings locked up – repressed, and hidden away. I suppose I get it honest, huh? Maybe it was simply God's amazing grace that put these letters in my hands at this time, but whatever it was ... I'm so thankful. I never knew where the anger came from. I do now. I understand, and I forgive you. Now that IS amazing grace! So, I'm letting you go, Dad. I'm ready now. I'm setting us both free. But before I do, I have one more thing to say to you because, just like you, I felt these words were hard to say ... I love you. I just hope you know how very much.

Be at peace, Dad. I'll see you when I get home!

All the love I possess I send you ...

Belinda

CHAPTER 33

LOVE'S PURE LIGHT

Neither shall they say: Behold here, or behold there.
For lo, the kingdom of God is within you.

Luke 17:21

If we but only knew
The power of God's Love
And that in sacred silence
Is the kingdom He spoke of,
Then we would seek within
To find Him waiting there
To ease our every burden,
Our pain and our despair.
The joyful soul would sing
In His love divine delight
And we would be transformed
By the power of Love's pure light

*I*n sharing my story, I've relived the darkest and most humiliating moments of my life, revealing secrets I never thought I'd find the courage to divulge. But it seems like it's my prayer life that's the most daunting thing of all for me to share. In part that's because there are not adequate words to describe the ineffable – the great mystery of God. Equally challenging is the fact that my prayer life speaks to my very private relationship with the Lord. For me, sharing such an intimate relationship feels a little like sharing experiences and feelings you might have about your significant other; such things are personal and are just not meant to be shared with the world at large. Besides that, I am an ordinary woman, not a theologian or a religious expert. My viewpoint comes from nothing more than my own experiences in prayer. But these prayer experiences not only healed my life but also transformed it, so I need to share them so that readers will understand how this healing miracle came about.

Sharing my prayer life is only part of the challenge here, because I also need to communicate the most miraculous moment of all – the miracle that stilled the Voice. That is nearly impossible. It is *the* single most profound moment, the single most indescribable moment, the single most extraordinary moment of my life. It was an encounter with God – a supernatural experience of how my soul was touched by the Divine that went beyond words.

After living with the Voice for so many years, I never thought it possible that I would one day know life without it. I had pretty much assumed that at some point the eating disorder would prove to be the death of me. I knew that to be truly free of it would take a miracle, but never did I entertain the idea that I'd get one! Nor did I pray for one. My miracle came simply by way of God's grace.

My fiftieth birthday was nearing. I'd struggled with the

eating disorder for thirty-eight years – all but twelve years of my life. Although the disorder had been a constant presence, there was something else that had also been a constant in my life for even longer than the eating disorder – that fervent childhood devotion I possessed for Jesus.

I can still see in my mind's eye the five-year-old I once was who so often imagined running into Jesus' loving arms. For that frightened child, my imaginary friend Jesus was the only love, comfort and safety that existed in my life. Jesus was my everything. I adored and worshipped Him with every fiber of my being. I wanted nothing more than to live for Him alone, never wanting to hurt Him, but pleasing Him in all I did. Discouraged as I was as a seven-year-old by my mom's strong rebuttal of my plans to be a nun, I wasn't about to give up my desire to serve the Lord. No, I wouldn't give up that desire, but instead I chose to keep my wish to serve God a safely guarded secret. After all, I'd had a lot of practice as a child at keeping secrets, and this would be no different. My ardent childhood devotion led to my eagerly watching whatever Easter movie was televised of His Passion each year, always with the same result. I found myself sobbing uncontrollably. Witnessing His Crucifixion ripped at my heart. How could "they" do this horrible thing to my beloved Friend, I wondered as a child. I came away from these movies with a new prayer in my heart, that Jesus would somehow open a way to make me His disciple. I would have followed Him anywhere or have done anything for Him. My love for Him and my desire to please Him were so strong as a child that in elementary school, when I innocently discovered what the "birds and the bees" were all about from a fellow classmate, it seemed natural that I'd choose to immediately profess a silent vow of chastity to the Lord. No boy would touch me inappropriately, I vowed. I would stay pure and chaste – a virgin.

The devotion that burned in my soul never died, no matter how dark my life became or how distant and silent God seemed to become. Even when I doubted His love or was angry and hurt at His apparent absence, I still loved Him. There was a place deep in my heart that had always been reserved just for Jesus. I knew I had to follow Him ... to seek Him ... to know Him ... to be as near to Him as I could in this life, because I'd always love Him more than anything else in this world.

Maybe what seemed like mere fantasies conjured up in a little girl's imagination were in fact more than meets the eye. Maybe they were a gift from the Holy Spirit to comfort a terrified child. It would be those imaginings that pointed me in the right direction all along to find the love I sought, the One who is all Love – a path that always pointed within. Without those childhood reveries, without my imaginary friend Jesus, I have to wonder what would have become of me. Early on in life I had established a firm foundation of deep devotion and love for God within myself, a foundation that gave me something to hold onto when I had nothing else. I believe those childhood imaginings were crucial to my survival later in life, and marked the beginning of a spiritual journey that would one day lead me into the interior life where I'd be blessed with healing and my own personal resurrection.

In those cherished childhood reveries, God's presence was as real and near as if He was standing before me in the flesh. He was never an angry, far-away or unapproachable God. He was never someone to fear, as Grandma Ruby's minister had often preached of from his pulpit. He was a kind and loving Father – the father that I cherished, adored and had always desperately needed in my life. As a child, my relationship with Jesus was playful, loving and deeply affectionate. I was the apple of His eye, and I could find Him simply by imagining Him there with me. Those reveries were so powerful in my mind that they carried with me into my day where the feeling of His presence so close became my lifeline.

But with the onset of the eating disorder around the age of twelve, that changed. The Voice grew louder and louder, coming to dominate my life. I became more and more isolated, not only from friends and family, but from God. The thick, dark cloud of anorexia and depression hung over me, obscuring any awareness I had ever had of God's presence within me. As the eating disorder slowly encroached into every area of my life, my thoughts and my world grew darker than ever before. I felt cut off from the Light that was my lifeline. Adding to my inner torment was the Voice telling me that it was my only friend now that Jesus had abandoned me. With my connection to Jesus gone, my place to run for solace was blocked, and the place of comfort to which I ran was the eating disorder. There were no longer words of comfort and love from my divine Friend, but words of chastisement and abuse from the Voice. My imagined hillside sanctuary with Jesus was now a bottomless black hole. What little light there'd been in my life because of my relationship with the Lord had been snuffed out. I had become immersed in a terrifying darkness that I didn't understand in the least.

I was just a young, naïve girl. I didn't understand what was happening to me or why. Having no one in my life to offer me any spiritual guidance, I spent years feeling hurt and angry with God for the pain of abandonment I felt so deeply. At that moment I thought He'd deserted me, and as an adolescent I didn't understand why. Why had He disappeared? Didn't He love me? Was I really that unlovable? I questioned everything. Had I made Him angry? Had I invented Him? But there was still this tugging deep at my heart, a longing in my soul that wouldn't let go. Although I remembered the love, the comfort, the joy of His presence in those imaginary childhood encounters, the eating disorder had become so powerful that such warm thoughts were pushed aside, leaving me feeling more alone than ever. But those fond memories of that time in my childhood when His loving presence was with me always seemed to resurface, a gentle reminder of His love. So I kept pursuing Him, reaching out in prayer in an effort to find Him again. But God remained silent and distant while I kept crying out – abandoned, betrayed and lost. That sense of abandonment continued until around the age of thirty-five, when the divine intervention occurred. A suicide attempt that could have been a tragedy for my husband and children was instead – by God's grace – a miraculous event, and the first time I'd felt God's presence in twenty years. Not only did this experience renew my faith in His presence with me, but it also set me on a life-transforming prayer journey – one that I eventually came to know as the path of contemplative prayer – a prayer journey that would one day save my life.

I never set out deliberately seeking a contemplative life-style, even though I always seemed to gravitate to my own interior path, as evidenced by the way I'd naturally sought out Jesus in my imagination as a child. I didn't even begin to explore contemplative spirituality until I was in my late thirties. Through my teens and twenties I had been so caught up in the eating disorder and the depression that staying alive and fighting the Voice daily consumed the majority of my time and energy. The first steps that would ultimately lead me to a contemplative discipline weren't ones by which I was following a method, a guide, a book or anything else particularly. For the first time in a long time I was listening to my heart rather than the Voice of an eating disorder in my head. I desperately missed the Jesus of my childhood, and it was as if this tugging at my heart was saying "Seek Me within." Unaware, and with no good understanding of contemplative spirituality, I thought that must mean meditation, so meditation became my focus.

At first I found meditation quite difficult. The Voice, as you would expect, fought back hard against my feeble attempts to shut it out, screaming all the more loudly in the stillness. So I prayed, asking God to help me find a way to shut down the Voice in order that I might find a few minutes of peace of mind. It was in this way that God led me to reading scripture and memorizing Bible passages. Then, when the Voice rose up and tried to disturb my few moments of peace and quiet in meditation, I was armed with scripture verses that I repeated, as if they were my spiritual armor against a demon I was trying to exorcise. Often, I would begin the quiet time with one of my favorite prayers, the Jesus Prayer: *Lord Jesus Christ, Son of the living God, have mercy on me, a sinner!* The prayers or the verses seemed to quiet the Voice, if only temporarily. As my thoughts settled down I praised and thanked God for the blessings of the day, following that with a mental dialogue – a spiritual colloquy of sorts – in which I'd pour out my love for Him. When I'd emptied my heart and soul and there were no more words to say, I'd rest, breathing the name "Jesus" or Abba" in and out, as I simply imagined I was gazing lovingly at Jesus as He gazed lovingly back at me.

As time went on I began to fall deeper into the prayer, and with God's grace and a lot of practice I learned to let random thoughts pass by without getting caught up in them. It wasn't so much that I was trying to empty my mind of thoughts, I wasn't. But rather, I was simply allowing them to pass by like clouds floating across the sky without allowing them to distract me from keeping my focus on gazing at Jesus. Spending time with Jesus in this way gave me great comfort for however long I could remain connected to Him, and with God's grace leading, I'd finally found a way to quiet the Voice temporarily. What I experienced in this silence was peace ... utter and complete peace, and after putting up with the Voice for so long, those precious few minutes of peace seemed heaven-sent. All I knew was that I was following my heart and taking the path I felt called by God to take.

My prayer practice soon became a devout discipline, and the time I spent with the Lord in deep inner silence became the most important and eagerly anticipated part of my day. As time went on, my prayers deepened. Some days I seemed to find myself so thoroughly absorbed in prayer that an hour or two would slip by unnoticed. The Lord's loving consolations were often the only thing that kept me going amid the turbulence of my life. God and this prayer of quiet was my anchor, my companion, my North Star. The acute loneliness I had felt so profoundly due to my troubled marriage and the illness only kept me seeking a closer daily companionship with the Lord, drawing me ever nearer to Him.

But despite all this, the eating disorder persisted. The depression came and went. Nothing in my outer life had changed to any large degree. My husband and I were still as distant from one another as ever. We lived from paycheck to paycheck in a desperate struggle to make ends meet. The wounds from my past were deep, and carried over into every area of my life. But there was one major change in the midst of it all – I had found a limitless divine source of strength to draw from, and this made all the difference. These daily periods of contemplation gave me courage and strength that I'd never had before to carry my cross without giving up.

The inner transformation continued. In the midst of those prayer periods, Jesus took away that void of loneliness by becoming my dearest companion, filling my heart with profound peace and soothing my troubled soul with a contentment and joy the like of which I'd never known. The emotional support and intimacy that I didn't have with my husband, and so sorely needed, I found in prayer in the arms of Jesus. He truly became my comforter and confidant. The divine friend and Father I remembered from childhood was once more a tangible presence in my life. No longer did I feel alone. These consolations that came early on in my prayer life were sorely needed, and God in His goodness was gracing my soul with what He knew I needed most – His loving presence to soothe my wounded spirit. Psalm 34:8 says, *"Taste and see that the Lord is good!"* Yes, I had tasted of the Lord's sweet consolations, and He was exceedingly good!

But the consolations I had come to look so forward to in prayer soon came to an abrupt end. The prayer began to change, and there came a long period of dryness. Once again, God was silent. But I was older now, and I'd had experience with His silence in the past, so I didn't panic. Past experience had taught me that when God was silent, it didn't mean He wasn't near. Rather than feeling hurt or angry at God and just giving up on prayer and assuming He'd abandoned me yet again, I stayed with the prayer day in and day out. It didn't seem to matter whether I felt or experienced anything at all in my quiet prayer-time now, because after experiencing those initial consolations in prayer, and getting a taste of how sweet His presence was, I possessed a hunger and thirst for the Lord that pushed me through those dry periods. Jesus was my center of gravity as He'd always been, so I simply refused to give up my quest of seeking His face. Whether I felt Him near or not, I *believed* He was there, and continued showering Him with love, remaining faithful to my daily quiet prayer in spite of how unrewarding that dry period may have been.

Time passed and the dryness passed with it, and I began to feel His presence with me once more. Often, it was fleeting – here and gone. Occasionally, it felt as if He stayed a bit longer, but it didn't matter, because I knew His love had touched my soul in a deeply profound way. This inner stirring was accompanied by a love that welled up from deep within and which overpowered me emotionally. My tears fell in abundance – but these were tears of jubilation! These were moments in which my helpless soul was given over totally to Him. I found myself both in awe and in adoration of His presence that was so real and near. Such moments when my soul was seemingly caught up in the Lord's presence are not easy to describe in words because they are beyond description in any language. But these experiences had moved something deep within me as well – the depth and breadth of my love for Him. I had fallen helplessly and hopelessly head-over-heels in love with God. Yes, I'd always loved Him, but this was something different. This was a fire burning – an all-consuming love. Jesus had become not just my friend, my Lord, my Savior, my God and my divine Father – *but my Beloved*. It was fifteen years after I began my contemplative practice, while in the midst of prayer one evening, that I experienced His presence in a way that stilled the Voice forever.

I was deep in silence when I was suddenly swept up by the powerful presence of all-encompassing love. To describe this experience so that it makes sense at all, let me compare it to something most people today are familiar with, the near death experience. Most of us have heard NDE stories. You probably know that one of the key features present in them is the brilliance of the light and the exquisite love that exists within the light. I simply call it Love's pure light. It is Divine Light, and it holds the essence of God ... His love. It is this indescribable love I found myself immersed in. Words simply cannot explain the ineffable, and this presence – this love – is beyond any words that exist in our language. Perhaps this entire experience could be explained more easily by simply saying that I was engulfed in the presence and power of the Holy Spirit. Maybe that's really what this experience was. But whatever way I choose to try and describe it, it was an experience in which I was caressed and tenderly held in God's embrace, and it was undeniably the most unforgettable and magnificent moment of my life. Caught up in His spirit, I was experiencing how real, true and indescribably wonderful His love was. All my life I had quite literally been dying to know what it truly felt like to be loved, but never did I expect a love like this to envelop me – never did I expect to *feel* His embrace or know first-hand what it meant to be truly cocooned in a divine hug! In the midst of God's love, I knew to the very core of my being that for the first time in my life, beyond any doubt, *I am loved!* This was the love my heart and soul had always craved. In that instant, swept up in His presence, overwhelmed by emotion, I could neither speak nor move. Honestly, I don't believe I would have wanted to even if I could have, for fear of losing this exquisite moment in time with my Beloved. When it ended, I knew I had just experienced something truly incredible and deeply profound, although I wasn't at all sure what had happened. But as profound as the experience itself was, it wasn't the experience in and of itself that was the miracle, but the transformative effects it had on my life.

The first thing that became apparent to me was that the Voice had been stilled. It was simply gone. Days went by and the shrill sound of the Voice that had been in my head for decades remained silent! No longer did I feel driven by it or its obsessions, and I realized that just as Jesus had commanded the sea to be still, so too had the Voice been stilled! Without the Voice, the eating disorder no longer had any power over me. The Voice was history – after thirty-eight years! In His presence and by His amazing grace I had been healed! I was at last free. But the miracles didn't end there.

This extraordinary spiritual experience restored, renewed and transformed me. I had been radically changed by it. Not only did I love Jesus desperately, but my sole desire in life was now to serve Him. I longed to be used as God's instrument, and so I prayed and prayed that He'd open a way to use me. I knew I wanted to help those who suffered, especially those suffering from emotional and mental issues the way I had. Since my time in Fairhaven all those years ago, I had always felt a strong solidarity with those who suffered from emotional disorders and mental illness. So many of these souls are lost, forgotten and misunderstood by society. So many feel nothing but hopelessness. But there is hope! God heals! I am a real and powerful testimony of hope – of His love and grace at work to share with the world for all that were suffering. Perhaps my story could help someone else to hold on and find hope in the face of despair through seeking a deeper relationship with God in prayer. Perhaps I could inspire those who were suffering as I had by telling them that God lives and His love transforms – our hope and healing is found in Him! I had a message to share with the world about how a living God is still with us, healing just as He did when He walked the earth among us. I felt as if I was on a mission, and I needed all who would listen to know how real and transformative His love truly was. God had performed a miracle – in me! He had delivered me from an eating disorder that everyone had said was hopeless after nearly four decades. I had to share the good news!

The poetry I'd written on and off since I was a teenager poured forth as verses about heaven, angels, God's love, forgiveness, His mercy and grace. I began to write prayers and devotionals with the intent of helping other hurting souls find a deeper intimacy – a deeper relationship with God through prayer. Bursting with joy, I wanted to shout from the rooftops about His amazing love and how He'd miraculously healed me. Free from the eating disorder and depression, my life was no longer centered around my illness. Nor was my life any longer about my own will – now it was about His. God had given me my life back, and now I wanted nothing more than to give that life back to Him.

Seeking an outlet for my joy, I soon found myself guided to create an artist website and a social media page focused on prayer, with the sole purpose of sharing that divine love with the world. To tell my story, I began writing this book in earnest, and my life started to unfold in unimaginable ways – ways I'd never dreamt possible. Sometimes I wonder if this path I'm now on is God's answer to a child's fervent prayer many, many years ago, "Dear Jesus, make me Your disciple."

Let me say again, I am just an ordinary woman. I am no one special to have had these experiences, nor to have such an incredible miracle occur in my life. I was simply a broken soul who set out to find my Jesus – the One I'd loved and adored since childhood – in prayer. As I said, I didn't set out seeking to live a contemplative lifestyle, but that is the great gift God graced my life with. I never expected to be given these spiritual gifts; the divine intervention, the dreams, the chance to feel His presence so tangibly or receive a healing miracle, yet by grace this is where God has led me. My only intention from the beginning was to love the Lord, and know Him as deeply as I could. It was purely God's grace that led me to the path of contemplative prayer, where I not only found the intimate relationship with God, and the love that I'd so long sought, but a healing no one ever believed possible for me. It would be in the midst of this prayer that I'd be given the greatest blessings in my life.

Today, the precious time I spend each day seeking the Lord in the Prayer of Silence –while among one of the most important parts of my prayer life – isn't the only way in which I seek God. I still spend time in spiritual reading, mental prayer, the Daily Examen and Imaginative Contemplation, practices which I began soon after I stepped onto the Contemplative Path nearly twenty-five years ago. I also spend time each week praying before the Blessed Sacrament, and this particular devotion has become the most cherished time of my week.

I also believe it important to mention that although my eating disorder and the depression are now a thing of the past

– something I absolutely attribute to God's grace and the Holy Spirit in prayer – living a contemplative lifestyle doesn't mean I no longer suffer or have problems. We all suffer, no matter who we are. I still struggle with emotional wounds that are so deep that without God's grace intervening, they may never completely heal. There are also physical ailments that are a direct result of the damage the eating disorder did to my body over all those decades of abuse, and if this be God's will, then let me not waste that opportunity to offer up that suffering for the good of another soul. I no longer waste the suffering God sends my way.

It is precisely because we do suffer that a deep and intimate relationship with God becomes all the more imperative, because through it God gives us all we need to be faithful and stand strong in the midst of our sufferings. That fidelity and strength can only come through building a deep abiding relationship with God, and spending time alone with Him in prayer is the only way to do that. I found that relationship through Contemplative Spirituality, and it has changed who I am in untold ways. Where once I would have continually worried and bemoaned my troubles, the path of contemplative prayer has given me a peace despite my suffering, and a deep resolve that all is well regardless of life's trials. Truly *feeling* His presence is with me, and knowing beyond a shadow of a doubt I'm never alone, especially in times of great adversity, is to me the pearl of great price.

Today, I would like nothing more than to spend the rest of my life proclaiming to all who are suffering and feeling lost, alone and hopeless, "You aren't alone in your darkness, because God never abandons you! Even in your dark night, when He is silent, He is with you, and if you but knew how much He loves you, then you too would weep tears of great joy! His is a love grander than anything imaginable, and His grace *is* the stuff of miracles! Come to Him, and simply love Him, as

He loves you! In the sacred space within, in the little Heaven of your soul, the Creator of the Heavens and the Earth abides. Seek Him there just for Himself and see if you too don't come to know and fall in love with Him in a whole new way. Will you get a miracle of your very own? Only God knows the answer to that. But I do know that His grace is amazing, His love is transforming, and with Him all things are truly possible to those who believe. Our Heavenly Father is waiting for you to come to Him – to know Him in an intimate relationship. All He asks is that you love Him with all your heart. Will you answer His call?

I WAIT

I wait
Just for you,
Far from the day's clamor
And yet
I'm so close,
Closer than your very breath.
I dwell within you,
In the secret place;
In the depths of your being
I wait
Just for you.

I wait
Just for you,
So close your eyes,
Fall into the silence,
Seek Me there.
Rest in My presence.
Know Me
As Friend, Abba, the Beloved.
Just for you
I wait.

I wait
Just for you.
Love Me
Just for Myself.
Fall into My embrace,
Give Me your heart,
And experience My Love.
Come ... enter into the silence.
Just for you
I wait.

CHAPTER 34

ALL IS WELL WITH MY SOUL

O Lord my God, I will give thanks unto thee forever.

Psalm 30:12

Abba,
the war is over
all is well with my soul.
the little girl crying ... cries no more
because
divine light triumphed over darkness
in an outpouring of heaven's
perfect and divine
Love.

Next to my computer sits the burgundy journal that I began nearly forty years ago while under the care of Dr. Kraft. Until I started writing this book it has remained closed since that last session with Sister Anne twenty years ago – archived on a bookshelf between the Bibles my husband and I had placed our hands on as we repeated our wedding vows. Revisiting it meant not only revisiting the memories of the pain and horror of one of the darkest periods in my life, but sharing those memories with the world, and that thought was just plain scary. Did I dare relive those terrifying memories – those moments when I'd first written those anguished heartfelt passages? I knew this was something I must do in order to share the whole of my message with you – a message of hope that says, in our greatest suffering, God is in our midst. I wasn't sure I was up to the task, but with God's grace, I found the courage needed. In turn, that burgundy journal became an essential tool in piecing together the times where my memory was impaired, such as that period of drug-induced psychosis.

I see my burgundy journal as a kind of war journal, because its pages tell of some of the toughest battles I fought with the eating disorder. Between its pages I unleashed the outpourings of my heart and soul, allowing expression to some of the deepest pain and greatest suffering of my life. Entries this grim and dark were meant for my eyes only – with perhaps a trusted therapist such as Sister Anne the exception. Yet by God's grace, I've shared some of the most poignant moments, some of my hardest and most shameful memories with you.

To this day not all its pages are filled. Many blank ones remain, and perhaps that is deliberate too. Could it be that those empty pages are waiting to be filled with words that tell about the most important part of the battle that for decades raged in my soul – the victory won? Maybe those pages have been reserved all along for the express purpose of giving thanks to the One who ultimately saved me from destruction, and for sharing stories of the wisdom and lessons I've learned along the way. I can only think of a single way to do that – writing a letter to the therapist who was ultimately responsible for giving me back my life – the Divine Therapist. Though the words I wrote on the pages of my journal in the past were meant for my eyes only, the words I write today are not. Although this letter is deeply personal in that it speaks from my heart and soul to my divine Father – the One who led me through the war to victory – it isn't meant to glorify my life. The glory resides in God alone! He is the hero of this story. Without His hand in my life there wouldn't have been a happy ending or a victory to speak about, of that I am sure. So, let this final entry in my burgundy journal be shared with the world as a testament of God's power, goodness, love, mercy and grace at work in the life of one suffering soul – resurrecting it against all odds. For with God all things are possible (Matthew 19:26). May my testimony give those who are suffering the courage to face tomorrow with a steadfast faith in the knowledge that beyond their pain and suffering lies the hope of their own personal resurrection.

My Dearest Jesus,

All is well with my soul! I never thought I'd say those words, my Jesus, when for nearly forty years – most of my life – my soul was in such agony. Not for one second did I dream that such a long, dark and difficult journey would turn out in such a miraculous way. Dear Shepherd of my soul, You took my hand and led me through it all, and for that I am eternally thankful. As I look back over the years, there have been so many moments of grace and light that I failed to notice in the midst of all those dark nights – and those moments were essential to eventually winning the war against my enemy. While that exquisite moment of prayer in which the healing occurred was by far the most extraordinary moment of my life thus far, it was but the triumphant final victory of a spiritual battle within my soul. It was the small moments of grace I experienced along the way that taught me invaluable life lessons, where wisdom was gained and unseen blessings were bestowed. So, I'd like to go back in time to my childhood, and reflect on where it all began, taking note and giving thanks for these small and seemingly insignificant victories along the way.

Even after so many years have passed I can still feel the terror of the little girl I once was, hiding beneath the bed clutching a Sacred Heart prayer card next to her heart after one of Dad's irrational and brutal whippings. How I pleaded with You over and over to "make it quit hurting" and "make the mean man go away". I believe You heard that little girl crying because the thought popped into my head immediately after that heartfelt plea to close my eyes and imagine You with me. I did, and I knew, Jesus, that I wasn't alone beneath that bed – You were right beside me, answering my prayer.

So, our friendship began with a child's game of finding You in my mind's eye when I was afraid. I ran to You in my imaginings and found You waiting for me in our special place with Your arms open wide, ready to scoop me up in a hug anytime I needed You.

Beneath the shade of that oak tree You'd hold me until my fears vanished. You pushed me high into the air on the old wooden swing that hung from that oak tree, and it felt so real. I was sustained by Your presence with me … if only in my imagination. All these years later, I can tell You unequivocally that those special moments with You on that hillside are my favorite childhood memories. You were the loving father I didn't have and desperately needed. You became my place of sanctuary – my world – my imaginary friend. My whole heart and soul belonged to You – only You, from that moment forward. That has never changed. Thank You, Jesus, for holding my hand and loving me through the most terrifying moments of my childhood.

But then the eating disorder began to take control of my thoughts around the age of twelve, and I could no longer find You or feel Your presence no matter how

hard I tried. My mind had been seemingly invaded by a foreign entity – an almost demonic voice determined to destroy me. I would not understand until years later that this was the voice of an eating disorder.

I was lost and alone in this crushing, impenetrable darkness that often felt as if it had swallowed me whole. Although the love I felt for You was as strong as it had ever been, You were gone, or so it seemed. I felt abandoned and alone. For the next twenty-five years, I wandered, seemingly alone in that darkness. You were silent. In that dark, silent abyss I still clung to You, wrongly believing I was alone in that clinging. Little did I know it wasn't just me holding onto and loving You, but You holding onto and loving me as well. Now I understand, Lord, that never once was I alone through any of it because You were there all along, keeping Your divine promise to be with me through the suffering. Sometimes I kicked, screamed, cursed and blamed You for all the pain in my life, and I'm sorry for that. I just didn't understand. I do now. I understand that You never promised that we won't be hurt or have bad things happen to us, only that when the suffering comes You will walk with us, giving us the courage and strength to endure it. Those times when You were silent, You were teaching me that I must walk in faith, trusting in Your presence beside me. For Your Holy Word reveals that "we walk by faith, not by sight" ... (2 Corinthians 5:7). Now I know that even when You are silent in my suffering, I needn't fear, for "Yea, though I walk in the valley of the shadow of death, Thou art with me" ... (Psalm 23:4). These verses are not simply beautiful words, Lord, but truth meant to sustain us.

Then came that defining moment in my mid-thirties when in great despair I sat huddled, contemplating sui-

cide in the corner of the bathroom with a knife blade to my wrist. Your grace found and saved me from myself through the whisper of an angel that opened my eyes to the reality that I had something bigger than myself to live for – my children. I shudder to think what would have happened to them if You hadn't intervened. Something deep within shifted at the moment of that divine intervention as I felt Your presence again after all those years of silence. It was then that the recurring dreams of angels began. O Jesus, thank You for loving me so much that You would send my guardian angel to minister to me in my dreams. At that point, I had lived with the illness for about twenty-three years, and I was beaten down and exhausted mentally, physically and spiritually. I just wanted it to end – one way or another. Only through Your grace was I lifted up and given enough strength and courage to go on, for the sake of my children.

Soon after that, Your grace was once more at work in my life, leading me into a deepening prayer experience. I felt You tugging at my heartstrings, calling me into the depths of the silence, and I followed You gladly into that silence in prayer. At the same time I had been reading some of the writings of St. Ignatius of Loyola and felt particularly drawn to a prayer he taught – Imaginative Prayer. That prompting seemed to guide me into using that big imagination of mine yet again! In so doing, it helped me to understand my own suffering in a new light. What happened was one of the most memorable experiences in prayer I'd had thus far. It began as I opened my Bible to John 19:24, and placed myself at the Foot of the Cross – the gospel scene of Your Crucifixion.

I envisioned myself beside our Blessed Mother Mary and Saint Mary Magdalene. In that moment, I imag-

ined their anguished cries, and then, I gazed up at You, bloodied and dying an excruciating death. You looked down at me with eyes that pierced right through my soul – the same beautiful eyes I recalled smiling at me as a child on that hillside. But now pain filled them – You wept, and my heart broke.

I understood with crystal clarity that if such suffering could happen to You, the Son of God, then pain and suffering could happen to any of us. We are not above the Master. I don't know why I'd never grasped that before. I guess I was too lost in self-pity, too exhausted, and too caught up in the long years I'd spent fighting against my adversary to see past it. But in that moment, I understood. We have been sent into a broken world of sin

where suffering is the reality, and no matter how much we try to avoid it entering our lives, or how good or holy we try to be, adversity will find us. Suffering is the way of this world. It is only when we enter into Heaven that we are free of it. I needed that wake-up call, Lord, because the reality that I had lost so many years to illness – my entire youth, in fact – was beginning to make me a bitter and angry woman.

I saw in that illumining moment of prayer hanging on that Cross not just my Lord and Savior, but the very One who truly knew what pain and suffering was. You endured the worst imaginable agony, and You did it willingly for all humanity, and that included me. Now it had become personal. No longer was the Passion just a Bible story, but a real living truth I felt in my heart and soul, and though my love for You was never in question, that epiphany drew me to You in a deeper and more profound way than I can ever describe. The Sacred Heart image I'd been so drawn to my entire life suddenly hit home as the words on that prayer card I'd recited daily rang in my head: "Sacred Heart of Jesus, filled with immense Love; broken by our ingratitude and pierced by our sins; yet loving us still..." Still, in spite of my wretchedness, and my unworthiness You loved this broken, pitiful, wounded soul enough to die for it.

It was a moment I'll never forget. Not only did I grasp the depth of Your love for me, but the depth to which You understood my emotional and often physical torment. I had grown so accustomed to my husband's insensitivity and Mom's detachment that I felt no one was capable of empathy or compassion, and that made the loneliness unbearable. But as I looked into Your eyes so filled with pain and agony ... as Your precious blood fell in a pool at my feet, the realization hit me – You got it! You were the One I could truly share my pain with because You alone understood in a way others could not. Jesus, all the things I'd suffered, You'd suffered before me – betrayal and humiliation, great physical pain, great mental and emotional anguish, and You'd even experienced the darkness and pain of abandonment. In the days to come You continued to open my spiritual eyes to the understanding that we all have crosses to bear, and the eating disorder, depression, and even the marital discord were mine. You helped me to understand that I could offer that suffering up to You – unite my suffering with Your suffering, that it might have a purpose. So, I began a daily prayer, saying, "Use this pain, Lord, for Your glory." That prayer soon became the most fervent cry of my heart. If I had to suffer... if there was no way out, then so be it, but at least let it mean something. Somehow ... some way, Jesus, use it for Your glory. Use it in building Your kingdom. Thank You, Jesus, for leading me into that prayer, for meeting me there, for taking me beyond myself, and thus forever transforming my outlook. You used my hopelessness and despair to lead me to You at the Foot of the Cross, where I saw suffering in a new way. I realized that all the years I'd lost to the illness didn't need to make me bitter any more than they needed to be a total waste of my life. All the suffering could have a redemptive value and be used for a greater good if I'd just surrender to You.

So many times over the years I'd asked myself why You didn't stop the rape, the bullying or Dad's abuse through some mighty divine intervention. Why did You allow so many people to hurt me in such despicable ways? There were times when I was so angry with You for not intervening. How could a loving God – a God I so loved – allow this? How could this be Your will for my life? I think I understand now, Jesus. It was never Your will that these horrible things happen to me. Your will is that we love one another. But You gave us free will, and there are many that choose to use that gift of free will in direct opposition to what You will for us. They choose to murder, rape, steal, and hurt one another. It is clear to me now, Jesus. Divine Providence allows all things to work for the good of those that love You, those who have been called according to Your purpose (Romans 8:28). Yes, through a mystery that I'll never understand, these difficult and painful things came into my life. My prayer is that I can accept and grow from them. By Your grace, I believe I have. I see now, that often the cup the Father asks us to drink from is bitter, as it was for You, my King. But God has allowed that bitter cup to be placed before us - a plan for our good that we cannot understand. But even so, I know with every part of my being that when bad and evil things occur, we aren't alone, even if we feel as though we are. You, precious Lord, are with the victims in their suffering, as You were there with me. I believe that You cry with us, feeling our pain and heartache, and that You catch our tears as You bear witness to our sorrow. Your Holy Spirit is in our midst to comfort and see us through those sorrows and tragedies, if we will only lean on You and not turn away. This is the way of a broken world of sin, and only – as the Book of Revelation tells us – "in the New Jerusalem, when you dwell among us, will every tear be dried from our eyes" (Revelation 21:4). I for one Lord can't wait for that day!

Thank You dear Jesus for also continuing to teach me the lesson of forgiveness, and for granting me the grace to let go of my persecutors. Through the dreams of Dad and the letters I received after his death I was not only able to forgive him, but to feel real compassion for him, and understand that he was broken too. It didn't make what he did right, but I could understand and let go. In so doing, You healed a wound I never thought could possibly be healed. I finally felt his love for me, and I was at last free to love him in return. I found the anger and conflicted feelings of love and hate I'd struggled with for a lifetime transformed, and that too seems like a miracle to me! Thank You, dear Lord, for only Your grace made that possible.

Your grace also allowed me to find the same place of forgiveness for the young man who raped me as a teenager, and the kids that bullied me so mercilessly in school. I hold no grudges towards any of them, and that includes Brian, my husband. While I have forgiven him for his past behavior and the deep pain it caused both my children and me, I admit, I struggle at times with forgetting. So my Lord, I'll continue to pray that You will graciously grant me the grace of forgetting, that these and other painful memories of the past will one day no longer even cross my mind.

Thanks to You, so much of my past has been healed through the power of forgiveness. But I know there's still more work to do. That will take Your grace once more because if I've learned one thing about forgiveness it's that it's a state of grace. Never would I have been able to forgive so many for so much, if not for You making it possible. You've granted me enough wisdom to know that the path to healing and to setting myself free is to let go of old grudges and past pain, and so I know I must do this no matter how hard or painful. You've showered that much needed grace upon me time and again so I might find that place of forgiveness. In doing so, You've already set me free from so much of my traumatic past – thank You for this priceless gift.

Lord, I've witnessed in my own life how You take the trials, suffering and pain and find a way to use it for a greater good. The isolation and loneliness that has been a constant companion in my life due to both my illness and my difficult marriage, is one such example. Although feeling so utterly alone in life has often pushed me into a place of great despair, You somehow found a way to use even this for a greater good. No, that loneliness didn't drive me into the arms of another man, but it did drive me into Your arms, where I found refuge. In Your Divine Embrace, I found not only comfort, but the love and companionship I hungered for. You took the greatest pain I'd ever known, and turned it into one of the greatest blessings I've ever been given – the blessing of Your love. I don't believe there exists a greater blessing than knowing You and truly experiencing Your love.

And Your blessings still continue to flow, Jesus, in ways I never thought possible. I see how You've been moving in my husband's heart, and I am overjoyed! I've prayed for so long that Brian would come back to You - become the man I married, and now, I actually see him praying again! Not only that, but he has embraced my Catholic faith, the beauty of the Latin Mass and the sacred silence of Eucharistic Adoration, attending both with me. Brian has always said he'd never have anything to do with Catholicism, and now here we are going to Mass and Adoration together. Jesus, that is Your mighty hand working in truly amazing ways! While our relationship sorely lacks the emotional connection I crave, and thus the physical connection he craves, there is still love between us. It's just a very different type of love than when we walked down the aisle all those years ago. Perhaps as Brian continues to draw closer to You, we will grow closer to one another. Only time will tell that story. But with Your grace leading, maybe we will find a path revealed to begin the hard work of rebuilding our relationship. I still believe there is hope for healing the wounds that divide us. These wounds are deep, I won't deny that. But even wounds stemming from emotional abandonment, and a lack of trust and communication, can be healed if both of us want it, are willing to work for it, and You are finally at the center of our marriage. I know first-hand that You are a God of miracles! I won't give up hope, or stop praying for a healing for our marriage. No matter how painful this relationship has been, I am still grateful for Brian. At heart, he is a decent man and a hard worker. He has mellowed over the years, and no longer does the wild, crazy and even cruel things he once did. I know that he loves me in his own way, even if it isn't in the way I need to be loved. Besides, without him Lord, I wouldn't have my three precious boys whom I love more than my own life.

Thank you Lord, for instilling in the depths of my soul, a love so strong for You, that not even the demons of despair could prevail against it. As I look back over my life to this point, I see so clearly that it is this great love and devotion I have for You that has always been my saving grace. Throughout my life, it has been this love that has helped me to hold on, if sometimes, only by a thread. Eventually, that love would lead me to seek You in the depths of my being, and there, through the gift of contemplative prayer, I would experience the power of Your divine love in such a way, that it would not only heal me, but transform my life in unimaginable ways. Is it any wonder, that although I may never have become the nun I so often dreamed of being as a child,

or officially professed vows to be Your bride, I am as de-voted to You today as though I had. You are the love of my life, and You always will be. In the depths of my soul, my love for You is deeper and stronger than ever. So my Jesus, between You and me, I feel I am Your bride, and You my Bridegroom regardless of religious vows I may have never professed. You are my Beloved. I feel it to the very depths of my soul.

I'd also like to thank You for opening my eyes to Your presence with me, Jesus – a presence I so often missed. There were the times I was locked away in psychiatric facilities, and the sense of abandonment I experienced while there was overwhelming. Unfortunately, I didn't have eyes to see at the time that You really were with me, and making friends with Jilly wasn't mere coinci-dence. Your presence was there in the midst of that brief but warm friendship, easing that deep sense of aban-donment that nearly consumed me. Then there was the angel in my midst, Nurse Karen. She listened to my fears, wiped away tears, gave hugs, saved me from Dr. Kraft once or twice and literally held my head up when I was deathly ill with the stomach flu. She was com-passionate, kind and loving always, and I believe that was Your sweet presence with me again. So many times You were present in those around me, and I missed it in that moment. When Dr. Duprow wanted to commit me to the state psychiatric hospital and Mom stood up to him ... that was You present in her. When my five-year-old son was frantically rapping on the bathroom door and the baby was crying as I sat on the bathroom floor contemplating ending my life ... that was You present in them. Even as far back as junior high when Eddie was calling me Freak, You were present in my best friend Valerie, who did her best to protect me from his vile mouth. I could go on, Jesus! I see You so clearly now, reflected in the words, gestures and faces of people who have crossed my path. I don't know, maybe I've just grown up! But I understand now that it is through people that You dwell among us and minister to our suffering. It can be as simple as a kind word, a smile or hug, or a simple deed – and this is but one of the many ways You are with us. Sadly, Lord, I was too blinded by and caught up in my own pain and the illness to see Your presence always in my midst.

I couldn't write a letter of thanksgiving to You without speaking about one of the greatest blessings in my life – contemplative prayer. It was this discipline that led me into the intimate relationship with You that my heart and soul longed for, and eventually led me to a miracle that healed me. All along, Lord, from my late twenties forward, Your grace was gradually leading me nearer to You on the path that led to the prayer of contemplation. All I knew at the time was that I still loved You desperately. I wanted to find that cherished relationship I'd had with You as a little girl once more, and I'd have followed You wherever You led to have it back again. You answered my prayer by first leading me to spiritual reading, and then to seeking You where You dwell, in the little Heaven of my soul!

Although it would seem that healing me from the illness would be what I would have prayed for, it wasn't. More than healing the eating disorder I simply wanted You. I was determined to pursue You above all else. Perhaps that loneliness I'd lived with for so long was more painful to me in many ways than the eating disorder. I believed You could fill that gnawing emptiness in my heart and soul. I wasn't disappointed, because You did just that. So really the loneliness wasn't a curse, but a blessing, only serving to send me on a relentless search for the One I instinctively knew did love me – the One I believed could cure the ache in my heart and fill the emptiness in my soul. So, I tirelessly sought Your Face. I was so thirsty for You. I had drunk from Your cup of love as a child, and my soul remembered well the joy, happiness and completeness it had found in Your divine presence. Night after night, when prayer seemed so dry and empty for so long, I persisted for one reason. I simply couldn't rest until I found what my heart kept telling me it needed most – You – and it told me I'd find You within my being. Contemplative prayer had been my daily practice long before the moment of the healing ever happened. Yes, I had felt Your sweetness stirring deep in my soul many times. My life has been graced by many cherished moments in prayer. But that one mystical encounter with You was unlike any previous experience I'd had. It was as if all those years that I'd reached out in prayer with my arms open, all those years of loving You, had been returned in one unimaginable life-altering moment with an unfathomable divine hug – a Love that literally transformed my life!

From that transforming spiritual experience, not only was the Voice miraculously stilled, but You also set me on a new path of service; a ministry of prayer, with a message to inspire the hurting – the forgotten ones who think no one understands or cares about their pain – who often wrongly believe there is no hope. But there is hope, healing and comfort for their suffering. It is found in an intimate prayer relationship with You, where Your love transforms all things. Jesus, through this miracle, You've given me a testimony to share with those souls that walk the same dark path I've walked. I pray my story may be a message of light, hope, healing and miracles for all that suffer – an inspiring message that leads them into Your embrace.

I don't know where this journey will take me, Jesus, but I am excited to follow the path, and humbled and thankful that You would use me in this way. You have indeed given all those years of suffering a purpose. There is no way to adequately express my gratitude, Lord, for this gift of healing and transformation. In so doing, You scattered the darkness with Your light and resurrected my life in unimaginable ways. So, what more can I do other than devote this life You saved to You. I live today for You, to grow in holiness, and to strive to be a saint as You ask of us. I do this Lord because of my love for You, and my burning desire to one day I fall into Your embrace and hear You say, "Well done!" Use me, Lord, and let me share my story with the world to those that will hear. Let me dedicate every remaining breath I have here on this earth in service to You; the One I love and adore above all things.

Jesus, in spite of the long years of suffering, I see how blessed my life is. I can't believe I'm saying this, but I'm thankful for all of it, no matter how dark or how difficult this journey has been. Not in a morbid or masochistic way, but because of the blessings You've created because of it. So many of the wounds of the past that were the cause of so much of my suffering, You've healed by transforming them into blessings. I can look back now at the precise moments in time when I was hurt, and no longer view those moments with a heart of bitterness. Instead I see them as divine moments - moments of grace. Lord, You took away the bitterness - such as my bitterness towards Dad - and turned it into fruitful suffering by teaching me compassion. This Lord is Your grace again poured out and overflowing.

While no one wants to suffer, Jesus, and we in our humanity recoil at the thought of it, from great suffering great good can come. We've only to look to the Cross to see the blessings that come out of suffering. Without Your surrendering and dying on the Cross, humanity wouldn't have been given salvation, and the opportunity for Eternal Life with You. Suffering and adversity are harsh teachers, to be sure, but perhaps it is also the greatest teacher of wisdom there is. I have grown and learned in ways I likely never would have without it. Although none of us want to suffer, when it does come, we mustn't run from it. Instead, we must embrace our own cross, our own suffering, following Your example. If we choose to run to You, and not away, the cross and suffering we bear can make us better for having carried it. It is by the cross, and through the fiery furnace of affliction we are transformed as Isaiah 48:10 tells us: "Behold, I have refined you, but not as silver; I have tested you in the furnace of affliction." So it is through the furnace that our dross is purged and turned into gold – our souls are refined and sanctified. The trials we must endure are but preparation for our souls to manifest Your glory and divine love anew – to become more like You. So in the end, Jesus, I have learned and grown from the painful experiences I've been through in ways that I likely never would have any other way. How can I regret that? Thank You for teaching me the tough, but invaluable lesson that the greatest blessings often come from the greatest pain.

This long, dark path I've traveled has in the end given more than it's taken. I've only to look to the profoundly deep and intimate relationship I have with You, my sweet and precious Jesus, to see this truth. The adversity I've experienced has only fanned the flame of my love for You. Though I have been devoted to You for as long as I can remember, along the journey I fell so deeply in love, that I came to know You as my Beloved. If not for this long difficult journey – from childhood onwards – would I have pursued You so tirelessly in prayer? Would I know what an inner peace in the midst of life's storms is? Would I have ever had the profound experience of being embraced by Your love, a moment I will cherish for eternity? I believe it's precisely because of the pain, trauma, and suffering I've experienced, that today I have this steadfast faith and immovable trust in You. I've a prayer life that's deep and strong, and a relationship with You that is deeply personal. I look for and find Your presence in things I never did before, realizing that You are not only among us, but within us – in the quiet whispers of our hearts You speak, and so we are never alone. There are no treasures on earth comparable to the blessings of experiencing Your love and presence with me. You, my precious Jesus, are the King of my heart, my treasure, my Hero, and the love of my life. Your love and presence is worth more than any riches this world has to offer. It is only because of You, dear Lord – Your transforming love and all-sufficient grace – that I survived the dark war that ravaged my soul for so many decades of my life. You, Lord, restored my soul, and that too was only by grace. As St. Therese of Lisieux said, "Everything is grace." Yes, Jesus, everything is indeed grace! For, in the end, it is only by Your amazing grace that the little girl crying cries no more.

Jesus
my treasure
I shall love You always
every heartbeat ... every breath
for You
may each precious moment of life
be lived to glorify
and honor You
Amen.

PRAYER OF SURRENDER

Teach me Heavenly Father to let go
Of everything, even that which I think I know
To fall freely into Thy loving arms
Knowing in all ways I'm safe from harm
The tiny sparrow does not fuss or fret
With its every need in perfection met
The willow tree gently bends and flows
Sustained by grace through her roots below
Help me Divine Father to ever rest in Thee
Knowing Thy love is even greater for me

Teach me Heavenly Father to learn to 'Allow'
'What is' to be embraced in each moment of 'Now'
Oh! That I may at long last see
Each precious moment as a gift from Thee
As I lay my trembling hand in His
Relaxing into the 'Now' and 'What is'
A newfound peace washes over me
As I learn to breathe and simply 'Be'
O Divine Father, how could I foresee
That in surrendering I'd be set free

Teach me Father to surrender all to Thee
For my will is not what's best for me
Alone I'm blind to what lies ahead
I'll trust in Thy vision of my Higher Path instead
The bigger picture of life I do not know
Nor what my soul needs to learn and grow
So, to divine will I surrender all this day
Asking Thee to lovingly guide my way
With Thy presence may I be forever one
Today and always may Thy will be done

Amen

Belinda Rose

THE TAPESTRY OF LIFE

"Life is a tapestry,"
I heard the still, small voice say,
A canvas intricately woven
as the soul travels life's highway.
Each thread is carefully chosen
with God's love and care,
weaving an original masterpiece
that is beyond compare!

Both threads of exquisite joy,
and threads of darkest gloom
Are skillfully intertwined
on the Divine Weaver's loom.
The sorrows and the trials,
the tears of yesterday,
He spins as threads of splendid gold
in a masterful display.

Each thread tells its story
in the tapestry of life,
From tales of great victories
to tales of greatest strife.
The Divine Hand weaves each canvas
as part of the grand whole,
Each tapestry a life journey,
a unique story of a soul.

It's not for us to question
His higher vision or grand design;
Let's leave the artistry of weaving
in the Hands of the Divine.
Only the Divine Weaver can spin
the frayed threads into silk and gold;
Creating a tapestry of each soul's journey,
that's a vision to behold.

In the midst of our suffering, life can appear to be darkness and utter chaos, a mishmash of tangled knots and loose threads just like the back of a tapestry. But then through God's grace a miracle happens; a life is healed, transformed and resurrected. Perhaps through God's grace He allows His divine light to shine through the tapestry of our lives, giving us a glimpse of how He is weaving the dark and light threads into a divine design. We are reminded to have faith and trust, and hold onto a steadfast belief that amid the chaos of our lives the Divine Weaver is at work creating a masterpiece, even if we can't see the intricacy of the pattern being woven. It isn't for us to know the divine design but for us to stop doubting that His artistry is at work amid life's turmoil, and to simply with childlike faith, let go and surrender, trusting everything in our life to His divine will.

Heavenly Father,
In Thy infinite grace, grant us a simple childlike trust and
faith in Thy presence abiding with us amid the storm. Despite
our greatest suffering may we experience the deep peace Thy
presence within us instills, that we may say, believing from
the very depths of our souls, "Lord, Thou art with me, and so I
shall not fear my Enemy. All is well with my soul."
In the Name of the Father ... the Son ... and the Holy Spirit.
Amen

EPILOGUE

*S*tanding at the foot of the driveway of my childhood home, I watched contentedly as Dad tended a colorful display of deep purple and yellow irises that lined the walkway to the front door. But that contentedness soon gave way to an overwhelming urge to race up the familiar path and greet him with an enormous hug, saying, "Dad, I'm home! It's so good to see you, and the yard looks just beautiful!" But I couldn't. In the middle of this incredible dream came the intuitive understanding that I was only observing Dad from the other side of the veil. I could go no further, because I was still very much alive. Still, seeing him again made me realize how terribly I missed him, and I longed to penetrate the barrier of the veil that kept us separated to deliver my heartfelt greeting.

Perhaps Dad had sensed my presence and desire to greet him. He turned towards me with a warm and welcoming smile. In that moment he smiled I understood he had come to deliver a message via this dream. At the time I didn't fully grasp that this message wasn't to be conveyed in words spoken, as my prior dream visitation with him had been, but through the scene before me. I just seemed to understand that I was to pay close attention to what Dad was doing, so I watched his every move intently.

Dad was obviously gardening, and there was nothing out of the ordinary about that. Frankly, if there is a Heaven in which we can do those things we love, this is what I'd have expected him to have been doing! His green thumb had been one of his greatest gifts in life and one of his greatest joys. Our yards, front and back, had always burst with flowers of every color and variety. But this time he'd really outdone himself! Deep crimson roses that hung in large clusters from dark green foliage were interspersed with giant white peonies in a row of exquisite color and fragrance that lined one entire side of the hill leading up the driveway. It was a vision to behold! But my attention was continually drawn back to Dad and the flowerbed of irises where he was so meticulously working the ground.

His beloved daffodils – the crown jewels of his garden – had once grown where these lovely irises now grew, so I was more than a little surprised to see he'd planted something else in their once sacred spot. But then it occurred to me ... these weren't just any variety of iris ... these were Mom's favorite ... the deep purple variety, and they now graced the entire walkway to the front door! If only she could see this, I thought. She would absolutely love how Dad had planted a divine combination of both purple and yellow irises to create a glorious path of magnificent color.

Dad rose from his stooped position over the flowerbed, turned and once more flashed that same radiant, welcoming smile, and in that instant, I got it! The smile ... it was welcoming ... that was the clue. He was preparing a welcome – a celebration! Dad was getting the yard ready to welcome one of us back home.

The next morning, I called Mom to share both my excitement and concerns about the dream. I told her the positives first – how good Dad looked and how happy and contented he seemed. I shared how amazing Dad had the front yard looking, and that he'd put her favorite purple and yellow irises where his daffodils had once grown. Her reply left me stunned.

"It's so odd you'd say that, Belinda. Your Dad and I had planned on planting yellow and purple irises in the bed along

454

the walkway to the door before he began having his strokes."

"You never mentioned that before, Mom."

"Yeah, I always thought it would just be so beautiful. But you know how he was ... just couldn't part with those daffodils."

"Mom, there's more. I think maybe Dad was giving me a message. I think he was getting the yard all spruced up because one of us is coming home."

"What do you mean by 'coming home'? As in *die*, Belinda?"

"Yeah. Mom, maybe *I'm* going to die. You know I've been having problems with the mitral valve stuff. Maybe my heart is going to finally give out."

"Oh, Belinda, don't say that," she said. "It was only a dream. Forget about it."

I tried to take Mom's advice and forget about it. But after what she'd said about the irises I wasn't so sure that it was only a dream. Maybe it really was a message I should listen to. For the next few weeks, I tried to push the dream out of my mind, but it kept tugging at me, begging me to pay attention to what it was trying to tell me. Then one morning, from out of the blue, its real intent was revealed.

I woke that morning to find a devastating voicemail on my phone; Mom had been rushed to the hospital suffering from a brain bleed. She was unconscious and her passing was imminent. As I rushed to the hospital, that dream from just a month before came flooding back. I hadn't understood it at the time. I thought it was me that the message was meant for, because I hadn't been feeling good while Mom had been doing much better. But I'd had it all wrong. Dad, knowing how close I'd always been to Mom, had come to prepare me for her passing, to soften the blow, to give me time to say and do the things I needed to before she was gone, and I had totally misunderstood. My beloved mother passed away suddenly on April 28, 2015, a month to the day after I'd had that dream.

We all have differences with our loved ones, and my relationship with Mom was no different, but my love for her far exceeded those differences. I had no greater advocate in life than Mom. Acknowledging her passing during the writing of this book seems appropriate because she was my biggest cheerleader in getting it written. Daily she'd call and ask how the book was coming. "Keep going," she'd say.

After she died, rather than quit and give in to my sorrow, I wrote. I kept hearing her words in my thoughts, "Keep going," as if her presence was beside me to encourage me not to grieve, but to go forward. As I shared some of the most painful parts of my life – even events she never knew happened and feelings she didn't know about – it seemed at times as though I could feel her comforting me.

Mom believed sharing my story was important – not only because she felt I could help others struggling with eating disorders, but because she believed my story could help their loved ones understand the illness in a way she hadn't. All the years I battled against the eating disorder Mom had a ringside seat to the horror. Although she didn't always do the right thing or make the right decisions, she was still my only ally. Deep in the trenches she'd been the one holding my hand, sitting by my bedside, accompanying me to every single doctor appointment and even defending me against them a time or two. But the one thing she found the most upsetting was that she couldn't understand the eating disorder so she could help me like she wanted to. It was as if a foreign entity had invaded my body and stole her little girl away. It broke her heart to witness my suffering while she sat by so helplessly, without a clue to understanding who or what the enemy we were fighting against was. What she didn't realize is that I never needed or expected her or Dad to understand the eating disorder, I only needed them to love me. I needed them to hug me once in awhile and express their love and concern. I needed a loving and safe environment in which to share my feelings without fear of judgment or condemnation so that the trauma could be addressed. Love – it might have made all the difference for me.

Today, if the parent of a child or adolescent with an eating disorder would ask me how they can best help their loved one my answer would be simple. From the viewpoint of a recovered anorexic I'd say, give them all the love you can. Be their arm of support so that they know they aren't all alone in the throes of this illness. Make them feel cherished, and allow them to speak their thoughts and feelings free from criticism. Of course, it goes without saying anyone dealing with an eating disorder needs the help of a qualified therapist, and in my opinion, spiritual guidance as well. For me, this was an illness of mind, body and soul and should have been dealt with in that way.

Even though my parents were unable because of their own wounds to give me the love I so desperately craved, or to understand that my eating disorder was an illness about unbearable feelings, emotions and pain, I still believe they cared and tried to help. I also still believe Mom is my number one advocate even from the other side. I hope she is pleased with this effort, just as I hope she is enjoying that grand heavenly garden Dad planted especially for her to welcome her home. "Enjoy those gorgeous purple irises, Mom, in all their stunning glory! And Momma ... know I miss you and love you every single day, with all my heart"

BE LOVE

Love is patient, and is kind...

1 Corinthians 13:4

It can be difficult knowing how best to support and care for a loved one suffering with an eating disorder. Rightly so, eating disorders now called ED in the medical and therapeutic communities are difficult to understand. Unless you are a trained health professional or have had a firsthand encounter suffering with one yourself, you may be at a loss in trying to help a loved one with an eating disorder. Although I am not a health professional, I have spent most of my life battling anorexia nervosa, and so, I can certainly tell you the things that would have helped me had my own parents, or even the doctors of that time understood more about ED.

I am often asked the question, "I know someone that has an eating disorder. How can I help them?" I'd like to answer that question here and have it to go out to the world as part of my message. It's a message that is simple really, and is encompassed in an acronym I've created to spread that message ... "BELUV" ... Be Love.

To those in a battle with an eating disorder, the love, support and understanding of family and friends play a much more critical role in recovery than anyone can imagine. I often compare those long years I spent lost to anorexia as being caged in the lair of a demon, and I would have given anything if I'd had just one person in my life in whom I could have confided, who loved me unconditionally, who listened and didn't judge, condemn or blame. The letters of the acronym themselves encompass its overall meaning – *be* love, and represent tangible actions anyone can take to emotionally support someone battling an ED. Unfortunately, my own family was too dysfunctional to have given me the blessing of much needed emotional support. But perhaps from that loss and that dysfunction in my own family, I can help someone else find action steps in how to better help and support someone fighting a battle with ED. My prayer is that from sharing my dark but triumphant journey and spreading the message of BELUV, I can bring light and hope to another's suffering.

The letters in BELUV stand for: Blame Not, Empathy, Love, Understand, Validate.

B is for Blame Not. Don't blame them for their illness. It's not their fault. Don't lash out in frustration with comments such as: "Just stop doing it!" "Just eat!" "It's up to you to think different!" "You just wasted that whole gallon of ice cream!" All things I've heard many times over. Don't give them the icy stare as my Dad was prone to do as I exited the bathroom because he knew I'd been purging. Blame, shame, and guilt only make an anorexic loathe themselves all the more, thus giving more power to the Voice. Remember, it's an illness and not a choice.

E is for Empathy. Be compassionate, and listen with an empathic ear and a caring heart to anything they are willing to share. Offer a safe and compassionate space of sharing.

L is for Love. Make them feel loved and cherished. Let them know you are worried, concerned and it hurts you to see them suffering because you love them. If you are a family member offer to attend family counseling with them. Help them seek out qualified spiritual guidance. Let them know they are not alone. If you are able, pray for them. Pray for them fervently, and let them know of your prayers. Go deeper into your own spiritual life.

U is for understanding. You likely won't understand the thoughts that ED has convinced them is truth, and they likely won't expect you to. What is important to understand is that these thoughts – ED's Voice - this illness, is causing them great emotional and physical suffering, so don't chastise them for what you feel are irrational thoughts. Understand that an anorexic saying, "I'm so fat!" at 70 lbs. might be irrational in reality, but to the one battling ED it is truth. Such seemingly irrational comments carry with them great fear for the anorexic. This is the illness speaking. The voice of ED is real, sinister, and powerful.

V is for Validate. As they express their feelings to you listen and stay present. Let them be heard, and know what they think and feel is important. You don't have to agree with them for their emotions to be valid.

Heavenly Father,
Thank you for delivering me from the voice of ED.
May other sufferers seek and find healing and comfort in
Your sweet embrace of love. Grant those suffering the
courage and strength to fight their battle. By Your grace,
grant those that love them support, strength and compas-
sion, and let them truly be love that they may lift up the
suffering, becoming a reflection of You.
Have mercy on all who suffer. Grant them peace.
In the name of Jesus ... Amen.

The VOICE of ED

It's not my fault so don't blame me,
For the skin and bones I appear to be.
I naively followed as ED lured me in,
Promising to be both savior and friend.
But on ED's friendship I can't depend.
That voice named ED ... that voice lied.
"You're a worthless pig," that voice now chides.
"From my dark agenda you can't hide."

By this hound of hell I've been pursued,
With evil intent that won't be refused.
Now I'm ED's slave, a victim abused,
Even my spirit's battered and bruised.
There's no escaping the voice in my head.
Life with ED brings nothing but dread,
So I'm pretty sure I'd be better off dead.
You'd agree if you heard what ED said.

"Hello Fatso, welcome to my lair.
Sorry, but you're not going anywhere.
But don't lament, and don't despair.
I'm your champion," ED declares.
"For that angst and pain, bingeing is key.
Thin and beautiful you'll soon be!
I love you the best, Little Piggy you'll see.
So why would you ever want to leave me?"

MY BELOVED

How is it my Beloved,
You love me as You do?
If I searched the whole world over,
Ne'er would I find a love so true.
Some people love you in the good times
Fewer love you when you fall
But my Beloved loves me
Anytime at all!
You know my heart's desire
From You nothing can I hide.
Yet no matter what I say or do
You stay right by my side.
In moments when I stumble
Those times I fall from grace
I hear Your sweet voice whispering,
"Meet Me in our silent, secret place."
It's there I feel Your Presence
In harmony one with mine
It's there I find in Your embrace
A love that's ever so divine!
There's no place on this earth
That I would rather be
Then in divine communion
With my Beloved close to me!
For in our holy secret chamber
All heartache and loneliness are gone.
Healed by the power of a love
I can always count upon!
How is it my Beloved,
You love me as You do?
If I searched the whole world over,
Ne'er would I find a love so true!

You listen to my troubles
You know my every doubt and fear.
And when my heart is breaking
You wipe away each tear.
When the path grows dark before me
And I can't find my way
I hear Your sweet voice whispering,
"Come Child, let Me carry you today."
So, I helplessly surrender
Into Your divine embrace
Trusting though the storm may rage
I'm safe beneath Your grace.
You are my Rock and Fortress
So through all I can and will prevail
I've safe passage through life's storms
Because Your love ... it never fails.
And You have promised my Beloved
To make the crooked places straight
Until the hour I come Home
And I walk through Heaven's Gate!
So until I hear the angels calling
And my time on earth is through
I'll face what life brings with courage
Because I walk this path with You.
If I searched the whole world over
Ne'er would I find a love so true!
How is it my Beloved
You love me as You do?

ACKNOWLEDGMENTS

I would like to express my gratitude to the following people, each of whom contributed in his or her own unique way to the writing and publication of this book:

Genny Boehmer ... as my spiritual director, you've provided endless support, encouragement and a non-judgmental ear through the emotionally exhausting parts of this story. Thank you for your love and priceless friendship.

Joann Deck ... my friend, publishing consultant and kindred spirit on this spiritual journey. I am so grateful to you. Thank you for your belief in me and in the value of my story right from our first phone conversation. Your help has been invaluable in bringing this book to publication so that my story might be shared.

Perry Iles ... my always brilliant and humorous editor. With such subtlety you took just enough of that creative control I'm always so determined to hang onto and thus found a magical way of making my words even more powerful. Thank you for making the editorial process painless and fun. I'm grateful for all you've done to make this book its very best.

Gail McMeekin ... as my friend and creativity coach, you instilled within me the courage and confidence I needed to move forward and share my poetry and writing with the world. Thank you for your encouragement when I needed it most.

Jim Parsons ... my writing coach and mentor. Your guidance was perhaps the most critical factor in bringing this book into being. I will be forever grateful to you. I was in overwhelm when I found you, and your guidance and direction helped me sort through the decades of my life to tell this story. Without that mentoring process, I would have been lost in overwhelm by the details of the story, and this project would likely never have come to fruition.

Jane Dixon-Smith ... Jane, thank you. You are such an incredibly talented graphic designer. I'm so very grateful for the beautiful cover design, and the many painstaking hours spent formatting all those poems, prayers and illustrations to perfection! Thank you for your help and guidance in making the finished vision I've long held of this book a reality.

A special word of thanks to my husband Brian for his courage and humility in allowing me to share with honesty and openness the most private and personal parts of our relationship.

To my three wonderful children for allowing me to take time away from family so that I could fully immerse myself in this project. I love you guys with all my heart.

ABOUT THE AUTHOR

*B*elinda Rose is an inspirational author, poet, and creative. She is the author of the vibrant on-line prayer community *Illustrated Devotions,* a prayer ministry where she shares daily prayers and devotions, and offers intercessory prayer for those in need. Through her ministry she seeks to inspire those who suffer by ultimately leading them into a deeper intimacy with God through prayer. As a Christian Contemplative, she believes it is by resting in God in the silence – the journey within – that sets God's divine action to work within us to allow true healing of the wounded heart, mind and soul to occur.

Belinda Rose is devoted to her Catholic faith, the Sacred Heart of Jesus and Eucharistic Adoration. She loves spending quiet time in nature and adores animals of every kind. Born and raised in the Midwest, she still lives there with her husband and three sons. Together they enjoy the companionship of their five cocker spaniels, three cats and Buster the parrot.

To become a part of her devotional community,
visit her Facebook fan page:
www.facebook.com/illustrateddevotions

Belinda's devotional writings and art-prayers
can be found at: www.belindarose.com